FORMER PRIME MINISTERS IN JAPAN

Power, Influence and the Role
of Informal Politics

Hugo Dobson, Karin Narita and Caroline Rose

First published in Great Britain in 2025 by

Bristol University Press
University of Bristol
1–9 Old Park Hill
Bristol
BS2 8BB
UK
t: +44 (0)117 374 6645
e: bup-info@bristol.ac.uk

Details of international sales and distribution partners are available at bristoluniversitypress.co.uk

© Hugo Dobson, Karin Narita and Caroline Rose 2025

The digital PDF and ePub versions of this title are available open access and distributed under the terms of the Creative Commons Attribution-NonCommercial-NoDerivatives 4.0 International licence (https://creativecommons.org/licenses/by-nc-nd/4.0/) which permits reproduction and distribution for non-commercial use without further permission provided the original work is attributed.

DOI: 10.51952/9781529206852

British Library Cataloguing in Publication Data
A catalogue record for this book is available from the British Library

ISBN 978-1-5292-0683-8 paperback
ISBN 978-1-5292-0686-9 ePub
ISBN 978-1-5292-0685-2 OA PDF

The right of Hugo Dobson, Karin Narita and Caroline Rose to be identified as authors of this work has been asserted by them in accordance with the Copyright, Designs and Patents Act 1988.

All rights reserved: no part of this publication may be reproduced, stored in a retrieval system, or transmitted in any form or by any means, electronic, mechanical, photocopying, recording, or otherwise without the prior permission of Bristol University Press.

Every reasonable effort has been made to obtain permission to reproduce copyrighted material. If, however, anyone knows of an oversight, please contact the publisher.

The statements and opinions contained within this publication are solely those of the authors and not of the University of Bristol or Bristol University Press. The University of Bristol and Bristol University Press disclaim responsibility for any injury to persons or property resulting from any material published in this publication.

Bristol University Press works to counter discrimination on grounds of gender, race, disability, age and sexuality.

Cover design: Lyn Davies
Front cover image: Getty/Junko Kimura
Bristol University Press uses environmentally responsible print partners.
Printed and bound in Great Britain by CPI Group (UK) Ltd, Croydon, CR0 4YY

Bristol University Press' authorized representative in the European Union is:
Easy Access System Europe, Mustamäe tee 50, 10621 Tallinn, Estonia,
Email: gpsr.requests@easproject.com

'You are very ex as an ex-prime minister'
Kenneth Clarke, 2007

'Even from my sickbed, even if you are going to lower me into the grave and I feel that something is going wrong, I will get up. Those who believe that after I have left the government as prime minister, I will go into a permanent retirement, really should have their heads examined'
Lee Kuan Yew, 1988

'We've never experienced such a thing as an ex-President'
Protestor in Cairo, 11 February 2011

'I have a message to … the Prime Minister of Japan who I don't know because it's like that in Japan – you say "good morning" to one Prime Minister and "good afternoon" to a different one!'
Luiz Inácio Lula da Silva, October 2009

'Japanese prime ministers are just like tissue paper'
Koike Yuriko, 5 February 2011

Contents

List of Abbreviations		vi
Glossary		viii
Acknowledgements		x
A Note on the Text		xii
1	Introduction	1
2	Former Leaders, Informal Politics and the Japanese Prime Minister	10
3	Former Japanese Prime Ministers, the Meiji Period to World War Two	33
4	Former Japanese Prime Ministers, 1945 to 1989	59
5	Former Japanese Prime Ministers, 1989 to 2024	91
6	Analysis and Conclusions	128
References		149
Index		174

List of Abbreviations

APDA	Asian Population and Development Association
CCP	Chinese Communist Party
CDP	Constitutional Democratic Party of Japan
DPFP	Democratic Party for the People
DPJ	Democratic Party of Japan
DSP	Democratic Socialist Party
G7	Group of Seven (Canada, the EU, France, Germany, Italy, Japan, the UK and the US)
G8	Group of Eight (the G7 plus Russia)
G20	Group of Twenty (the G8 plus Argentina, Australia, Brazil, China, India, Indonesia, Mexico, Saudi Arabia, South Africa, South Korea, Türkiye and the African Union)
GEA	Global Environmental Action
GHQ	General Headquarters, Supreme Commander of the Allied Forces
IMF	International Monetary Fund
IMTFE	International Military Tribunal for the Far East
JCP	Japan Communist Party
JSP	Japan Socialist Party
LDP	Liberal Democratic Party
MITI	Ministry of International Trade and Industry
MOFA	Ministry of Foreign Affairs
MRA	Moral Re-Armament movement
NATF	Northeast Asia Trilateral Forum
ODC	Oriental Development Company
SDP	Social Democratic Party of Japan
TICAD	Tokyo International Conference on African Development
UK	United Kingdom
UN	United Nations

LIST OF ABBREVIATIONS

UNCED	United Nations Conference on Environment and Development
US	United States
WEF	World Economic Forum
WW1	World War One
WW2	World War Two

Glossary

chōtōha gaikō	bi- or non-partisan foreign policy
Daikun'i Kikka Saijushō	Grand Cordon of the Order of the Chrysanthemum
donchō naikaku	curtain cabinet
Furusato Sōsei	Hometown Revitalization Programme
Gakusei Kokubu Kenkyū Kyōkai	Student Defense Research Association
genrō	elder statesman
habatsu	faction
heiwa-kyō	peace teaching
honne	true feelings
Hoshutō	Conservative Party
Jiyū Minshutō	Liberal Democratic Party
Jiyūtō	Liberal Party
Jūshin	Council of Elders
Kaishintō	Reform Party
kakushin-ha	reform-minded group
Kenseikai	Constitutional Political Association
Kenseitō	Constitutional Party
kōhai	junior
Kokumin Minshutō	Democratic People's Party
Kōmeitō	Clean Government Party
kozō naikaku	apprentice cabinet
kuromaku	black curtain
lao pengyou	old friends
Minseitō	Good Governance Party
Minshatō	Democratic Socialist Party
Minshintō	Democratic Party (2016–18)
Minshu Jiyūtō	Democratic Liberal Party
Minshutō	Democratic Party
nejire kokkai	'twisted' Diet
Nihon Minshutō	Democratic Party (1954–55)
Nihon Shintō	Japan New Party
Nippon Kaigi	Japan Conference

niryū naikaku	second-class cabinet
nisei	second generation
rachi jiken	abduction of Japanese citizens by North Korean agents
Rikken Dōshikai	Association of Comrades of the Constitution
Rikken Minseitō	Constitutional Democratic Party
Rikken Seiyūkai	Association of Friends of Constitutional Government
Seiwakai	Seiwa Seisaku Kenkyūkai, faction in LDP
senpai	senior
Shakai Minshutō	Social Democratic Party (1996–)
Shakai Minshūtō	Social Democratic Party (1926–32)
Shakaitō	Japan Socialist Party
Shaminren	Socialist Democratic Federation
Shin Gunbi Sokushin Renmei	New Armament Promotion Association
Shin Hoshutō	New Conservative Party
Shinpotō	Progressive Party
Shinseitō	Japan Renewal Party
Shinshintō	New Frontier Party
Shintō Sakigake	New Harbinger Party, New Party Sakigake
shō-Yamagata naikaku	mini-Yamagata cabinet
Shōwa no yōkai	monster of the Shōwa era
sokkin	right-hand man
sūmitsuin	Privy Council
Taisei Yokusankai	Imperial Rule Assistance Association
Taiyōtō	Sun Party
tatemae	surface
tōnaitō	party within the party
yami shōgun	shadow shogun
yūtōsei	honours student

Acknowledgements

This book would not have seen the light of day without the support of a number of people to whom we owe thanks and apologies in equal measure.

At Bristol University Press, we would like to thank Stephen Wenham for his infinite patience and good humour. At times, he must have regretted meeting Hugo at the 2017 Political Studies Association's annual conference in Glasgow and taking an interest in Japanese prime ministers. Many thanks also to Zoe Forbes for her support throughout the process of writing this book. We are deeply grateful to the referees for their generosity in reading and commenting on our work.

At the University of Sheffield, Hugo would like to thank all his colleagues in the School of East Asian Studies, Faculty of Arts and Humanities and Faculty of Social Sciences who helped in various ways to get this project started and finally complete it. An extended community of scholars, including Christopher Hughes, Patrick Köllner, Ian Neary, Arthur Stockwin and Dennis Yasutomo, all provided food for thought at various points. In Japan, he is equally grateful to the late Professor Takahashi Susumu, Professor Uchiyama Yū and Wada Keiko at the University of Tokyo and Professor Takayasu Kensuke at Waseda University for welcoming him to Japan on numerous occasions, as well as Ishiguro Kuniko at Tokyo International University for sourcing materials.

At the University of Leeds, Caroline would like to thank her colleagues in East Asian Studies and the School of Languages, Cultures and Societies for their support over the years and for enabling the research that made her contribution to the book possible.

At Queen Mary University of London and the University of Sheffield, Karin would like to thank her old and new colleagues in the School of Politics and International Relations and the School of East Asian Studies for providing stimulating research environments. She is grateful to her co-authors, Hugo and Caroline, for bringing her onboard the project and for their generous support.

Beyond Bristol University Press and our respective universities, there are a number of people whose contribution we would like to acknowledge. The work of Kevin Theakston at the University of Leeds on British ex-prime ministers provided the initial inspiration for us to focus on Japanese former prime ministers. We would like to thank the Japan Foundation Endowment Committee and GB Sasakawa Foundation for funding research trips to Japan. We are grateful to libraries in Hull, Leeds, Sheffield and Tokyo that gave us access to materials and a place to think and write. The Japan Society and the Japan Research Centre at SOAS provided us with an opportunity to present and road-test our evolving ideas. We are particularly grateful to all the former Japanese prime ministers and their families who agreed to meet and speak candidly, and give a first-hand view of events.

We would also like to thank the University of Sheffield's Open Access Fund for its support in making this book freely available. Apologies to the many family, friends, colleagues and organizations who were generous sources of helpful advice and concrete assistance, whether they were aware of it or not, but have not been namechecked here.

This book comes with the rider that we claim the credit if it proves to be of interest to anybody and blame everyone else for any errors in fact or interpretation.

Hugo Dobson, Karin Narita and Caroline Rose
April 2025

A Note on the Text

Throughout this book, Japanese names are given in the correct order, namely the family name first and the given name second, except when referencing works by Japanese scholars written in English.

As regards pronouns, he/him/his are used with reference to the former prime ministers discussed in this book, as they all were, or are, male. This is not to assume or imply that there will be no non-male Japanese prime ministers in the future.

Long vowels are expressed in the form of a macron, except in the case of place names like Tokyo and, once again, when referencing works by Japanese scholars in English.

The structure of Japan's ministries and agencies has changed over the decades and centuries and inevitably many of their titles have changed. The usage in this book observes the official title in use at the specific period in question.

1

Introduction

Why former leaders?

As 2023 turned into 2024, Japanese politics underwent a dramatic turn. Earlier in 2023, Prime Minister Kishida Fumio, generally regarded as a safe pair of hands, had hosted a seemingly successful G7 summit in Hiroshima, with pundits wondering if he would call an early election and capitalize on his position. However, by the end of the year the governing Liberal Democratic Party (LDP, *Jiyū Minshutō*) was embroiled in scandal over political fundraising that led to the resignation of several cabinet ministers and the collapse of popular support for Kishida, contributing to his decision in August 2024 to not seek re-election as LDP president and prime minister the following month. The reverberations continued to be felt in the October snap election for the House of Representatives and the LDP's loss of its overall majority.

Scandal is nothing new in Japanese politics, but the intensity and fallout of this particular scandal was different. By mid-January 2024, in an attempt to stem popular distrust, the largest LDP faction – led by former prime minister Abe Shinzō from 2021 until his assassination in 2022 and colloquially called the 'Abe faction' – decided to disband after the fourth and fifth largest factions had made similar announcements. Factions – one of the long-standing structural features of Japanese politics – have served as a source of prime ministers, a mechanism to raise and distribute campaign funds, as well as a key consideration when appointing ministers. During this extended political drama, three former prime ministers played high-profile roles. Asō Tarō, who served as prime minister for just shy of a year in the 2000s, continued to lead one of the remaining factions and stubbornly refused to disband. Mori Yoshirō, who also served for just over one year at the turn of the millennium and once led the 'Abe faction', sought to shape the faction's leadership and future direction before it disbanded. Similarly, Suga Yoshihide, who took over the premiership from Abe when he stepped down in 2020, piled pressure on the incumbent Kishida Fumio to resolve the influence of factions in party politics. In short, Japanese politics experienced a structural shift and former prime ministers were at the centre of these events.

To lose power is one of the pivotal events in any leader's political and personal life. The Ronald Reagan Presidential Library includes a full-scale replica of the Oval Office, a fact that was parodied in an episode of *The West Wing* suggesting that former leaders struggle with the loss of power. Combining comedy and tragedy, Václav Havel returned to playwriting after stepping down as president of the Czech Republic in 2003 with *Leaving*, which premiered in Prague in May 2008. The play portrays the personal and professional difficulties associated with leaving office, in addition to the relationship between an outgoing chancellor and the incoming regime (Cameron, 2008; Havel, 2008). Havel's motivation in writing the play was to explore the existential crisis that lay at the heart of a leader losing power and influence:

> I was interested – and indeed am still interested – in the more general, existential side of things. I was interested in how come when someone loses power, that person also loses the meaning of life? How come power has such charisma for some people that its loss means the collapse of that person's world? (Cameron, 2008)

Beyond the individual's own lived experience, their departure from power can become part of the news cycle and capture the public's attention. Several factors will contribute to this interest: the leader in question, the country they lead and the circumstances of their departure, to name a few of the obvious variables. Some of these departures have become iconic political moments. As researchers who work in and have been trained in British universities, the UK is a natural point of reference. Furthermore, UK prime ministers have often provided a logical point of comparison with their Japanese counterparts (Burrett, 2023; Dobson et al, 2023). In any case, UK prime ministers have provided moments of high drama over the decades (Topping, 2022). In November 1990, after 11 years in power, Prime Minister Margaret Thatcher tearfully departed Downing Street. This event and the associated imagery divides people today as it did then, much as her personality and policies did and still do. For some, her departure was a cause of celebration regardless of the emotion, while for others it represented a national and personal tragedy.

Fast-forward almost 20 years to May 2010. New Labour's Gordon Brown resigned after failing to prevent the formation of a Conservative–Liberal coalition government following the inconclusive 2010 general election. One of the most striking things about his farewell speech outside the door to Number Ten was that he and his wife chose to leave hand-in-hand with their two young sons, who had previously been kept deliberately out of the public eye. Possibly for the first time for many voters, Brown managed to project a human face to the country. The post-Brexit revolving door of UK politics has provided us with more tearful departures (Theresa May), apparent apathy (David Cameron) and resignation speeches that were proportionally as brief as the time in office (Liz Truss).

However, this interest and drama are often fleeting. The news cycle moves on and the public's attention wanes. Nevertheless, former leaders continue to be active. Returning to the example of Brown, he moved to the backbenches, representing the constituency of Kirkcaldy and Cowdenbeath until he chose not to contest the general election of May 2015. During this time he was touted as a possible but ultimately unsuccessful candidate for the position of managing director of the International Monetary Fund (IMF) in Spring 2011 in the aftermath of Dominique Strauss-Kahn's sudden resignation. He took on roles with the United Nations (UN), World Economic Forum (WEF) and New York University. He also emerged as an active campaigner in the Scottish independence referendum of 2014, arguing to remain in the UK. After resigning as an Member of Parliament (MP), Brown published his memoirs and several polemics, and has continued to be active in public life by promoting various causes with his wife.

Other examples abound of former UK prime ministers developing an afterlife that goes beyond the ubiquitous book contract and public-speaking circuit and instead seeks to exert political influence, whether it be John Major and his campaign against Brexit, Tony Blair and sporadic speculation around a possible return to front-line politics, or David Cameron's surprise appointment to the position of foreign secretary in November 2023.

These experiences and vignettes of former UK prime ministers raise the first-order questions that this book seeks to ask in the case of Japanese prime ministers – where are they now and what are they doing?

In addition to the simple curiosity of a political biographer keen to answer these questions, Kevin Theakston and Jouke de Vries (2012a: 1–2) provide sound justification for the study of former leaders. First, they have the ability and potential to still exert some kind of leadership across a range of different areas, not just political, and at different levels. Second, their existence and activities bring controversial issues into relief regarding their ongoing relationship with government, as well as their political, private and financial interests. Third, the norm of leaders' retirement is a sign of a healthy democracy. As John Keane has written:

> [d]emocracies specialize in bringing leaders down to earth. They manage to do this by using a variety of formal methods and informal customs that require leaders to leave office peacefully, without staging ruthless comebacks, so enabling other leaders to take their place without kidnappings or gunfire, bomb blasts, or street upheavals. (2009: 279)

Or, as the outgoing chancellor in Havel's play *Leaving* says: 'We are living, sir, in a democracy, and in a democracy it is quite normal and common for people to hold certain positions, and then leave them again' (Havel, 2008: 77).

Recent developments reinforce this justification for focusing on former leaders. With the exception of the US and the Trump–Biden–Trump presidencies, leaders are becoming younger across the world. As a result, they are stepping down at a younger age than previously, in good health with longer life expectancies and a considerable period of time remaining in their careers. For many former leaders, their post-resignation lives will be substantially longer than their periods in power. The image of an elderly grey-haired leader retiring quietly into retirement and obscurity is increasingly unlikely to dominate the popular imagination. Moreover, in addition to the increasing youth of former leaders, globalization is exerting its influence: '[i]n the digital age, the concept of a former head of state slinking quietly into the post-presidential night is drifting into obsolescence' (Benardo and Weiss, 2009: 5). In short, former leaders (and more of them) are here to stay.

Why Japan?

Returning to the example of Japan as mentioned at the outset of this chapter, most researchers of Japanese politics will own a mug depicting caricatures of all the Japanese prime ministers to date that is on sale at the Diet building and some department stores in Tokyo. With the high turnover rate of Japanese prime ministers, at some point most of us gave up on attempting to replace it, so only a minority is likely to have an up-to-date mug. Nevertheless, this is a tangible and readily understandable manifestation of the questions posed previously – where are they now and what are they doing?

Usually when a Japanese prime minister resigns, it will dominate the news for a day or two, but the levels of media and public interest are barely comparable to other countries, like the UK, and soon wane. The reasons behind this may be related to the 'revolving door' of Japanese politics, famously captured by Brazilian President Luiz Inácio Lula da Silva's comment at the 2009 G20 summit in Pittsburgh that you say 'good morning' to one Japanese prime minister and 'good afternoon' to another (Soble and Dickie, 2010). In other words, the Japanese electorate and media are inured to the regular churn in the country's leadership. It may also be explained by the absence of an emotional farewell with spouse and/or family in supporting roles. For example, Abe may have bucked the trend of short-lived Japanese prime ministers, but when he resigned in August 2020 after almost eight years in power citing ill health, he gave a standard, stage-managed, hour-long press conference as part of the working day that dealt with other issues alongside his resignation, including North Korea and COVID-19. On the surface, it appeared to be little different from the many other press conferences he gave during his long tenure except for its content and the fact it was televised live.

Despite the banality of Japanese prime ministers' resignation speeches, the manner of departure still has the power to capture attention and linger in the memory. For example, Abe is a rare example of a prime minister who resigned twice – in 2007 and 2020 – both times citing health reasons. In contrast, Prime Minister Uno Sōsuke is known as one of Japan's shortest-lived prime ministers having served for just over two months in the summer of 1989. However, the scandal that erupted around his affair with and treatment of a *geisha* received national and international attention. There was even speculation as to whether Margaret Thatcher as the only female leader would shake his hand at that year's G7 summit in Paris (Shima, 2000: 66–7). Ultimately, Uno's position was untenable, and he resigned.

As regards their afterlives, Japanese prime ministers demonstrate the full gamut of activities. At one end of the spectrum sits Abe as the only post-Occupation prime minister to serve two non-consecutive terms of office ranging from a return to the position of prime minister. Several other ex-prime ministers have returned to power in ministerial positions. Moving from formal political positions, other ex-prime ministers have continued to exert influence in domestic politics through party political factions, protégés and family connections. In this context, Tanaka Kakuei stands out as an oft-cited example of an éminence grise. Other ex-prime ministers have established themselves as elder statesmen, or *genrō*, offering pearls of wisdom with Yoshida Shigeru as a representative example. At the other end of the spectrum, some ex-prime ministers have received passing attention for activities with no connection to their political roles. For example, Hosokawa Morihiro trained and exhibited as a potter, whereas Koizumi Junichirō provided the voice of Ultraman King in 2009's *Mega Monster Battle Ultra Galaxy: The Movie* (Dobson and Rose, 2019). Regardless of the nature of these afterlives, whether political or apolitical, they can still pique public interest.

At the time of writing, Ishiba Shigeru is serving as the 65th prime minister of Japan, despite losing the LDP's majority in a snap general election in October 2024, leaving us with 64 former prime ministers – for the time being. On the one hand, as will be discussed in the following chapter, traditional studies of the role of the Japanese prime minister have stressed his position as a compromise figure, the product of inter-factional negotiation, and, as a result, essentially a transient figure. However, this has not prevented the extant English and Japanese literature from according him considerable attention, and more recent studies have begun to revise this traditional position by highlighting changes in the institutional framework, personality and media perception of the prime minister to argue that he has come to play a much more influential and central role in Japanese politics.

One contribution of this book to the literature on the role of the Japanese prime minister will be to highlight the role he continues to play and the influence he continues to exert after retirement.

On the other hand, as will also be explored in the following chapter, although some academic literature has focused on how leaders leave power and what they do thereafter, it has predominantly focused on Western examples with the US president understandably capturing most of the attention. In an effort to address this bias, some initial efforts have been made to understand the Japanese case, the applicability of the Western-focused literature, where it falls short analytically and what adaptations are required (Dobson and Rose, 2019; Tsuda, 2023). So, the other objective of this book is to continue addressing this gap in the literature and do for Japanese prime ministers what Cooper (2014) has done for former leaders in general, and Theakston (2010) has done for former UK prime ministers specifically, by detailing their post-retirement lives and making sense of them through a range of categories drawn from the extant literature but also generated by the specific case of Japan.

As regards the relevant literature in the Japanese language, numerous biographies of individual prime ministers cover their periods in office and the formative years but ignore the question of what happens next. Uji (2001), for example, provides a comprehensive review of Japanese prime ministers but each individual entry begins with their background and ends with their resignation. Some recent works, especially by Chūō University professor Hattori Ryūji, have begun to account for post-prime ministerial activities, as for example on Shidehara Kijūrō, Satō Eisaku and Nakasone Yasuhiro (2021a; 2021b; 2023, respectively) and have been translated to English. Some works provide a thick contextual analysis on a particular event, for example Yoshitake Nobuhiko's research on the politics of former prime minister Yoshida Shigeru's Nobel Prize nomination (2016; 2017). However, this focus on individual prime ministers is not comprehensive. Most often when the Japanese literature does focus on former prime ministers, it tends to be quasi-academic or journalistic. Mikuriya Takashi, emeritus professor of Japanese political history at the University of Tokyo, conducted a series of interviews with former prime ministers since 2001 that were published in the journal *Chūō Kōron*. These interviews were more academically focused but neither analytical nor comprehensive. In addition, former prime ministers in Japan are comparatively reticent when it comes to writing their memoirs (Nakasone Yasuhiro and Kaifu Toshiki being the main exceptions). In short, no systematic and comprehensive analysis of the role of former prime ministers exists in Japanese or English.

Contribution and structure

Japan's modern political history is a well-researched field presenting little opportunity for new perspectives. However, this book makes two contributions. First, it shifts our attention from the usual concerns of political biography, which focus primarily on the time in power with some consideration of the formative period, towards the question that has tended to lie on the margins of our attention of what happened next *after* the prime minister has stepped down. In this way, it provides an alternative political history of Japan from the perspective of the former prime minister and his post-premiership.

Second, this book appeals not only to political historians but also to political scientists by categorizing and evaluating the various roles and activities of an often overlooked informal actor in domestic and international politics, specifically, former Japanese prime ministers. There is no formal template for what prime ministers do after retirement, so the post-premierships under examination in this book can be varied and overlapping. Former prime ministers may continue to exert influence behind the scenes; they may return to the top job or a ministerial role; they may assume an unofficial role but still be actively engaged in the political process; they may make a career break and move into a new field; they might publish their memoirs; or, they may even retire completely from the limelight. With a particular interest in sources of continued power and influence, official or unofficial, formal or informal, this book categorizes the activities of Japan's 64 former prime ministers. An emerging question at this point, which will be introduced in Chapter 2 and answered in Chapter 6, is how similar and different Japan and its ex-prime ministers are from other, particularly Western and democratic, countries.

To these ends, the book is structured as follows. Chapter 2 explores the extant literature on former leaders and the various categories that have emerged to capture their activities. As mentioned previously, this literature has traditionally been overshadowed by the attention accorded to the US president. However, recently it has expanded to cast light on the various roles played by former leaders in other democracies, including Japan, and non-democratic countries across the world. The chapter then takes a slight sideways move to explore the literature on informal politics and the role therein of informal political actors, before moving on to focus on the position of the prime minister in Japanese politics and the power he exerts – both formally and informally – in order to locate this study within that specific literature. This exploration is partly informed by the belief that what a prime minister does after his resignation is shaped to an extent by the position he occupies while in office, his achievements and failures, and the way in which he leaves office.

Chapters 3 to 5 constitute the empirical contribution of this book by detailing the afterlives of Japan's prime ministers. Chapter 3 is historical in nature and covers the period from the appointment of Itō Hirobumi as Japan's first prime minister in 1885 through to the end of World War Two (WW2). This is admittedly a substantial slice of history. However, when dealing with

64 former prime ministers from Itō to Kishida Fumio, arbitrary lines have to be drawn in order to make the empirical material manageable. It also makes sense to deal with Japan's pre-democratic period in a single chapter that provides the historical context behind the postwar period during which Japan's present-day democracy was established. This book does not seek to be comprehensive and capture every aspect of all Japan's ex-prime ministers' afterlives. Rather, Chapters 3 to 5 will focus on populating the categories highlighted in Chapter 2 with examples that best illustrate the former prime ministers' activities during the period under examination. Each category in each chapter is thus structured around the most significant cases, rather than slavishly following a chronological order.

Chapter 4 takes a similar approach based on categories to the 17 prime ministers who served during the postwar period from defeat in WW2 through to the end of the Cold War. Chapter 5 highlights the fates of the 18 prime ministers that served after the end of the Cold War, which conveniently coincides with the Heisei period from 1989 to the present day. These three chapters are based on a wide range of English and Japanese newspaper articles, obituaries, memoirs and interviews with living former prime ministers, in addition to a range of secondary sources.

Chapter 6 provides the main analytical contribution of this book. It returns to the categories identified in Chapter 2, highlights those that are helpful in the Japanese context as well as those that do not apply, and brings into relief any new categories suggested by Japan's former prime ministers and their activities. It also explores which categories have greater or lesser analytical power over time and why. It will argue that the case of Japan illustrates, as does the wider literature on former leaders, that there is no one-size-fits-all afterlife for its prime ministers. They actively engage in a wide range of public and private activities that exhibit a strong interpersonal element, and to the wider argument of this book, reinforce the importance of embracing informal actors and spaces in our understanding of politics. What is striking in the Japanese case is the longstanding and ongoing tendency for ex-prime ministers to continue dabbling in politics. Furthermore, this tends to cut across the other activities that might make up a prime ministerial afterlife. Finally, this chapter will point to possible areas of future research.

In short, this book makes a genuinely original contribution by focusing our attention on former leaders as a distinct category of political actor, and in so doing it provides an alternative and unique political history of Japan. It integrates a wide range of literatures and evidence, unifying an otherwise diffuse and fragmented sub-discipline, to advance our understanding of elite-level, but also informal, politics in Japan.

One clear and ever-present danger exists in writing a book of this nature. Whether the focus be Japan or Italy with their reputations for revolving-door prime ministers, or the US where, barring assassination, resignation or impeachment, the president's term of office is predictable at either four or eight years, or even France and Germany where the leader tends to be in power for relatively longer, there is always the chance that they will resign while the book is being researched and written. Several Japanese prime ministers left office during this time thereby adding to our 'data points'. In addition, some former prime ministers passed away, including Nakasone in 2019, Kaifu in 2022 and most tragically with the assassination of Abe also in 2022. As much as possible, any recent changes in the leadership of Japan have been taken into account within the empirical chapters. Even if events have moved on between submission of this manuscript and its eventual publication, the conclusions drawn here from across 64 former prime ministers are valuable in and of themselves and are likely to be borne out, rather than undermined, by future developments.

2

Former Leaders, Informal Politics and the Japanese Prime Minister

Overview

At first blush the activities and roles of former leaders across the world, on the one hand, and the position, power and influence of the Japanese prime minister, on the other hand, may appear to be unlikely bedfellows. However, where they overlap is that they have both experienced a recent upsurge in academic interest and require us to think about the informal nature of politics. This chapter reviews these literatures, thereby locating the original contribution of this book as it relates to both our understanding of the role of former leaders more generally as well as the Japanese prime minister specifically. Reviewing these literatures also frames the empirical focus of the following three chapters, as well as the conceptual analysis of the final chapter. It does this by highlighting a range of categories that can be applied with varying degrees of explanatory power to make sense of the roles played by Japanese former prime ministers. Thereafter, by exploring our understanding of informal politics and locating the various actors who operate in this space (including the Japanese prime minister), this chapter will demonstrate that informal influence continues to be exerted in the absence of formal power.

Former leaders

Biographies, autobiographies, memoirs and biopics are replete with leaders' formative experiences and their time in power but are often silent when it comes to the period after resignation and/or retirement. This is a shame and often misses the opportunity to flesh out the leader's life story. After all, one of the inescapable truths of life and politics is that all leaders eventually become former leaders one way or another, and this period of their lives should not be overlooked. In some cases, they can even come to overshadow the time in power. For example, in his account of Jimmy Carter's post-presidency, Douglas Brinkley details his initial experience of researching Carter's early life for a traditional biography and encountering the rare example of popular interest focusing on the story of what happened next: '…few seemed interested in Carter's early years; people were far more curious about the political resurrection that had turned 1980's malaise-ridden loser into 1994's distinguished global peacemaker' (1998: xii). In Carter's case, his humanitarian activities and diplomatic efforts in later life were more memorable than achievements in power: '[r]ejected by the voters in 1980, he was at best an average president; yet Carter has emerged as perhaps America's greatest ex-president with his strengths generally outweighing his weaknesses … As an ex-president, Carter seems somehow more presidential' (Chambers, 1998: 405).

However, for most leaders stepping back from power is challenging. For example, Manfred Kets de Vries (2003) has highlighted what he calls the 'retirement syndrome', which is shorthand for the various difficulties and barriers – both real and imagined – that exist to leaders eventually leaving office; specifically, feelings of nothingness, the talion principle of falling victim to revenge (and taking measures to stave this off) and the edifice complex of creating a legacy. The manner of departure will often influence the retirement plans and the psychological well-being of the ex-leader in question. Several examples of the culture shock experienced by former leaders as they adjust to their new lives can be observed. On a practical level, Charles Powell, private secretary to UK Prime Minister Margaret Thatcher, remembers:

> being rung up by Margaret Thatcher a week or two after she left Number 10 and being told on a Sunday she had a plumbing problem. And I said 'oh dear, better get a plumber in'. And a long silence. 'How do I do that?' 'Well', I said, 'try the Yellow Pages'. And that's the way we had to go. I ended up ringing the plumber in the Yellow Pages. (*BBC News*, 2007)

John Major, Thatcher's successor, captured the challenges in finding an appropriate role having stepped down from power:

> An ex-prime minister's a rather unusual fish in politics. If they say nothing, what are they doing there? If they say something, there's every chance it will be construed as an oblique attack on your successor. So it is extremely difficult to have a role that isn't capable of severe misinterpretation. (*BBC News*, 2007)

US President Richard Nixon felt that his life after resigning had become a 'life without purpose, [an] almost unbearable' existence (Chambers, 1979).

According to Don Watson, Australian Prime Minister Paul Keating's speech writer, the loss of power was visceral:

> Paul Keating, while maintaining an admirable dignity and despite his depression, felt each blow on his good name as it said people continue to feel a limb after it has been amputated ... Political death is like the other kind – the body keeps twitching after the head is cut off. (Watson, 2002: 732, cited in Strangio, 2012: 90)

Over recent years, the academic literature has begun to pay more attention to these opportunities and challenges. This is both an academic and a practical issue, as John Keane has written, '[t]he subject of ex-office holders is under-theorized, under-researched, under-appreciated, and – in many cases – under-regulated' (2009: 282–3). What leaders may do after resigning from the top job raises not only practical existential issues, such as what they will do next and how they will survive financially and emotionally, it also raises ethical questions around whether they should benefit financially from their time in power. Then there are political questions, such as the kind of ongoing influence they may or may not have, where their legitimacy resides, what their relationship with the incumbent regime might look like and whether they should comment on their successors' policies either supportively or critically.

These questions by no means represent an exhaustive list and will not disappear any time soon. Although Kevin Theakston (2006: 448) has written quite rightly that '[f]ormer prime ministers are members of a small, exclusive club' (and this is the case even in Japan, where the turnover rate of prime ministers is considerably higher than other countries, for reasons that are discussed later), this exclusive group is getting progressively larger. As Andrew Jack (2007) has argued, the topic of former leaders has increased in salience over recent years and by this very fact is set to continue: '... growing numbers of successful politicians are leaving office younger, more energetic, keen to do more in the future, propelled by their recent predecessors, precedents and increased chances to consolidate their legacies and to continue to make a difference'. We are going to have to live with the presence of more former leaders in the future.

Traditionally and unsurprisingly, the former US president has dominated the academic literature; ultimately, '[a]n ex-President of the United States occupies a unique position in our national life. As one of a select few he has held the highest position in the gift of the people, an office with which, perhaps, none other in the world is comparable for power and influence' (Sheldon, 1925: 3). Much of the literature is mostly descriptive in its accounts of the post-resignation lives of ex-presidents. For example, Asa E. Martin (1951) dedicates a chapter to each post-presidency from George

Washington to Herbert Hoover. Homer F. Cunningham (1989) takes the same approach, taking the story through to Lyndon B. Johnson. James C. Clark also has a similarly modest aim of 'tell[ing] the stories of the men who served as president and how they spent their lives after leaving the White House' but extends the coverage through to Jimmy Carter (1985: vi). Mark K. Updegrove (2006) provides similar accounts but of a more limited number of former presidents from Truman to Clinton.

Others have explored the post-presidencies of individual, high-profile ex-presidents. For example, Patricia O'Toole (2005) and Edmund Morris (2010) explore the eventful post-presidency of Theodore Roosevelt. Douglas Brinkley (1998) provides a detailed account of how Jimmy Carter, as mentioned previously, forged a successful ex-presidency out of what was regarded as an unsuccessful single-term presidency. The focus here is on the establishment and the activities of the Carter Centre, the Habitat for Humanity programme, diplomatic and peacemaking activities in Haiti and North Korea, and ultimately the award of the Nobel Peace Prize in 2002. Although Carter regards his post-presidency as a continuation of his presidency, he is more widely seen as the apotheosis of what an ex-president can achieve regardless of his time in power, in fact '[n]othing about the White House so became Carter as his having left it' (Brinkley, 1998: xviii).

As informative as these biographies may be, inevitably they tend to be descriptive. Winthrop Dudley Sheldon's work (1925) represents an early attempt to also tease out some categories from the descriptive account of 23 post-presidencies. These include: (1) quiet seclusion; (2) has-been; (3) resuming a previous profession; (4) becoming a national figure; (5) offering wisdom and advice; and (6) engaging in (or rising above) partisan politics. Marie B. Hecht (1976) provides detailed historical reviews of post-presidencies that highlight contributions to both warmaking and peacemaking, attempts to run for the presidency again, engagement in partisan politics or serving the incumbent president, as well as the financial position of an ex-president, his international status and literary contributions. John Whiteclay Chambers II (1979) traces the evolution of the ex-presidency from its rather ad hoc historical development but also the more recent interest in the role, and along the way he highlights many of the possible post-retirement lives that emerge elsewhere in the literature. Alan Evan Schenker (1982) argued for the more systematic study of former presidents and consideration of their instrumentalization as a national resource. As part of this initial study, Schenker highlighted three scales of activity for understanding the behaviour of former presidents along these spectrums: '1) orientation of personality and activities from private to public; 2) involvement in government which ranges from none at all to seeking and possibly obtaining formal positions; and 3) active pursuit of a post-presidential career vs. a more passive approach to retirement: a "summing up", if you will' (1982: 547). These scales provide a useful and parsimonious way of plotting and comparing the activities of former leaders, while at the same time avoiding simplistic labelling and pigeon-holing, and recognizing that former presidents can exist on one or more scales. Three years later, Schenker (1985) extended this preliminary analysis in the direction of a comparative study with UK prime ministers.

Max Skidmore (2004) provides detailed historical reviews of post-presidencies but places greater emphasis on the extent of post-presidential influence through the four categories of attempting to regain the presidency, seeking an alternative political office, contributing to education and public understanding, and, finally, pursuing humanitarian causes. Similarly, Leonard Benardo and Jennifer Weiss (2009) present their narratives of US post-presidencies more thematically by organizing them under the categories of the financial concerns and affairs of ex-presidents, their efforts to maintain their legacies particularly through presidential libraries, their provision of support, advice or criticism during times of conflict, supporting or campaigning on behalf of a successor, protégé or even family member, returning to some form of political office (both successfully and unsuccessfully) and/or engaging in some kind of public service or humanitarian work. Lisa Anderson (2010) highlights the options of continuing in public service (either domestically or internationally) and sometimes planning a return, campaigning on behalf of a successor or mentee, genuine retirement, humanitarian work by which ex-leaders may establish their own foundations and sometimes verge on becoming celebrity diplomats, returning to former jobs, ensuring financial security through lecture circuit or well-paid jobs in the private sector, writing memoirs to also do this in addition to security a legacy.

Further analytical work can be found in an article by Thomas F. Schaller and Thomas W. Williams who ask how influential ex-presidents can be in a postmodern world. They argue that '[t]he heightened role of electronic media, the globalization of politics, the successes of governors winning the presidency, and the increasing significance of campaign finance are just a few recent developments that combine to give postmodern ex-presidents unprecedented opportunities to influence politics and policy' (2003: 188–9). The post-presidency roles of influence include electioneering, surrogate diplomats and legitimizers, 'ex-bully pulpit' advocates, as well as a source of advice and annoyance to incumbent presidents.

Paul B. Wice (2009) provides a social-psychological understanding of US presidents' lives after retirement arranged by activities and roles such as: running for president again (with Grover Cleveland, and more recently Donald J. Trump, as the only successful examples of a return to the presidency after defeat); assuming another official role in Congress (John Quincy Adams); advisory roles to incumbent presidents, whether the advice be solicited or unsolicited (such as George Washington or Harry S. Truman);

public service (Jimmy Carter as the obvious example but also John Quincy Adams' contribution to the abolitionist movement); economic pursuits that might include writing the ubiquitous memoirs or becoming a prolific and profitable author (Theodore Roosevelt and Richard Nixon); leisure pursuits such as playing golf (Dwight Eisenhower) or parachuting (George H.W. Bush); and health concerns (Ronald Reagan's battle with Alzheimer's disease and James K. Polk's briefest of post-presidencies after contracting cholera).

One strand of the literature focuses on the connection between ex-presidents and democracy. In her brief study of the post-retirement careers of 35 former US presidents, Anderson (2010) highlights the fact that:

> democracy imposes some difficult demands. Among others, it asks its leaders to risk defeat in elections or (perhaps even more boldly) to retire from office at the end of a limited term … This is not an easy thing to do in the best of circumstances – that is, when two centuries or so of practice have made it routine. In new democracies, it is even harder … Indeed, democracy depends on the willingness of its most faithful servants to abandon their roles. (2010: 64–5)

In the case of George Washington, not only the first president but the first ex-president:

> a man relinquishing power over his countrymen and systematically giving it over to another was a radical concept when Washington did it on the eve of the nineteenth century. Just as novel was the notion of a supreme ruler in open retirement, relieved irrevocably of the power he once wielded. (Updegrove, 2006: xi)

The existence of former presidents as a symptom of democracy is all well and good, but the literature has identified a number of challenges. As regards continuing in some kind of political role, in the words of Bill Clinton, 'you lose your power but not your influence'. In his book *Mr Citizen* (1961), Harry S. Truman captured the difficult transition into retirement and supposed normality:

> [a]lthough the responsibility was no longer mine, how could I detach myself from events with which I had been so intimately associated for so long? The truth is that it was impossible for me to withdraw myself from the world and its activities, as former Presidents are supposed to do. (Truman, 1961: 19–20)

He also expressed his frustrations with his successor: 'it was most trying for me to restrain myself from making the comments I wanted to make when the President [Eisenhower] took certain actions and made certain statements' (1961: 95). The polar opposite can be seen in Woodrow Wilson, who did little in his few years as a former president and was conscious of this: 'I am showing President Harding how an ex-President should behave' (Bailey, 1978: 118). Equally, on a practical level, *Forbes* magazine even published a list of ten rules for former presidents by President George H.W. Bush, including advice that can be summarized as: disappear from public view as quickly as possible, try not to shape history and stay out of the way (Bush, 2000).

However, this is easier said than done as the existence of former presidents cannot be denied, and their activities in retirement inevitably reflect upon the office of president, if not the individual incumbent. In his exploration of presidential greatness, achievements and reputations, Thomas A. Bailey (1978: 114–26) dedicated a brief chapter to 'the post-presidential glow' and how their activities ranging from continuing or rejecting political lives through to publishing their memoirs may influence a presidential reputation either positively or negatively. Thus, in 1958 the Former Presidents' Act allowed ex-presidents to draw a pension. The goal was to prevent ex-presidents falling into penury and preserve the dignity of the post by providing some support. Three years previously in 1955, the Presidential Libraries Act provided the basis for the creation of a series of libraries that would provide important historical materials on specific administrations but also burnish the reputation of individual presidents (Hufbauer, 2005).

One practical question that a strand of the literature has explored is how to make the most of ex-presidents' experience and expertise as 'they are typically the only individuals who might be able to share with the incumbent a full appreciation of the tremendous, often oppressive, burdens that must be shouldered' (Schenker, 1985: 499). In this vein, Stephen W. Stathis (1983) explored the occasions upon which former US presidents have chosen to appear before Congressional committees and provide 'unique insights ... both worthwhile and meaningful' (1983: 476). Sheldon (1925: 3–4) pondered the best way in which the experience of ex-presidents could be harnessed, citing proposals to give them a seat in the Senate or an advisory role. Truman certainly regarded them as an important resource and supported something similar to the UK's Privy Council to provide informed advice to the incumbent administration based on experience of former leaders (1961: 96). Clinton suggested the creation of 'a council of sorts for active ex-presidents to encourage national discussion regarding the serious issues of the day' (Skidmore, 2004: 172). Updegrove (2006: xvii) argued in colourful terms that the regular and often supportive gatherings of presidents have served to forge close links among them resulting in the 'world's most exclusive trade union'. However, the following question was posed in an essay by Alexander Hamilton published in 1787–88 as part of a series of essays promoting the Constitution and federal government:

> Would it promote the peace of the community or the stability of the government to have half a dozen men who had had credit enough to be raised to the seat of the supreme magistracy, wandering among the people like discontented ghosts, and sighing for a place which they were destined never more to possess? (Hamilton, Madison and Jay, 1948: 370–1)

Hecht has argued similarly that:

> [i]n the Senate, with no specific constituency and no vote, he would be a tolerated anomaly. Any artificial position that would be created for the retired chief executive would upset the careful constitutional balance and cause awkwardness and, possibly, embarrassment to the elected President. (1976: 311–2)

This is a question that inevitably emerges outside of the US. For example, in France, Article 56 of the Constitution of the Fifth Republic states that former presidents of the republic shall be *ex officio* life members of the Constitutional Council. Article 59 of the Italian Republic's Constitution explains that former presidents are senators by right and for life unless they renounce the office. Similarly, ex-presidents in Burundi were appointed to the Senate for life until the practice was revised in 2018. As regards commercial activities, Wong (2002) has noted that former leaders in the UK also have to abide by the Ministerial Code for two years after leaving office and seek advice on their taking up of any appointments, although they are free to ignore this advice with impunity. In both the US and France, former leaders are not limited by law in their commercial undertakings but rather by convention, as well as media and public attention.

The literature beyond the US has also taken up some of the categories highlighted previously and sought to apply them. In the case of the UK, in his manual of advice to the ambitious statesman, originally published in 1836, Henry Taylor dedicated a chapter to being out of office and the opportunities this period afforded with one eye on returning to power:

> Let him consider, therefore, what are the defects of knowledge which have been most sensibly felt by him when in office, and which he had then no time or opportunity to supply; and let this be his season of such preparation as shall enable him to resume office at a future time with more ample resources. (1957: 127–8)

Taylor also argued that continued influence even during retirement was nothing new:

> it will very often happen in this country that a leading statesman's loss of office is attended with but little loss of political importance. Even for the activity which is directed to immediate effects he may have no inconsiderable scope in the conduct of a parliamentary opposition; and he will continue to cover a space in the public mind proportioned to the reputation which he has acquired. (Taylor, 1957: 128–9)

Fast-forward to the current millennium and a number of studies have appeared on the subject of former British prime ministers from Walpole onwards. In particular, Theakston's work (2006; 2010) is meticulously researched and has served to establish a sub-field of research on former prime ministers. Although he acknowledges that '[r]eviewing the experience of former prime ministers in the twentieth century suggests little in the way of a common pattern' (2006: 448), in his 2006 article Theakston uses the labels of 'in government office after being prime minister' by serving as a minister in another prime minister's cabinet; 'honours' including serving in the House of Lords; 'setting the record straight' by putting pen to paper; 'money matters' or securing financial solvency in their retirement; and 'outlive the bastards' by recovering from the exigencies of the position, attending to health and ageing issues, and not succumbing to illness for as long as possible.

These categories are slightly adapted in Theakston (2010) but by citing Belenky (1999) the roles of ex-presidents are expanded upon:

> 1) still ambitious (who long for a comeback); 2) exhausted volcanoes (who quietly retire); 3) political dabblers (who give advice, campaign and fund-raise for their party); 4) first citizens (who engage in dignified and non-partisan public service); 5) embracers of a cause (usually a big humanitarian and/or global 'cause'; and 6) seekers of vindication (those aiming to reverse history's likely negative verdict on them). (2010: 226)

The edited volume by Theakston and de Vries (2012b) expands the country-specific analysis by building on the US (Morgan, 2012) and looking at the UK (Theakston, 2012) but also other democracies including Canada (Azzi, 2012), Australia (Stangio, 2012), Germany (Paterson, 2012), France (Bell, 2012), Ireland (O'Malley, 2012), the Netherlands (de Vries, 't Hart and Onstein, 2012), Belgium (De Winter and Rezsöhazy, 2012) and Israel (Korn, 2012). This collection of essays represents a welcome extension of the focus beyond the US and UK. It also provides a template to explore both beyond Europe, on the one hand, and the understandable focus on democracies, on the other hand.

The case of African states embraces both aspects but represents an extreme example 'due to the indisputable fact that, unless one is talking of a metaphysical after-life, in nine cases out of ten it is a rhetorical question; there was no Afterwards' (Kirk-Greene, 1991: 183). However, more recently, Southall and Melber have described the presence of former heads of state in the countries they once governed as 'an increasingly common phenomenon' (2006: xv). Their edited volume focuses attention on the way in which political systems and the manner of leaving office shape outcomes so that in a presidential system leaders tend to withdraw from public attention whereas in parliamentary systems leaders seek to regain power. Across Africa, where many of the regimes have made the transition from authoritarianism to democracy, the added difficulty exists of trying to balance the desire for justice with the need for stability. They conclude that:

> First, the continuing engagement of former presidents in day-to-day politics, even if constitutional, tends to provoke conflict with new regimes and may well provoke an autocratic response which may test the limits of tolerance in a new democracy. Second, the better their record in office, the more likely presidents are to facilitate a relatively easy transition from one government to another and to play a constructive post-presidential role domestically and internationally. Finally, it is almost inevitable that any difficult transition, involving the potential or actual standing down of an authoritarian and corrupt dictator, will inform construction of some form of what Jennifer Widner refers to as a 'reform bargain'. Or, to put this in a more popular parlance, the crafting of stable democracies will usually require that democrats have to hold their noses and make important concessions protective of incumbent power-holders if they wish to fashion a political transition and subsequently consolidate democracy. (2006: xviii)

Shifting the focus to Asia, the tradition in China was similar in that former leaders had no afterlife to speak of. However, this was challenged as various restrictions and limitations on the length of service were introduced in the 1980s resulting in an uptick in the number of former leaders:

> Before they go to meet their Marx, most are keen both to continue exerting political influence and to go on protesting the (business or less often political) interests of family members, along with their vast networks of protégés ... When former leaders have kept a hand in things, they have usually done so from behind the scenes. Most maintain offices and large staffs. They get copies of official documents and are quietly consulted on important matters – not least on the promotion of future leaders. (*The Economist*, 2011a)

Zhu Rongji as a former prime minister broke this mould by publicly criticizing the incumbent regime both in print and through speeches. Former president Jiang Zemin's attendance at the 100th anniversary of the 1911 Revolution and his proximity to Hu Jintao, the incumbent president, led some China watchers to conclude that he was attempting to have some input into the post-Hu transition of power (*The Economist*, 2011b). In 2018, Xi Jinping abolished limitations on the president's length of service so we can expect to see fewer former leaders as Xi will serve as 'president-for-life'.

In Singapore, Lee Kuan Yew went through various stages of retirement. He served as prime minister until 1990 after which he still sat on the cabinet as senior minister, and in 2004 he was appointed as minister mentor in his son's cabinet. He continued to play a number of roles: a power broker unable to let go of power, '[f]or decades he has been a loose cannon in Singapore's foreign relations with a bad habit of offending neighbours like Indonesia, Malaysia, Thailand and the Philippines' (Barr, 2011). By contrast, and at the same time, he served as a goodwill ambassador in the region defusing tensions. On 14 May 2011, he announced his final retirement, although the reaction of some was incredulous: 'He will surely continue speechifying from the backbenches, as he did in the previous parliament, on almost every topic under the sun. He will intervene in public debates and write more books, all in his quest to keep Singapore on the straight and narrow' (*The Economist*, 2011c).

Cutting across the national borders, several examples exist of former leaders assuming a diplomatic role and exerting informal soft power on the international level (Cooper, 2015). For example, the Vail Group was founded in 1982 and chaired by Gerald Ford until his death in 2006 to encourage informal discussion among government and business representatives on the pressing issues of the day (Morgan, 2012: 24). Former German chancellor Gerhard Schmidt flippantly referred to it as 'a conspiracy of former world leaders against present world leaders. But thank God none of us has the power to do anything anymore' (Ford, 1990: 173, cited in Theakston, 2006: 448). Club de Madrid was established in 2001 and describes itself as the 'largest forum of democratic former presidents and prime ministers', addressing 'issues of global concern and provid[ing] peer to peer counsel, strategic support and technical advice to leaders and institutions working to further democratic development', offering 'today's leaders an unequalled body of knowledge and political leadership' (Club de Madrid 2024). Although not exclusively made up of former leaders, the Elders was established by Nelson Mandela in 2007 to provide 'independent moral voices for peace and ethical leadership' based on the 'individual and collective wisdom' of a group dominated by former presidents and prime ministers (The Elders, 2024). These groups function on the basis that ex-leaders can exhibit authority and legitimacy as peers with experience, even if they are retired. As regards their impact, Anderson argues that:

> The increasing density of the global relationships of national leaders and the proliferation of international roles and responsibilities suited to the dignity of officeholders at the pinnacle of national governments are reshaping the opportunities to which such officeholders will be responding. This international web of ties and opportunities, though it is not without the potential for abuse, will increasingly make it easier for elected leaders to play by the perverse rules of democratic politics—'to accept political defeat: to leave office upon losing an election, to follow rules even when they work against one's own interest'. (2010: 76–7)

Bringing the focus to the case of Japanese prime ministers and their afterlives, the literature has been thin. Although former prime ministers have been a constant feature of Japan's modern political history and often significant figures in their own right, Dobson and Rose's article (2019) represents the first attempt to explore the afterlives of Japanese prime ministers in an academic and systematic way. Their starting point was to review the existing literature and apply it to Japan for the first time. Dobson and Rose also highlighted three additional categories that were relevant to their initial exploration of Japanese ex-prime ministers: 'acolytes and protégés', who feel indebted to a former leader and mentor and continue to burnish his reputation; 'family affair', in an attempt to capture the generational nature of Japanese politics; and 'celebrity', which can be leveraged as a form of soft power or an end in and of itself (Dobson and Rose, 2019: 133–6).

Tsuda (2023) has engaged with Dobson and Rose's work by asking for clarity and further delineation on some of the categories employed, such as 'still ambitious' and 'first citizen'. He also seeks to highlight Japan-specific categories, specifically around the importance of factions (*habatsu*), to be discussed later, and factional lineage beyond the sideways reference that Dobson and Rose make by highlighting 'acolytes and protégés'. Similarly, these categories can be further developed by taking up Tsuda's call for comparison with other Asian countries, rather than relying solely on the Western-centric academic literature, in order to tease out the importance of Confucianism as manifested in seniority, patriarchy and patron–client relations.

Tsuda adds further to the typology in fascinating detail by focusing on the case of Satō Eisaku. Despite a short-lived post-premiership suggesting that Satō was an Exhausted Volcano, especially in contrast to his longevity in office, Tsuda argues convincingly that he provided political stability in the three years between stepping down as prime minister in July 1972 and his death in June 1975, a period of instability captured by the normalization of relations with the People's Republic of China (PRC), the 1973 Oil Shock and the divisive premiership of Tanaka Kakuei. The role of an 'anchor point' during times of upheaval and crisis is redolent of the monarchy in the UK and is a categorization that can be added to the earlier list.

In summary, the extant literature – in particular Belenky (1999), Theakston (2010), Dobson and Rose (2019), and Tsuda (2023) – coalesces around ten categories. These ten categories will provide both a structure and analytical focus for the empirical chapters and are understood as follows.

First, the category of Still Ambitious captures a politician who longs for some form of official political office. This might include becoming prime minister again, returning to cabinet in a ministerial role or in opposition. This category could apply to both successful and unsuccessful returns to power, whether desired or reluctant. The official political office in question could be at the national or international level through multilateral organizations. The level of ambition may also vary from returning to the top job at one end of the spectrum and seeking to influence through official political channels as a backbencher at the other end. The emphasis here is on official roles and public channels.

Second, Exhausted Volcanoes captures departure and disengagement from political life. This may be sudden or terminal as a result of ill health, exhaustion or personal temperament. It may also manifest within an official role such as a continued parliamentary position. However, the former leader is not particularly ambitious and is effectively seeing out their days.

Third, a Political Dabbler is still personally ambitious and a political animal by nature but operates in the background rather than through official public channels, even if they occupy a formal political office. The Japanese phrase *kuromaku* (literally, black curtain) conjures up the image of a puppet master and captures the space in which this kind of former leader is most comfortable operating. Their dabbling could be an end in and of itself or it could be a kingmaking role to maintain some continued influence. It could even be to set the scene for an official return to power, thereby connecting with the first category. As the following chapters will demonstrate, this category is salient in Japanese politics due to the structural role of factions. Again, the extent to which former leaders can effectively play this role will vary widely for a range of reasons.

Fourth, former leaders can establish themselves as First Citizens or elder statesmen with a general sense of duty not focused on any single cause with which they wish to be closely associated. They will seek to appear non-partisan, sitting above day-to-day political concerns. The Japanese term *genrō* captures this group of elder statesmen – many of whom, but not all, were prime ministers – who continued to provide advice and guidance to the Emperor in the latter half of the 19th century and first half of the 20th century. This does raise the question of agency in that not all former leaders can become an elder statesman. It is a category that some former leaders might be born to (as a result of family connections or celebrity status, to be discussed later) or have thrust upon them by circumstances, rather than attained.

Fifth, Embracers of a Cause devote their energies and resources to a specific issue or cluster of inter-related concerns. What distinguishes this from the previous category is the specificity of the cause. Although examples like Carter emphasize the humanitarian nature of the cause in question, it need not always be a 'good' cause. Embracing a cause could also be a first step towards eventually becoming a First Citizen or elder statesman.

Sixth, Seekers of Vindication seek to present their side of the story of their time in power, possibly responding to a need to put the record straight and reestablish a tarnished reputation at the point of resignation. Writing memoirs is one means of doing this that has proved popular across time and space. These efforts might seek to maintain or polish an existing reputation as well as restore a damaged one. This raises a challenging question around the point at which a Seeker of Vindication can be reassured that they have been successful.

Seventh, some former leaders have nurtured Acolytes and Protégés on a level that is more personal and less structural than through factions. This can be motivated by several reasons mentioned previously including a desire on the part of a former leader to ensure a perceived line of succession, a form of political dabbling or burnishing a reputation.

Eighth, generational politics is a feature of many political systems but one that has been highlighted as particularly prevalent in Japan alongside the role of factions. This provides former leaders with an opportunity for leveraging Family Affairs. This can be associated with an element of celebrity (mentioned later) as seen in the Kennedy political dynasty, with which the Hatoyama family in Japan has been compared. It can also be relatively banal. In the Japanese case, family connections proliferate extensively and can often manifest publicly in the passing on of a constituency from one generation to the next. Either way, the effect is that politics is seen as a family business enabled by the former prime minister.

Ninth, having once occupied the top job imbues an individual with a degree of celebrity and the opportunity to leverage it. This category of Celebrity has become more of an option over recent years with the proliferation of social media and reality TV. This could be a soft power means to a political end or an end in and of itself as an alternative career opens up.

Finally, an Anchor Point provides a sense of continuity and security. This role is often, but not always, required at a tumultuous moment in a nation's history. In some countries, this role will be played by the head of state and requires a high degree of gravitas, legitimacy and neutrality. For example, Queen Elizabeth II during a series of postwar crises from Suez to Brexit.

Tsuda (2023) explains how Satō assumed this role, but not all former leaders will have the required skills set or reputation to play this role effectively.

Informal politics and the Japanese prime minister

This literature on former leaders, outlined previously, is part of a wider interest over the last couple of decades in the informal aspects of politics and power. Pike (2000: 281) defines informal politics as 'interpersonal activities stemming from a tacitly accepted, but enunciated, matrix of political attitudes existing outside the framework of legal government, constitutions, bureaucratic constructs and similar institutions'. In the same book, Dittmer (2000: 292) argues that 'informal politics consists of *the use of non-legitimate means* (albeit not necessarily illegal) *to pursue public ends* [original stress]'. Dittmer, Fukui and Lee (2000) provide numerous examples of this in their edited volume related to how informal politics operates in East Asia. For example, Fukui and Fukai's chapter (2000) explores the informal aspects of electoral politics in Japan. Lee (2000) explores leadership succession in post-Mao China.

Similar to informal politics, but more a subset thereof, 'marginal diplomacy' has been highlighted as 'the performance of quasi-diplomatic functions of intelligence, promotion, and negotiation in the national interest by persons lacking the status of diplomatic representatives, and hence the degree of legal privilege and immunity accorded to officially accredited diplomatic agents' (Johnston, 1971: 470). Johnston pays particular attention to the ways in which China and Japan have utilized marginal diplomacy and non-state, non-traditional and private actors through which to conduct their immediate post-World War Two relations.

Alongside establishing definitions, exploring spaces of activity and outlining the way in which informal politics or marginal diplomacy are conducted, much of this literature focuses on the question of who is doing informal politics. Possibly one of the most salient examples of this recent turn in the literature is 'celebrity diplomacy'. In a book-length treatment, Cooper has shed light on the rise of 'celebrity diplomats' such as Angelina Jolie, Bono and Bill Gates, quite rightly claiming that '[s]uch a phenomenon cries out for conceptual clarification as well as extended analytical treatment. Teasing out the motivations and modes of operation of this emerging cohort of diplomats is important, but so is the task of finding out exactly who these new celebrity diplomats are' (2008: 1).

Finding out who they are is much less of a pressing issue in the case of former leaders. They need to have served in office making them much more readily identifiable. Furthermore, Cooper suggests that 'everybody has the potential to be an authentic diplomat' (2008: 2), but this does not apply to the same extent in the case of former prime ministers who have to negotiate higher barriers as a pre-condition to achieving their status. Moreover, former leaders will have received training and often operate in private, traditional diplomatic spheres, whereas celebrity diplomats have received no or little training and operate in public, non-traditional diplomacy. Nevertheless, there are many similarities as both former leaders and celebrity diplomats cannot claim to speak for a constituency; they have not been elected and suffer a considerable legitimacy gap that can often only be filled with their own personal moral capital rather than the institutional legitimacy of their positions (Cooper, 2008; 't Hart and Tindall, 2009).

Similar aspects emerge from the gendered work of Domett (2005) and Dobson (2012a) on another group of informal actors – political spouses and first ladies – particularly in their diplomatic roles. In addition to spouses, widows, sisters, daughters and granddaughters have also received attention as part of a growing trend of political dynasties maintaining a grip on the reins of power. This can be seen in examples such as Yingluck Shinawatra in Thailand, Marine Le Pen in France, Keiko Fujimori in Peru and Park Geun-hye in South Korea. Their activities suggest that '[f]amily name confers brand recognition, useful contacts and financial contributions – all of which are vital in democracies, and become more so as retail politics become more important ... [In addition], daughters seem to embody their male relatives' agenda – but with the rough edges planed away' (*The Economist*, 2011d).

So, former leaders, political spouses and families as well as celebrity diplomats have all received more academic and popular attention recently as there is a shared added value in understanding their roles. They each represent an 'emergent phenomenon that straddles "democracy's edges"' ('t Hart and Tindall, 2009: 257).

It might seem strange at this point in the discussion to return to the Japanese prime minister as he clearly occupies an official position, which is vested with a considerable amount of formal power. First and foremost, the Japanese Constitution confirms the central and influential position of the prime minister in the decision-making processes of Japanese domestic and foreign policies. For example, Article 66 states that the prime minister will head the cabinet; Article 68 gives him the power to appoint and remove ministers; Article 72 states that 'representing the Cabinet, [he] submits bills, reports on general national affairs and foreign relations to the Diet and exercises control and supervision over various administrative branches'; Article 74 requires the counter-signature of the prime minister on all laws and cabinet orders; finally, Article 75 protects serving ministers from legal action without the consent of the prime minister (e-Gov, 1946). In addition, Article 7 of Japan's Self-Defence Forces Law identifies the prime minister, representing the Cabinet, as the commander-in-chief of Japan's Self-Defence Forces (SDF); and Articles 76 and 78 give him the legal right to dispatch the SDF in a range of scenarios (e-Gov, 1954).

Moreover, the more recent literature on the Japanese prime minister has argued for a re-evaluation of his formal top-down role in decision-making. Shinoda (2007) highlighted the reforms that took place in the *kantei* (the prime minister's official residence that embraces members of the Cabinet Secretariat and the prime minister) at the end of 1990s and beginning of 2000s. These reforms created more robust support mechanisms, particularly in addressing the meagre resources and enhancing the support given by the Cabinet Secretariat to the prime minister and, as a result, the independent leadership role of the *kantei* in policy making, resulting in a top-down decision-making process in contrast to the previous bottom-up process. In short, Shinoda argued that 'the *kantei* has become Japan's new policy center in defense and foreign affairs' (2007: 15). Around the same time, Krauss and Nyblade (2005) highlighted the salience of a longer-standing trend of presidentialization of Japanese politics and the rise of personalized government whereby then-prime minister Koizumi Junichirō could appeal directly to the people, bypassing his own party and the bureaucracy. Although Koizumi was not the first prime minister to do this, his skilful handling of the media and the extent to which he utilized this resource was new. In short, the public face of the prime minister has steadily increased in importance over the last three decades. In addition, Krauss and Nyblade (2005) highlighted the impact of electoral reform whereby voters began to consider the party rather than the candidate bringing the image of the prime minister into play. Another effect of the reform was the rise of the floating voter, which created a space for the prime-ministerial leadership to fill in an attempt to appeal to this influential new group whose influence was obvious in the 2005 and 2009 elections although with different outcomes.

Others have also sought to identify examples and sources of prime ministerial leadership whereby the prime minister used councils, commissions and policy advisors to counter the bureaucracy and influence the policy-making process (Kabashima and Steel, 2010: 24). Similarly, Shimizu Masato (2005, cited in Kabashima and Steel, 2010: 21) traced the shift towards cabinet leadership with a strong prime minister. The resources available to the prime minister and the perceived importance of his role has increased over the years: '[n]ow the Japanese focus on the position to a degree not seen before, and evaluate the prime minister critically as the leaders of his party and of Japan' (Krauss and Nyblade, 2005: 368).

Despite a short-lived period in office from 2006 to 2007 that was widely regarded as a failure, Abe's return to power in December 2012 accelerated these developments and centralized decision-making authority within the *kantei*, resulting in the dominant position of the 'prime ministerial executive' and making his second term notably different from the first both in terms of substance as well as length of tenure (Burrett, 2017; Mulgan, 2018). As part of this process, for example, he established a US-style National Security

Council in the Prime Minister's Office in December 2013, which increased the prime minister's influence over defence and security issues. He also established structures and processes with the *kantei* to control ministers and senior bureaucrats more closely than had been the case previously and introduce robust personnel selection (Harris, 2020: 209–25). It has been argued that this set of wider reforms and the resulting stability he brought to Japanese politics represent his lasting legacy more than any other aspect of his time in office (Dobson, 2019).

However, these are recent developments, and for the most part the Japanese prime minister has been regarded as a marginal, transient and powerless figure in comparison to his international peers. Prime Minister Takeshita Noboru described his own role as 'not to pull people along, it is to get the consensus of the people' (Hayao, 1993: 7). Prime Minister Tanaka when serving as finance minister in December 1962 captured the nature of Japanese politics when he outlined to his private secretary and chief of staff various strategies for eliminating enemies with the ultimate goal that '[y]ou will then find a large group of open-minded people who will be somewhat favourably disposed to you. There arises the way that leads you up to the highest position' (Hayasaka, 1994: xv). Thus, rather than a capable, uncompromising leader providing vision (qualities that might antagonize, rather than appeal), the Japanese prime minister has been a compromise figure who avoids alienating too many people and has some appeal across a wide spectrum. Henry Kissinger went further, describing the Japanese prime minister as 'the custodian of the national consensus, not the creator of it' (quoted in Pyle, 1987: 245).

The academic literature on Japanese prime ministers mirrors these views of practitioners by traditionally portraying them as weak, short-lived, lacking in resources and ultimately occupying a less influential position than in other countries. Ian Neary points to cultural aspects and 'the often-cited tendency of Japanese leaders to avoid taking on an up-front role preferring to exercise power by manipulating events from behind the scenes' (1996: 11). Edström (1996) has explored the ability of Japanese prime ministers to exert leadership in foreign policy and concluded that a number of constraints exist that limit their agency. Descriptions emerge such as 'reactive', 'passive' and 'anonymous'. Fukai reviews the literature that stresses the leadership deficit among Japanese prime ministers and their tendency to seek compromise and defer to followers rather than shape the debate and policy agendas. She concludes that, '[t]he one-party dominant system has led to the institutionalization of the intra-LDP appointment and promotion practices based on seniority and factional balance rather than ability of expertise. This system has tended to breed mediocre leaders and led to a situation similar to a crisis of leadership' (Fukai, 1999: 179). Ultimately, the Japanese prime minister was traditionally regarded as a consensus builder who ultimately follows rather than leads.

Karel van Wolferen (1989) famously described the Japanese political system as having no point at which the buck stops, rather the buck continued to circulate in the absence of a centre. Arthur Stockwin similarly wrote that '[t]he view exists that in Japan it does not really matter who happens to be prime minister at a particular time because the whole of Japan works as a kind of "system" that is essentially without leadership' (1991: 90). In the absence of accountable central leadership, it was assumed that the bureaucracy was exerting decisive influence and that the role of the prime minister was to ratify legislation drafted by them or within the governing party (Richardson, 1997). The revolving door of prime ministers that followed the resignation of Prime Minister Koizumi in September 2006 reinforced the view that prime ministerial leadership was absent in Japan, amusingly captured by Lula da Silva's quip quoted in Chapter 1. Similarly, governor of Tokyo since 2016, and former LDP environment and defence minister, Koike Yuriko stressed the disposable nature of the office by claiming that 'Japanese prime ministers are just like tissue paper' (*The Economist*, 2011e). At the time of writing, Japan has experienced 65 prime ministers. This averages out in the postwar period as an average lifespan in office of around two years. This high turnover rate of Japanese prime ministers has proved to be problematic in a number of ways with the result that 'the [Japanese] prime minister was merely the representative of a faction in a system that placed the greatest emphasis on consensus formation and found the idea of the political leader as a figure able to take important decisions without prior agreement unacceptable' (Armstrong, 1996: 43).

In short, the extant literature on the position of the prime minister has traditionally emphasized his marginal position as a product of compromise while Japan was run by a stable political elite dubbed the 'iron triangle' or Japan Inc., formed of the LDP, the bureaucracy and big business.

Despite (and possibly because of) these constraints, the Japanese prime minister exerted influence in informal and creative ways, possibly more so than any of his counterparts across the democratic world. For some time, Hayao Kenji's 1993 *The Japanese Prime Minister and Public Policy* was the main treatment of the position of prime minister in Japanese politics and decision-making processes. He noted that Japan 'has no equivalent of such leaders as Franklin Roosevelt, Charles de Gaulle or Mao Zedong' (p 4). However, motivated by the questions of which issues Japan's prime ministers have been most involved in and how they have influenced the way in which these issues are handled and resolved, Hayao argued that there were three archetypes of the Japanese prime minister (technocratic leader, reactive leader and political leader), and although the position of the prime minister in Japanese politics may appear weaker in comparison to his peers, in fact he could be seen to be in a stronger position to influence issues, sometimes decisively. Hayao also demonstrated how individual prime ministers tend to be able to exert their influence, or moral authority, on at least one 'trophy' issue, whether it be the normalization of relations with the Soviet Union by Hatoyama or the reversion of Okinawa to Japan for Satō Eisaku.

Shinoda Tomohito highlighted four distinct leadership styles among Japanese prime ministers, the first three of which demonstrate his ability to utilize informal spaces and mechanisms to exert influence: (1) the political insider, typified by Takeshita who had well-established personal links with various political actors; (2) the grandstander, typified by Nakasone, who sought to mobilize sources of power outside of the political world, particularly public support. This example applies equally to Koizumi; (3) the kamikaze fighter, who sacrifices himself to achieve his objective, such as Hatoyama Ichirō and Kishi Nobusuke; and (4) the peace lover, typified by Suzuki Zenkō and Kaifu Toshiki, whose efforts to satisfy everyone results in failure (Shinoda, 2000: 205–11). Richard Samuels demonstrated in his case study of administrative reform how 'powerful individuals manipulate constraints in creative ways, tipping the balance of historical inertia in directions of their choosing – even in Japan' (2003: 1). He highlighted two examples in particular: a businessman – Dokō Toshio – and a prime minister – Nakasone. Takayasu Kensuke (2001; 2009) similarly argued that prime ministers could navigate obstacles by utilizing other resources and channels of influence beyond the officially sanctioned sources of power to play a key part. Domestically, this can be seen in the establishment of ad hoc study groups that bring outside experts from business or academia into government to promote a specific issue, as exemplified by Ōhira and Hosokowa. Internationally, the rise of informal summitry as typified by the Group of 7 (G7) and Group of 20 (G20) have provided proactive leaders with a space and opportunity to promote a range of initiatives (Dobson, 2004; Hook et al, 2011). Historically, Tsuda (2023: 5) captures the inherent role of informality in Japanese politics:

> From the 'rule of the cloistered ex-emperor' (*insei*) in the medieval period, to the advisors to the emperor in the Meiji and Taishō periods, Japanese history demonstrates that retiring or rejecting rigid institutional roles can at times liberate, rather than constrain, the hands of top power brokers. More broadly, the significance of elder statesmen suggests the richness and complexity of Japan's universe of informal politics, which has included fixers (*kuromaku*), criminal syndicates, secret societies, and other elusive pressure groups.

At this point, attention turns to some of the spaces and mechanisms that represent structural aspects of Japanese politics that are important in their own right but will also appear in the chapters that follow. First and foremost, as already mentioned earlier and in the previous chapter, the focus returns to factions. The tendency to group around powerful individuals exists in many, if not most, political systems but for a long time Japan represented the *ne plus ultra* of factional politics. Factions are parties within a party, usually associated with, but not particular to, the long-ruling LDP. Although their influence over members has waned over the last couple of decades, they are the mechanism by which support is garnered in return for the funds required to run for election and maintain a political presence. As mentioned previously, the need to balance between the interests of the various factions has been cited as one factor limiting the Japanese prime ministers' powers of patronage, inhibiting the emergence of strong leaders and resulting in mediocrity. This is exemplified by Kaifu, regarded as a compromise candidate not belonging to any of the main factions but beholden to them for his position. Nevertheless, several prime ministers have been key factional leaders or members. As seen in the vignette at the beginning of the previous chapter, there are several examples of leaders who have exerted a strong influence within their factions both in and out of power as prime minister. The factional nature of Japanese politics has provided a space in which mentoring across generations of politicians can take place, resulting in relationships of dependence that have been dubbed 'Acolytes and Protégés' previously. This is a complicated web of connections but can be captured in the nickname of 'Tanakasone' that demonstrates the relationship between Nakasone and his mentor Tanaka and the former's dependence on the latter for support in becoming prime minister.

At the same time, dynastic or hereditary politics is the second important feature of Japanese politics that will be relevant to the chapters that follow (Asako et al, 2015; Smith, 2018). Once again, this exists in several political systems across the world, for example the Bush family in the US and Le Pen family in France, and, once again, it is taken to an extreme in the Japanese case with relatively high numbers of second-, third-, fourth- and even fifth-generation politicians. Abe is one of the most prominent and oft-cited examples. His father, Abe Shintarō, was a long-serving Diet member who occupied several ministerial posts, his paternal grandfather, Abe Kan, also served as a Diet member, and his maternal grandfather, Kishi Nobuske, served as prime minister, as did his great-uncle Satō Eisaku (Harris, 2020). Other high-profile examples include the Hatoyama family, who were dubbed the Kennedys of Japan as mentioned previously, and Koizumi Junichirō and his son Shinjirō, long thought of as a successor to his father as prime minister. However, it is not so much the celebrity political families that capture the attention, it is rather the extent of dynastic politics in Japan that places it at the extreme end of the scale, comparatively (Smith, 2018). This important aspect of Japanese politics can shape ambitions, advantages, expectations, opportunities, resources and behaviours both personally and politically. As regards the top job, ten of Japan's 25 LDP prime ministers between 1955 and 1993, and nine of the 15 (LDP and non-LDP) prime ministers since 1993 have hailed from political dynasties (four with fathers or grandfathers who were previous prime ministers). As will be seen in the chapters that follow, dynastic politics can be an important aspect of a prime minister's experience both in and out of power.

The Japanese prime minister has continued to operate in these spaces and with these mechanisms in mind alongside the increased centralization of his role. Thus, he has to balance both the formal and informal sources of power. As the following chapters will demonstrate, these spaces, mechanisms and sources of power will often shape his political afterlife.

Summary

There are two distinct bodies of literature on the role of the Japanese prime minister. The traditional literature and, to a degree, popular first impressions have regarded him for the most part as a transient, marginal and, ultimately, powerless figure. The more recent literature does not deny this historic position of irrelevance but has argued that he now plays a more decisive role because of institutional reforms and the increased importance of political optics. In short, once regarded as largely irrelevant, the prime minister is firmly back on the radar of observers of Japanese politics.

Regardless of one's position in these debates on the role of the prime minister, the objective of this book – exploring his post-premiership – can be justified. On the one hand, from the viewpoint of the camp that would regard him as weak, it would be intuitive to expect former Japanese prime ministers to be similarly disempowered, especially considering their transient term of office. However, the informal nature of Japanese politics and some of its idiosyncrasies are enabling factors that allow an afterlife for former prime ministers in Japan and need to be acknowledged and brought into our understanding of the wider literature on former leaders. On the other hand, if we accept the recent increase in the profile and resources of the Japanese prime minister, asking the question of what he does after stepping down and exploring how he continues to exert influence despite losing power are valid fields of inquiry. As the literature reviewed previously makes clear, this is the case with former leaders in most countries. In short, whether he matters or not in power, what he does after losing it matters. At the end of the day, former prime ministers are still a member of an exclusive group. Within this group, some disappear from the spotlight completely to spend time with their families or pursue a pastime, some refuse to be written off and harbour ambitions of returning (successfully or unsuccessfully) to the highest position, some persist in interfering in or undermining their successors' affairs (often if they have not left office willingly), whereas some go about building their legacies and burnishing their reputations in various ways. Some exert indirect influence by retreating into the shadows or assuming the position of elder statesmen with domestic and/or international profiles. Although at first blush no discernible patterns may be evident, the following three empirical chapters and concluding analytic chapter will provide a systematic attempt based on the ten categories outlined previously to explore the roles, influence and power of former prime ministers.

3

Former Japanese Prime Ministers, the Meiji Period to World War Two

Overview

This first empirical chapter provides the historical context behind the post-World War Two (WW2) focus of Chapters 4 and 5 by exploring the Meiji, Taishō and early Shōwa periods. This is admittedly a very broad period that covers several pivotal events and developments in Japan's modern political history: from the Meiji Restoration in 1868, rapid modernization, colonialism and imperialism, transcendental governments sitting above party politics, experimentation (not always successful) with democracy, political scandals and economic recession, the shift towards militarism and authoritarianism, rivalry between the army and navy, war and, ultimately, defeat.

This is reflected in the profiles of the 29 prime ministers who served during this period from the leading lights of the Meiji Restoration, who dominated Japanese modern political development both as individuals and through their protégés, via advocates of democracy to the military leaders that dominated to the end of WW2. The specific prime ministers covered in this chapter are outlined in Table 3.1. In order to make this number manageable, the focus of this chapter is firmly on those who served as prime minister and will not include interim or caretaker prime ministers, such as Sanjō Sanetomi, the only statesman to occupy the position of Lord Keeper of the Privy Seal and prime minister concurrently, or Foreign Minister Uchida Kōsai, who served twice as an interim prime minister after the assassination of Hara in 1921 and the death of Katō Tomosaburō in 1923. However, it will include ex-prime ministers who served as acting prime ministers, such as Kuroda and Takahashi, as this activity was part of their afterlives.

One development, core to the theme of this book and specific to the focus of this chapter, is that the position of prime minister was established by imperial decree on 22 December 1885: '[f]or the first time, a Prime Minister was responsible to the Emperor for the administration of the entire country; moreover, all department ministers were subject to his direct supervision and were at the same time accountable to him for all the affairs of their respective departments' (Beckmann, 1957: 75–6). Itō, Japan's first prime minister, regarded the cabinet as 'the most important political body in the state and the Prime Minister the most powerful single figure' (Beckmann, 1957: 76).

However, there are several caveats that are specific to this era which justify a dedicated historical chapter rather than conflating this cohort of ex-prime ministers with those that follow, and they need to be stated at the outset. First, despite the prime minister being clearly at the forefront of Itō's mind, the position was not even mentioned in the Meiji Constitution. It was the postwar constitution of 1947 that spelled out the position and duties of the prime minister for the first time. Second, the position of former prime ministers was relatively well understood as a result of the existence of a group of elder statesmen known as *genrō*. For a period, several former prime ministers continued to exert influence, especially in selecting future prime ministers, through this exclusive clique, as will be explored later. Third, the post-premierships of the final prime ministers of this period were clearly shaped by the end of the war, Japan's surrender and the US Occupation. Konoe committed suicide while several were tried under the International Military Tribunal for the Far East (IMTFE), found guilty and executed, most notably wartime prime minister and general, Tōjō, as well as prewar prime minister and civilian, Hirota. There are other aspects specific to this period and its political context that will emerge later, including a higher number of individuals returning to the position of prime minister, but also more incidents of assassination in contrast to the postwar period.

So, on the one hand, an exploration of prime ministerial afterlives in this period allows certain traits of the prewar political situation and the position of the prime minister to emerge. In other words, understanding these afterlives allows us a fresh lens by which to view this well-researched period. On the other hand, understanding the prewar context and how the categories of prime ministerial afterlives are relevant (or not) allows us to better understand how the categories apply in the postwar period in the two chapters that follow, and the extent to which prewar norms persist in the postwar period and through to today.

Still Ambitious

Seeking a return to some kind of official political office, whether it be successful or unsuccessful, desired or reluctant, is a notable feature of this period. In the case of the position of prime minister, 13 of the 29 prime ministers under examination in this chapter returned to the top job at least once. One of the most prominent examples of ex-prime ministers returning to their former position is the period from June 1901 to February 1913, which was dominated by the alternation of power between two men. Katsura Tarō became 'the only soldier-politician in Japan ever to head three cabinets' (Lone, 2000: 1) and one of its longest serving prime ministers. These three cabinets were punctuated by the two cabinets of Saionji Kinmochi, resulting in this period being dubbed the *keien* period based on the alternative readings of their names.

Another prominent example of this in the popular imagination, if not in the traditional view of historians (Takii, 2014: 2–3), is Itō, Japan's first prime minister. One of the preeminent Meiji leaders and statesmen, he is popularly dubbed father of the Constitution (see Oka 1986 for his life and character). Itō became prime minister for the first time in December 1885 at the age of 46 and served 861 days. Thereafter, he served three more times as prime minister, resulting in four prime ministerial afterlives totalling 16 years (see Table 3.1). His second period in office lasted 1,485 days from August 1892 to September 1896 during which revision of the unequal treaties with the Western powers was achieved and Japan won the first Sino-Japanese War. His third and fourth terms in office were shorter, from January to June 1898 and October 1900 to June 1901 respectively. Between these four cabinets and after resigning for the final time in May 1901, Itō also served in several other official roles. When he first resigned his position as prime minister in April 1888, Itō assumed the role of first president of the Privy Council (*sūmitsuin*) (Beckmann, 1957: 82). He established the Privy Council to deliberate drafts of and approve the Meiji Constitution and Imperial Household Law. After the constitution's promulgation the following year, the council became the highest advisory body to the Emperor. According to Article 56: 'the Privy Councillors shall, in accordance with the provisions for the organization of the Privy Council, deliberate upon important matters of State, when they have been consulted by the Emperor' (Colegrove, 1931, p 591). In effect, Itō created an advisory body to regulate the Emperor's role in politics but also create some distance between the two (Takii, 2014: 53). He would go on to serve as president on three other occasions and under his successor, Yamagata Aritomo, the Privy Council's powers expanded considerably beyond this advisory role.

It was between his third and fourth cabinets that Itō, despite some failed previous attempts, established the *Rikken Seiyūkai* (Association of Friends of Constitutional Government) as a political party that would come to dominate Japanese politics. He spent much of 1899 conducting a speaking tour of Japan, partly to discuss politics and the Constitution, partly to disseminate his views, and partly with prefectural assembly elections in mind (Takii, 2014: 84–8). During this third interregnum, Itō was also active from August 1899 to September 1900 as President of the Imperial Household Research Committee charged with exploring ways and means to improve

Table 3.1: Former Japanese prime ministers, the Meiji period to World War Two

Name	Born	Party[1]	Tenure as PM	Days in office[2]	Former PMs alive	Age at leaving office	Died	Total post-PM years
Itō Hirobumi	1841	Independent (until 1900) and Rikken Seiyūkai (Association of Friends of Constitutional Government after 1900)	22 December 1885 to 30 April 1888; 8 August 1892 to 31 August 1896; 12 January 1898 to 30 June 1898; 19 October 1900 to 10 May 1901	861; 1485; 170; 204	0; 3; 3; 3	46; 54; 56; 59	1909	16
Kuroda Kiyotaka	1840	Independent	30 April 1888 to 25 October 1889	544	1	48	1900	11
Yamagata Aritomo	1838	Army	24 December 1889 to 6 May 1891; 8 November 1898 to 19 October 1900	499; 711	2; 4	52; 62	1922	29
Matsukata Masayoshi	1835	Independent	6 May 1891 to 8 August 1892; 18 September 1896 to 12 January 1898	461; 482	3; 3	57; 62	1924	30
Ōkuma Shigenobu	1838	Kenseitō (Constitutional Party); Rikken Dōshikai (Association of Comrades of the Constitution)	30 June 1898 to 8 November 1898; 16 April 1914 to 9 October 1916	908; 132	4; 5	60; 78	1922	22
Katsura Tarō	1848	Army	2 June 1901 to 7 January 1906; 14 July 1908 to 30 August 1911; 21 December 1912 to 20 February 1913	1681; 1143; 62	4; 5; 4	58; 63; 65	1913	3

Table 3.1: Former Japanese prime ministers, the Meiji period to World War Two (continued)

Name	Born	Party[1]	Tenure as PM	Days in office[2]	Former PMs alive	Age at leaving office	Died	Total post-PM years
Saionji Kinmochi	1849	Rikken Seiyūkai	7 January 1906 to 14 July 1908; 30 August 1911 to 21 December 1912	920; 480;	5; 4	58; 63	1940	31
Yamamoto Gonbei	1852	Navy	20 February 1913 to 16 April 1914; 2 September 1923 to 7 January 1924	421; 128	5; 3	61; 71	1933	18
Terauchi Masatake	1852	Army	9 October 1916 to 29 September 1918	721	5	66	1919	1
Hara Takashi	1856	Rikken Seiyūkai	29 September 1918 to 4 November 1921	1133	6	65	1921	0
Takahashi Korekiyo	1854	Rikken Seiyūkai	13 November 1921 to 12 June 1922	212	5	67	1936	14
Katō Tomosaburō	1861	Navy	12 June 1922 to 24 August 1923	440	4	62	1923	0
Kiyoura Keigo	1850	Independent	7 January 1924 to 11 June 1924	157	4	74	1942	18
Katō Takaaki	1860	Kenseikai (Constitutional Political Association)	11 June 1924 to 28 January 1926	597	5	66	1926	0
Wakatsuki Reijirō	1866	Kenseikai; Rikken Minseitō (Constitutional Democratic Party)	30 January 1926 to 20 April 1927; 14 April 1931 to 13 December 1931	446; 244	4; 5	61; 65	1949	22

(continued)

Table 3.1: Former Japanese prime ministers, the Meiji period to World War Two (continued)

Name	Born	Party[1]	Tenure as PM	Days in office[2]	Former PMs alive	Age at leaving office	Died	Total post-PM years
Tanaka Giichi	1864	Rikken Seiyūkai	20 April 1927 to 2 July 1929	805	5	65	1929	0
Hamaguchi Osachi	1870	Rikken Minseitō	2 July 1929 to 14 April 1931	652	6	61	1931	0
Inukai Tsuyoshi	1855	Rikken Seiyūkai	13 December 1931 to 16 May 1932	156	5	76	1932	0
Saitō Makoto	1858	Navy	26 May 1932 to 8 July 1934	774	5	75	1936	2
Okada Keisuke	1868	Navy	8 July 1934 to 9 March 1936	611	5	68	1952	16
Hirota Kōki	1878	Independent	9 March 1936 to 2 February 1937	331	4	58	1948	11
Hayashi Senjūrō	1876	Army	2 February 1937 to 4 June 1937	123	5	61	1943	6
Konoe Fumimaro	1891	Independent; Taisei Yokusankai (Imperial Rule Assistance Association)	4 June 1937 to 5 January 1939; 22 July 1940 to 18 July 1941; 18 July 1941 to 18 October 1941	581; 362; 93	6; 9	47; 50	1945	5
Hiranuma Kiichirō	1867	Independent	5 January 1939 to 30 August 1939	238	7	71	1952	13
Abe Nobuyuki	1875	Army	30 August 1939 to 16 January 1940	140	8	64	1953	13
Yonai Mitsumasa	1880	Navy	16 January 1940 to 22 July 1940	189	9	60	1948	8

Table 3.1: Former Japanese prime ministers, the Meiji period to World War Two (continued)

Name	Born	Party[1]	Tenure as PM	Days in office[2]	Former PMs alive	Age at leaving office	Died	Total post-PM years
Tōjō Hideki	1884	Taisei Yokusankai (Imperial Rule Assistance Association)	18 October 1941 to 22 July 1944	1009	9	59	1948	4
Koiso Kuniaki	1880	Taisei Yokusankai (Imperial Rule Assistance Association)	22 July 1944 to 7 April 1945	260	8	65	1950	5
Suzuki Kantarō	1868	Taisei Yokusankai (Imperial Rule Assistance Association)	7 April 1945 to 17 August 1945	133	9	77	1948	3

[1] Affiliation during tenure as prime minister.
[2] According to https://japan.kantei.go.jp/past_cabinet/index.html

the operations of the imperial system and clarify its legal status. He resigned this position upon the establishment of *Rikken Seiyūkai* but returned to the position in July 1903, a couple of years after stepping down as prime minister for the final time. In June 1906, Itō submitted to the Emperor several proposals that would form the basis for laws and regulations related to the functioning of the imperial institution and the peerage within the Constitution (Takii, 2014: 135–43).

In December 1905, Itō achieved another first when he was appointed resident-general of Korea, a post he had created himself (Uji, 2001: 10). Although his true Korean policy is unclear and contested (Kim, 2008), Itō appeared to have initially resisted formal annexation, preferring informal control as a protectorate, and instead attempted to promote Emperor Sunjong's image and authority within Korea and the resulting 'spirit of cooperation' with Japan through a range of nation-building techniques. However, this position had the unintended outcomes of stirring anti-Japanese nationalism and contributed, it has been argued, ultimately to the formal annexation of Korea in 1910 (Kim, 2009; Takii, 2014: 183–216; for an unashamedly pro-Japanese account, see Scherer, 1936: 122–3). After resigning from this position in June 1909 and becoming president of the Privy Council once again, Itō toured Manchuria in October of that year. Intending to meet Russian Finance Minister Vladimir Kokovtsov to discuss the position of Korea in Japan's East Asian policy, he was assassinated by An Jung-geun, a young Korean nationalist. Itō died at the age of 68 and received a state funeral on 4 November 1909 (Oka, 1986: 40–1).

Another preeminent Meiji leader and Itō's rival, Yamagata, also served more than one term as prime minister. Known as father of the Japanese Imperial Army, he was Japan's third prime minister from December 1889 to May 1891, during which time the Imperial Rescript on Education was issued and Yamagata's concept of security known as the 'line of advantage' beyond Japan's territorial borders and within which Japan would seek overarching influence, chiefly with Korea in mind, was developed. Yamagata resigned citing health reasons but returned to the top job on one more occasion between November 1898 and October 1900. As discussed later, during these two periods in office, Yamagata served for eight months in Itō's second administration as justice minister before resigning, appointing one of his protégés to the position and agreeing to become president of the Privy Council in March 1893, a position he would occupy on two further occasions.

Similarly, several other former prime ministers went on to serve either in a ministerial role or as president of the Privy Council. As regards the latter, Konoe resigned from his first cabinet in January 1939 and assumed the role before resigning it and returning to the prime ministership in July 1940. Hiranuma had served as president before his short-lived prime ministership in 1939 but returned to the role in 1945, helping to shape the first postwar cabinet of Higashikuni. Similarly, Suzuki served before and after his short, four-month prime ministership at the end of WW2.

As regards a ministerial role, it was not uncommon up until the turn of the 20th century for former prime ministers to serve in a ministerial role. As mentioned in passing previously, the first example of this was during Itō's second cabinet of 1892 to 1896. Obviously, Itō himself was returning to the role of prime minister but three other former prime ministers served for a time in his cabinet: Kuroda (Japan's second prime minister) as communications minister, Yamagata (Japan's third prime minister) as justice minister, and Matsukata (Japan's fourth prime minister and Ito's immediate predecessor) as finance minister. Matsukata would serve as finance minister again in Yamagata's second cabinet between 1898 and 1900 having served as prime minister himself for a second term prior to this. However, this phenomenon of former prime ministers returning in ministerial roles ceased for a while with the advent of alternating cabinets in the *keien* period and beyond.

Returning to the top job has not always been the ultimate objective and some former prime ministers have been more comfortable in a ministerial role. After Hara's assassination in November 1921 (discussed later), Takahashi, selected as Hara's successor by the *genrō* to provide continuity ahead of the upcoming Washington Naval Conference, only served as prime minister until June 1922 when he resigned. By his own admission, Takahashi was more comfortable in the role of finance minister, which he also occupied while prime minister. After stepping down as prime minister, Takahashi gave up his peerage so he could run and be elected to the House of Representatives in 1924 in Hara's parliamentary seat, just defeating a candidate from a breakaway party, *Seiyūhontō* (Orthodox Friends of Government Party). He served in various ministerial roles, charged with the remits of agriculture and commerce under Katō Takaaki's cabinet of 1924 to 1926 and was persuaded to return once more as finance minister under Tanaka for a brief period of six weeks before retiring again. He returned once more as finance minister across the cabinets of Inukai (December 1931 to May 1932), Saitō (May 1932 to July 1934) and Okada (July 1934 to March 1936) until his assassination on the morning of 26 February 1936 by ultranationalist young army officers as part of an attempted coup d'état (Smethurst, 1998: 227; Smethurst, 2007: 224–31). The role of finance minister is where his lasting reputation lies as Takahashi led Japan through the Great Depression as a Keynesian before Keynes (Smethurst, 1998; Cha, 2003; Metzler, 2006). Saitō was also assassinated in the 26 February Incident, the two being the last ex-prime ministers to be assassinated until Abe Shinzō in 2022. In the tense situation that followed, Takahashi was denied an official funeral but a private family funeral eventually took place on 26 March that still attracted considerable attention at home and abroad.

Although 'a persistent but unsuccessful candidate for Japan's major political offices' (Yasko, 1973: 112), Hiranuma only served as prime minister from January to August 1939 when he resigned over foreign policy and military issues, in particular the signing of a non-aggression pact between Nazi Germany and the Soviet Union (Oka, 1983: 87). However, not long after his resignation, in December 1940 he served as minister of state and home minister in his successor Konoe's subsequent cabinets. Through his conservative factional base, Hiranuma worked to neutralize the radical elements of the Imperial Rule Assistance Association, oppose the Tripartite Pact with Germany and Italy, and de-escalate tensions with the US (Yasko, 1973).

Hirota, a career diplomat, served as prime minister from March 1936 to February 1937, and although he initially retreated to his coastal villa after resigning, he was persuaded to serve again as foreign minister from June 1937 in Konoe's first cabinet. As part of a cabinet reshuffle in May 1938, Konoe dropped Hirota as foreign minister and was only able to secure him the privileges accorded to a minister-of-state, rather than a former prime minister. Hirota retired again to his villa but pledged to keep an eye on developments in China (Shiroyama, 1977: 202). His name was later put forward as a replacement after Hiranuma resigned as prime minister in August 1939; however, the military blocked this and General Abe Nobuyuki assumed the role. Abe was succeeded by Yonai who served through the first half of 1940 and was able to persuade Hirota to serve in his cabinet as a state minister without portfolio. Hirota advocated neutrality when war broke out in Europe and expressed misgivings as regards developments towards the signing of the Tripartite Pact in September 1940 but was ignored. In 1945, he was approached for his expertise in Soviet affairs to conduct peace talks with Jacob Malik, the Soviet Ambassador in Tokyo, and have Japanese proposals communicated back to Moscow, although these plans fell through (Farnsworth, 1974: 246; Shiroyama, 1977: 217–18, 221–3).

Yonai served as prime minister for only six months from January to July 1940 when he was ousted from the role by the army who were opposed to his pro-UK/US, anti-German/Italy stance. He returned to active service during the war. Although considered for another term as prime minister after Tōjō's resignation, he served as navy minister under the final two prime ministers of this period, Koiso Kuniaki and Suzuki Kantarō, and the first two prime ministers of the postwar period, Higashikuni Naruhiko and Shidehara Kijūrō (who are explored in Chapter 4) until December 1945 when Japan's armed forces were abolished along with the navy and army ministries (Krebs, 1990).

Konoe served as minister without portfolio under his successor Hiranuma's cabinet. In July 1945, he accepted the nomination and appointment as the Emperor's special envoy to the Soviet Union to request its mediation in bringing an end to the war; however, this initiative ultimately came to nothing (Oka, 1983: 175–8). At the request of Prince Higashikuni Naruhiko, he would serve as minister of state in Japan's first postwar cabinet, liaising with the US occupation forces particularly on constitutional revision and attempting to preserve the imperial institution. He also considered establishing a new political party. This return to politics appears to have been motivated primarily by duty rather than personal ambition, but he was open to the idea of forming his own cabinet after Higashikuni resigned in October 1945, although ultimately he was replaced by Shidehara (Oka, 1983: 183). Konoe's activities were cut short when his fears were confirmed and GHQ (General Headquarters, Supreme Commander of the Allied Powers) issued orders for his arrest as a war criminal on 6 December 1945. He committed suicide ten days later.

Exhausted Volcanoes

This brings us to the second category. A corollary of the tumultuous developments in this period are that many of the figures examined in this chapter were assassinated in office, executed as war criminals or committed suicide. These are the extreme examples of Exhausted Volcanoes. Hara was the first prime minister to be assassinated in office but not the last. He served from September 1918 to 4 November 1921 and was known as the 'commoner prime minister' having become the first prime minister not to hold a peerage (Najita, 1967; Duus, 1968). He was stabbed to death at the age of 65 at Tokyo Station by Nakaoka Konichi, a railwayman and nationalist, disillusioned with Hara's perceived corruption and diplomatic failures, including the response to the Nikolayevsk Incident of 1920, the mass killings by the Red Army in the Russian Far East during Japan's intervention in Siberia. Almost exactly nine years later in November 1930, Hamaguchi, who had served as prime minister since July 1929, was shot at Tokyo Station by ultranationalist Sagoya Tomeo. Although Hamaguchi did temporarily recover and resume some duties (Metzler, 2006: 236), he ultimately had to step down because of injuries and his cabinet resigned in April 1931. Hamaguchi died of his wounds in August of that year (Uji, 2001: 123). Inukai served as prime minister from December 1931, for a time concurrently as foreign minister, until his assassination the following year during the 15 May Incident, an attempted coup d'état led by radical elements in the Japanese Imperial Navy. This assassination represented the end of civilian control over the military until the end of WW2 (Oka, 1986: 172–4).

These are the examples of assassination bringing a sudden and tragic end to a premiership. There are other examples of prime ministers dying of natural causes while in office resulting in a similarly truncated post-premiership. Katō Tomosaburō died in office on 24 August 1923 of cancer at the age of 62, a week before the Great Kantō Earthquake. He was posthumously created a viscount and generally received positive evaluations of his abilities and leadership (Nish, 1996: 152). Katō Takaaki served as prime minister from June 1924 to January 1926. He collapsed in January 1926 and died in office a week later at the age of 66.

There are further examples of prime ministers stepping back from political life as a result of ill health and dying soon after. For example, after working to establish *Rikken Dōshikai* (Association of Comrades of the Constitution), the political party that supported his third and final cabinet, Katsura was forced to resign in February 1913, fell ill the following month and was mostly bedridden from April until he died on 10 October 1913 at the age of 65. Terauchi served as prime minister from October 1916 until resigning in September 1918 in response to the rice riots and citing ill health (Uji, 2001: 69). He died in November 1919.

Tanaka and his cabinet were forced to resign as a result of the assassination of Manchurian warlord Zhang Zuolin by Japanese troops on 4 June 1928. As details of the incident emerged, Tanaka lost the Emperor's confidence and resigned in July 1929. He returned to his hometown of Hagi and, having suffered for some years from angina, died of heart failure on 29 September 1929 at the age of 66: 'perhaps, it was said, because of the heartbreak of being rejected by his sovereign, or perhaps because of excessive drinking, feasting, and fornicating on the occasion of his homecoming' (Metzler, 2006: 202–3).

Koiso was appointed prime minister in July 1944 having been recommended by the elder statesmen known as *jūshin* (discussed later) as a compromise candidate that would placate the army (Browne, 1967: 169–70; Oka, 1983: 165–6). He served through to April 1945 when he resigned over the deteriorating war situation and divisions within his cabinet between the army and navy. He was arrested at the end of the war and detained in Sugamo prison during the IMTFE. Receiving a life sentence, he was allowed to return home temporarily due to his worsening health but died of cancer in Sugamo in November 1950.

Former prime ministers might aspire to the status of Exhausted Volcanoes and a complete withdrawal from politics but are prevented by circumstances. Konoe expressed the desire to leave the world of politics; before finally resigning in October 1941 having failed to resolve differences with the US and control the military, he is quoted as having said that he wanted to become a Buddhist priest (Uji, 2001: 185). However, even if these intentions were sincere, he continued to play an active role as minister, as explored previously, and First Citizen, as explored later.

After his resignation, Tōjō lived largely in obscurity and '[t]he speed with which Tōjō disappeared from public view, even in Japan, was the more surprising because of the role he had supposedly played as a twentieth-century shogun' (Butow, 1961: 433–4). Tōjō described his life to US reports as: 'I get up at 4:30 or 5:00 in the morning. Then I work in the vegetable field until breakfast. After that I read' (Hiraizumi, 1983: 268). However, as will be described later, his arrest, trial and execution by the IMTFE forced him out of this obscurity.

Suzuki served from April to August 1945 and led Japan through a tumultuous time that included the defeat of Germany, atomic bombings of Hiroshima and Nagasaki, the Soviet Union's entry into the war and Japan's eventual surrender. Suzuki's overarching goal was to oversee Japan's unconditional surrender and acceptance of the Potsdam Declaration, putting his own life at risk as hardline militarists opposed to these terms attempted a coup d'état. Suzuki survived but resigned as prime minister on 17 August, two days after Japan's surrender. After resigning, he once again led the Privy Council, tasked with assessing the new constitution, until June 1946 when he retired from public life. He died at his home in Chiba prefecture in April 1948, his last words being 'eternal peace, eternal peace' (Tadokoro, 2024).

Political Dabblers

As outlined in the previous chapter, Political Dabblers are the polar opposite of Exhausted Volcanoes. They cannot disengage successfully from politics and still seek to influence, preferring to do so from the sidelines rather than in an official capacity as somebody who is still ambitious might do. They may do this as an end in and of itself, or a means to an end related to their own or others' political futures. As an example of the latter, between his first resignation as prime minister in January 1939 and his return to the position in July 1940, Konoe articulated his vision for a new party that would promote a 'political order of national unity' (Oka, 1983: 91–4). This would eventually become the Imperial Rule Assistance Association in October 1940.

During the period under examination in this chapter, the high number of prime ministers returning to power (as explored previously) was accompanied by a high degree of political dabbling. For example, during the *keien* period mentioned previously, it is 'clear that throughout the period of the Second Katsura Cabinet, Saionji and Katsura corresponded regularly and met frequently to discuss political affairs' (Connors, 1987: 31). During Saionji's second cabinet, sandwiched by Katsura's second and third cabinets, Katsura continued to play a role in foreign policy by conducting secret negotiations in Moscow with German counterparts to explore a possible alliance (Dickinson, 1999: 45). Saionji's second cabinet was brought down by the role played by Yamagata, Katsura's mentor, in the Taishō political crisis of 1912–13. When

War Minister Uehara Yūsaku resigned in reaction to Saionji's refusal to fund the expansion of the army by creating two new divisions, Yamagata refused to nominate a successor. Unable to fill the position, Saionji was forced to resign, resulting in Katsura, Yamagata's protégé, assuming the role (Dickinson, 1999: 29). The cliques that existed among a tight-knit group of leaders also provided several opportunities for former prime ministers to maintain their influence through protégés and acolytes, as will be explored later.

However, continuing to dabble is not without its risks. For example, after stepping down as prime minister, Itō visited a number of European capitals including St Petersburg in the final months of 1901 and opening months of 1902 to discuss Russo-Japanese relations and a possible settlement over spheres of influence in Korea and Manchuria with the Tsar and his foreign and finance ministers (Hamada, 1936: 142–66). A former prime minister seeking to dabble can be unwelcome and Itō's visit has been cited as an example of his waning influence. The visit was conducted without the official sanction of the Emperor or Katsura's government and ran counter to the goal of negotiating an alliance with Britain, which had reached an advanced enough stage to preclude withdrawal. Thus, Katsura's government had to manage the indecisive and occasionally contradictory loose cannon that Itō was seen by some to have become (Nish, 1984: 90–1). The risks associated with continuing to dabble can also be seen in Ōkuma's failed attempt to try and anoint Katō Takaaki as his successor and inability to stop Terauchi, Yamagata's protégé, from establishing his cabinet from October 1916.

Continued political dabbling could also be a product of frustration. As mentioned previously, Tōjō's retreatment from public life, although not complete, surprised many. His wife, Katsuko, observed that 'he had too much time and didn't know what to do with it' (Browne, 1967: 170). Despite this, he emerged from time to time to support the war effort, including a private audience with the Emperor as an ex-prime minister and senior statesman on 26 February 1945 in which he disparaged the policies of the Koiso administration and the defeatism in Japan while he maintained a hawkish approach to Japan's prospects in the war (Butow, 1961: 440–2; Browne, 1967: 173–5; Coox, 1975: 145). Tōjō made a visit to War Minister Anami with a similar objective in June 1945. He was also involved in the discussion with the *jūshin* after Koiso's resignation in April, with Suzuki emerging as the reluctant successor (Browne, 1967: 177).

During this period, political dabbling was institutionalized within the structure of Japanese politics. A group of Meiji elder statesmen, including several former prime ministers, were members of the *genrō*, a group that continued to influence politics in a number of ways, most prominently through the selection of prime ministers. Later in this period, as the *genrō*'s power and their number declined, the Council of Elders (*jūshin*) emerged as a group of non-*genrō* elder statesmen, again many of whom had served as prime minister. These groups of elder statesmen provided an organized means by which to dabble, although they were not necessarily self-serving individuals seeking a return to office. They were closer to the next category: First Citizens.

First Citizens

First Citizens are elder statesmen motivated by a sense of duty and a higher purpose that stands above their own political futures or legacies. As mentioned earlier and in the previous chapter, the *genrō* captures this group of elder statesmen – many of whom, but not all, were former prime ministers – who continued to provide advice and guidance to the Emperor. Bailey (1965) has traced the development of the term during the Meiji period, demonstrating that *genrō* was not a retrospectively applied term and instead these First Citizens were conscious at the time of their collective status, role and responsibilities. Lesley Connors (1987: 43) describes the *genrō* as:

> a self-generated and self-limiting body of elder statesmen who chose to justify their power from their position vis-à-vis the Court. The group was not created at one time. In a sense it was not created at all, but evolved gradually, gathering members which it was necessary or useful to include and jealously excluding all others.

In addition to imperial advisers, the roles assigned to the *genrō* included recommending the selection of the prime minister and cabinet members. From 1898, the role of advising on foreign policy was also established with full access to all Foreign Ministry documents. However, this role was curtailed by the rise of a professional foreign service by the end of World War One (WW1) and the Paris Peace Conference (Connors, 1987: 46–7). Although definitions of *genrō* are contested, there are nine men who are without doubt regarded as *genrō* and six of them were former prime ministers: Itō, Kuroda, Yamagata, Matsukata, Katsura and Saionji (the remaining three were Inoue Kaoru, Saigō Tsugumichi and Ōyama Iwao).

Yamagata was one of the most dominant *genrō*, especially after his rival Itō's assassination in 1909, with 'a decisive voice in the formation of each new government, if not in day-to-day policymaking' (Dickinson, 1999: 41). He had access to Foreign Ministry documents, was able to observe developments and have an input into negotiations that resulted in the Anglo-Japanese Alliance of 1902 in addition to the negotiations in the run-up to the military phase and settlement of the Russo-Japanese War of 1904–05, Japan's response to the outbreak and development of WW1, the Twenty-One Demands, the secret alliance with Russia of 1916, the Bolshevik Revolution and consequent Siberian expedition.

Writing at the beginning of 1908, a contemporary political commentator observed that:

> Probably the most perplexing figure in modern Japan is Prince Yamagata ... [H]is character, ability and policy are not clearly known. The public knows he has power in the political world without any knowledge of his true worth. For example, it is known that he represents the most obstinate conservativism but no one understands the exact nature of his conservatism. Again it is known that he is a statesman opposing a party cabinet system yet who has ever heard him speak publicly as an advocate of non-party cabinets? Again, he is called crafty and an oppressor yet what is that actually based upon – the real facts? It is extremely doubtful. Nevertheless, his chief value lies in the fact that his real worth is not known. (cited in Hackett, 1971: 213–14)

Others noted that: 'Although detested by the people, Yamagata still is able to hold his political power because of his entrenched strength in the House of Peers ... [Pro-Yamagata groups] hold a position which prevents Itō's supporters from penetrating no matter how hard they tried' (cited in Hackett, 1971: 240–1).

His involvement in the day-to-day running of Japanese politics can be seen in June 1915 when he mobilized the other *genrō* in demanding that Ōkuma dismiss his foreign minister Katō Takaaki (who would go on to serve as prime minister) for ignoring the *genrō* and his pro-British position, that he always consult the *genrō* on the key matters of foreign policy and to seek diplomatic accommodation with Imperial Russia. However, Ōkuma was able to resist Yamagata and the *genrō* on this occasion (Dickinson, 1999: 112–13). Nevertheless, Yamagata's continuing influence was acknowledged by some: 'it remains true that no important decision is come to in Japan without his approval and sanction' (cited in Hackett, 1971: 341).

Another prominent *genrō* was Saionji. His appointment as prime minister for the first time in January 1906 captures the tone of the period. His assumption of power had been arranged among Katsura, Hara and himself, with Saionji liaising with each of the *genrō*, rather than convening a council meeting of all these elder statesmen. Katsura, Saionji and the *genrō* appointed the cabinet members, and Itō was consulted as Saionji's mentor (Connors, 1987: 23–4).

Although Saionji has been described as a 'languid prime minister' – 'in the policies of his first and subsequent cabinet, there is nothing that can be positively attributed to Sainoji, either as prime minister or party leader' (Oka, 1986: 190–1) – he was a key player in prewar Japanese politics after stepping down for the second and final time in December 1912. At the beginning of 1913, he became the last appointed member of the *genrō* to advise and assist the new Taishō Emperor on important matters. Saionji went on to become the longest living *genrō* until his death on 24 November 1940 at the age of 90, a year before the attack on Pearl Harbor. He advised the Emperor on matters of foreign policy and also influenced the selection of cabinets in line with his faith in a cabinet responsible to the public, a constitutional monarchy and the westernization of Japan. From his appointment, his influence can be seen in the selection of several cabinets, particularly the first Yamamoto cabinet from February 1913 to April 1914, dubbed by Hara as the 'third Saionji cabinet' (Metzler, 2006: 87). Saionji came to dominate the *genrō* as numbers dwindled, and he continued to play a key role in the selection of prime ministers, such as Takahashi in November 1921 after Hara's assassination, Yamamoto's second cabinet after Katō Tomosaburō's illness and Katō Takaaki despite some reservations (Oka, 1986: 198–220; Connors, 1987: 91–8). Saionji himself was approached on a number of occasions to become prime minister again, although he refused (Connors, 1987: 91).

In terms of foreign policy, Saionji was selected by Yamagata and Hara to be appointed as Chief Plenipotentiary to the Paris Peace Conference that opened in 1919 (Oka, 1986). Saionji sought to keep Japan in the conference when there had been talk of its withdrawal if its demands were not met. He was a convinced internationalist advocating cooperation with the European–US world order alongside Shidehara, Hara, Katō Tomosaburō and others but limited in his role at the conference as unlike other participants he was not the prime minister of the day. The following decade represented the high point of the dominance of his ideas on foreign policy, personified in Shidehara, foreign minister and favourite of Saionji, who would become prime minister after WW2.

In 1936, Saionji's influence was shattered by the 26 February Incident, an attempted coup d'état by young army officers that targeted leading figures sympathetic to Saionji, his internationalist outlook and liberal values, although ultimately not targeting Saionji himself. Connors characterizes this period as a shift in his role from political actor to political commentator (1987: 181–210). Saionji summarized his own position during these final few years of his life:

> It is evident when one looks at politics in Japan today that they are being dragged along by the right-wing. To me this seems a retrograde step and shows no hint of progress. It is a great pity, but even if I were to speak out now, it would come to nothing and it would not do to give forth vainly on this and that, without even limited power. There is nothing to do but to hold one's tongue and to watch the lay of the land. Within ten or twenty years, the atmosphere may change and more progressive politics appear, but at present, there is absolutely no alternative but to endure it in silence. (quoted in Connors, 1987: 208)

With the decline of both Saionji and the *genrō*, the *jūshin* group (which included former prime ministers) assumed the responsibilities of advising the Emperor and selecting the next prime minister (Grew, 1940). For example, from spring 1944, Konoe alongside other former prime ministers Wakatsuki, Hiranuma and Okada had been meeting to discuss the war situation and formulate responses, including the idea of instituting a cabinet of national unity (Oka, 1983: 165–6). This anti-Tōjō movement succeeded in forcing his resignation after the fall of Saipan in July 1944 and shaping the subsequent choice of prime minister (Browne, 1967: 169–70; Oka, 1983: 165–6; Yasko, 1973).

Embracers of a Cause

Several prime ministers have pursued a cause in their post-premiership whether it be educational, humanitarian, ideological or otherwise. In the process, several have become grand figures, mythologized and synonymous over time with their chosen cause. Ōkuma served twice as prime minister but between these two terms in office from 1898 to 1914, he focused on his role as president of Waseda University, which he had previously founded (Idditti, 1940: 344–9). He also served as president of the Peace Society of Japan upon its creation in 1909, as well as the Japan–India Society and Japan–Holland Society, chaired the committee planning and supporting the Japanese Antarctic expedition of 1910 to 1911, and also engaged in lecture tours and media commentator as part of his mission of educating the Japanese people (Lebra, 1973: 114; Idditti, 1940: 352–5).

In a similar vein, Matsukata served as the second president of the Japan Red Cross Society. After resigning as prime minister in July 1934, Saitō became president of the Japanese Boy Scout Association and the Japan Film Association (Kuramatsu, 1999: 194).

As regards an ideological cause, Katsura was an active promoter of Japan's colonization of East Asia. Having served as governor-general of Taiwan in June 1896 and helped found the Taiwan Association School (known today as Takushoku University), Katsura advocated for greater investment in Taiwan during his presidency of the Oriental Society (Lone 2000: 140–54). In October 1907, between his first and second cabinets, he visited Korean Prime Minister Yi Wanyong in his capacity as president of the Oriental Society. The following year, he secured Yi's agreement to the establishment of the Oriental Development Company (ODC) which worked towards the migration of Japanese farmers to Korea (Hyung 2005: 29–30).

Seekers of Vindication

Former leaders may often seek to present their side of the story of their time in power. Although the motivation and means will often differ, writing is a common approach to this across time and space. During the 16 years that separate his two periods in office, Ōkuma compiled and contributed to *Kaikoku Gojūnenshi (Fifty Years of New Japan)*, which was first published in 1908 and then translated into English, with a dedication to King Edward VII, and re-published in 1910. The aim of the book was twofold: to provide a first-hand account of developments in Japan's recent history since its opening to the Western world across a range of political, economic, social and cultural topics, as well as promote a broader understanding of Japan at that time. It included contributions from a number of former and future prime ministers, including Itō on the Constitution, Matsukata on finance, Yamagata on the army, Yamamoto on the navy and Saionji on education.

After resigning in October 1916 for the second time in the face of increased criticism, Ōkuma returned to his Waseda residence and his previous life of retirement highlighted previously. However, he continued writing and public speaking to reestablish his image after the damage done to his reputation by his second term of office. When he died at the beginning 1922, he was given a state funeral that came to be known as the people's funeral with 3,000 people paying their respects daily for a month afterwards (Lebra, 1973; Oka, 1986).

Yamagata's interest in waka poetry and role in establishing the *Tokiwakai* poetry group could be interpreted as an attempt to project a more cultured side to his martial reputation.

Writing need not always take place within the immediate afterlife of the former prime minister and can be posthumous. In the case of Hara, his diaries were not published immediately after his assassination in 1921 in line with stipulations in his will. The diaries were published eventually by two companies in the 1950s and 1960s, providing a detailed record and valuable source for historians of the prewar period.

The most contested reputations will often require the most vindication. The former prime ministers arrested as war criminals during the US Occupation of Japan are the most obvious examples of this. Although he was never tried, it was discovered after Konoe's suicide in December 1945 that he had underlined the following phrase in a copy of Oscar Wilde's *De Profondis* possibly as an attempt to seek vindication: 'people used to say of me that I was too individualistic … Indeed, my ruin came not from too great individualism of life, but from too little', sealing his reputation as a weak and ineffectual prime minister (Oka, 1983: 198). Konoe regarded himself as a victim of fate and was 'despised before the war as weak, criticized as a peace activist during the war, and accused of being a war criminal after the war' [*our translation*] (Uji, 2001: 185).

With the spectre of arrest hanging over him, Tōjō entertained a number of US journalists at his home in the Setagaya Ward of Tokyo. On 11 September, when military police eventually came to his home to arrest him, he attempted unsuccessfully to commit suicide (Browne, 1967: 194–9; Hiraizumi, 1983). During the IMTFE, which ran from spring 1946 to the end of 1948, Tōjō took the opportunity to defend his actions and the Japanese war effort but was found guilty and executed on 23 December 1948 (Butow, 1961). In his final days, Tōjō drafted a final testament for future publication in which he venerated and apologized to the Emperor, as well as the Japanese people, criticized the IMTFE and predicted a future war between the US and USSR. This was eventually published in 1961 (Browne, 1967: 221–2). It is not always the individual who seeks vindication for their actions and other agents can play this role; as will be discussed later, Tōjō's granddaughter also sought more recently to rehabilitate his reputation.

Acolytes and Protégés

As mentioned in the previous chapter, former leaders may nurture acolytes and protégés for a number of reasons: to secure a line of succession, a chance to continue dabbling or an opportunity to enhance their reputations. However, these relationships run the risk of turning sour.

During the Meiji Restoration, these relationships were evident within the two clans of Chōshū and Satsuma, who had initially allied to overthrow the Tokugawa Shogunate but thereafter saw the former dominate the latter. As Chōshū leader, Yamagata was able to disseminate his political views throughout government via the proxy of his active followers, most notably Katsura, Terauchi and Tanaka, who all served in the Sino-Japanese War of 1894–95 (Morton, 1980; Uji, 2001: 112). This represented the line of Chōshū leadership and all of these individuals would go on to serve as prime minister. In the bureaucracy, Yamagata was also able to rely on fellow Chōshū men, including a number of relatives (Hackett, 1971: 144–6). Tanaka, who served jointly as prime minister and foreign minister from April 1927 to July 1929 after Wakatsuki's resignation, is quoted as saying, 'Yamagata has achieved most of his successes through the willing toils of his loyal followers who would stick to him through thick and thin, but this could not be said of Ito who was very fickle in the treatment of his men, and consequently had no loyal adherents' (Saito, 1922: 4).

To give a specific example of Yamagata's continuing influence, upon resigning as prime minister for the second and final time in October 1900, he retired to his Kyoto villa, as he had done in 1891 after his previous resignation from the premiership. Nevertheless, Yamagata's acolytes and protégés could be mobilized for or against government policies that met his approval or disapproval. His protégé, Katsura, formed his first cabinet in June 1901, and although it was the first not to be led by one of the original Meiji oligarchs, Yamagata played a key role in shaping its composition to the extent that it received many disparaging nicknames, suggesting both its weakness and the true source of power: 'mini-Yamagata cabinet' (*shō-Yamagata naikaku*), 'second-class cabinet' (*niryū naikaku*), 'apprentice cabinet' (*kozō naikaku*) and 'curtain cabinet' (*donchō naikaku*) (Matsuoka, 1967; Hackett, 1971: 214). However, Yamagata and Katsura's relationship waned. A year after resigning from his second term as prime minister, Katsura departed for Europe in July 1912 and was in St Petersburg when he heard of the failing health of the Meiji Emperor. He returned to Tokyo but not before the Emperor's death on 30 July. Yamagata appointed Katsura as Grand Chamberlain and Lord Keeper of the Privy Seal to the new emperor in absentia, attempting to arrange for his protégé's quiet retirement into the Imperial Household and demonstrating the extent of their estrangement (Najita, 1967: 93–4).

Yamagata's great rival and fellow Chōshū man, Itō, was mentor to Saionji, whose time in power alternated with Katsura. In turn, Saionji also mentored Hara and Konoe. Saionji and Hara represent another example of the relationship between mentor and mentee becoming strained. Hara was Saionji's protégé but his 'acid descriptions of Saionji's ineffectuality' have been identified as one of the reasons that our historical understanding of Saionji's role has been warped (Connors, 1987: 1).

Family Affair

The oligarchs that dominated the many prime ministers across the Meiji, Taishō and early Shōwa periods fathered comparatively more children than was the case in the postwar period, providing a potential foundation for building political dynasties and family connections. Matsukata provides a notable example who was putatively unable when asked by the Meiji Emperor to identify how many children he had (Yoshida 2007: 250). In Matsukata's case, many of his children had high-profile careers in business, journalism and art collecting, as well as politics. Family connections between prime ministers through birth, marriage and adoption were evident. For example, Katō Takaaki's younger brother-in-law, Shidehara, served as foreign minister in Katō's cabinet. He served in the same role under the subsequent Wakatsuki and Hamaguchi cabinets and went on to serve as prime minister for a brief period during the postwar US occupation. Salient examples also exist of these family connections being leveraged by former prime ministers to continue exerting an influence and to give the impression of politics as a family business. For instance, Yamagata instrumentalized his adopted son, Isaburō, who served as minister of communications in Saionji's first cabinet, in an attempt to bring about its collapse in January 1908 and replace Saionji with his protégé, Katsura (Notehelfer, 1971: 157–8).

Two historically contingent aspects during this period should be noted: the existence of the peerage and the position of the military in the prewar period. These are many examples of the children and relatives of prime ministers following family traditions and serving in one or the other and often both. Itō's adoptive son, Hirokuni, served for several decades in the Imperial Household. Ōkuma Nobutsune served in the House of Representatives and as a personal secretary to his father-in-law up until Shigenobu's death in 1922, when he inherited a position in the House of Peers. Nobutsune's son, Nobuyuki, in turn served in the House of Peers but was elected to the House of Councillors in the democratic postwar period. Saionji was born into the longstanding noble Tokudaiji family and his brother served as Lord Keeper of the Privy Seal. His own children and grandchildren inherited the family headship and pursued political careers. As regards a military career alongside holding an aristocratic rank, Terauchi's son, Hisaichi, followed in the footsteps of his father by achieving the rank of field marshal and serving as war minister. Several other examples exist of the children of prime ministers such as Katsura and Yamamoto continuing the family tradition and serving in the Japanese Imperial Army or Navy and also being appointed to the House of Peers.

Rather than actively leveraging family connections to achieve a specific political goal, several prime ministers across the Meiji, Taishō and early Shōwa periods benefited from illustrious political backgrounds and the associated privileges of these inherited structures of power. Looking back, Konoe was born into one of Japan's elite aristocratic families. Hara's father-in-law was Nakai Hiromu, Meiji politician and diplomat, who played an active role in supporting Hara's career before he became prime minister (E. Yamaguchi, 2022). Looking forward, several former prime ministers during this period were the antecedents of politicians who would later occupy a range of roles from prime minister to cabinet minister and beyond. As a result, a number of origin stories can be highlighted. For example, Hosokawa Morihiro, who will feature in Chapter 5, became the first non-Liberal Democratic Party (LDP) prime minister in 1993 since the establishment of the party in 1955. He also ran unsuccessfully for the governorship of Tokyo in 2014. Hosokawa belongs to a formerly aristocratic family with ties to the Imperial family and is the grandson of Konoe. At the ministerial level, Hiranuma Takeo, an LDP politician who served in several ministerial roles through the 1990s and 2000s, was adopted into the Hiranuma family as a small child making him the grandson of Hiranuma Kiichirō. Tanaka Giichi's eldest son, Natsuo, served as a Diet member, as well as at gubernatorial and ministerial level.

At the international level, Ogata Sadako, who served as High Commissioner for Refugees from 1991 to 2000, and president of the Japan International Cooperation Agency, is the great-granddaughter of Inukai Tsuyoshi, who was assassinated in 1932. Ogata was at different times mooted as a possible prime minister of Japan and secretary-general of the United Nations (Kitaoka, 2019). In addition, one of Inukai Tsuyoshi's sons, Takeru, served as minister of justice from 1952 to 1954 in Yoshida Shigeru's cabinet. The spouses of diplomats and politicians have received academic attention for the political influence they can exert (Dobson, 2012a). Under this broader definition, we can mention Matsukata Haru, granddaughter of Matsukata Masayoshi, who married Edwin Reischauer, US Ambassador to Japan from 1961 to 1966.

Celebrity

As will be seen in the following chapters, especially Chapter 5, celebrity, and celebrity politics, have both recently and increasingly become salient phenomena. As a result, former prime ministers have engaged in non-political activities in the public eye by which they promoted their ideas, extended their influence or, in a few cases, reinvented themselves as celebrities. A more useful distinction that can be made during the period under examination in this chapter is the former prime minister being celebritized during his post-premiership and often after his death. With a considerable period of time in which to build a reputation and having been part of the oligarchs that led Japan through a pivotal period in its modern history, several of the prime ministers during this period have a present day reputation and degree of celebrity.

For example, before becoming prime minister, Ōkuma founded Tokyo Senmon Gakkō, which would become Waseda University and occupy some of his post-prime ministerial attention as discussed previously. This reputation forms part of his reputation today, symbolized by Ōkuma Auditorium, probably the University's most well-known building with its 125-feet high clock tower, whose height was meant to represent the age to which Ōkuma intended to live (Lebra, 1973: 131). In a similar vein, Matsukata is known today as the founder of the Bank of Japan.

Celebrity can go hand in hand with infamy and, as mentioned previously in terms of seeking to restore a reputation, Tōjō's legacy cannot be ignored as he continues to be a lightning conductor today for debates over Japan's role in WW2. This is despite the efforts of most of Tōjō's family, who '… set out on their postwar life with an obscure and heavy burden of responsibility on their shoulders' (Hiraizumi, 1983: 267). Their reaction for the most part was to respond evasively to curiosity and questions about their infamous relative. Tōjō's widow, Katsu, died in 1982 at the age of 91 having lived a reserved life since the end of the war, keeping the family home in its wartime state including the paper tape on the windows used avoid them shattering during air raids (Hiraizumi, 1983). Nevertheless, on the one hand, both at the time and still today, either within or outside Japan, Tōjō became the personification of Japanese militarism and its war of aggression. For example, the cover of an edition of A.J.P. Taylor's book *The War Lords* (1977), which focuses on Churchill, Hitler, Mussolini, Roosevelt and Stalin, also features

Tōjō. On the other hand, he captures nationalist sentiment in Japan, whether this be focused on Yasukuni Shrine where he was enshrined alongside other Class A war criminals in 1978, or in popular culture with the release of the sympathetic and revisionist biopic *Puraido* (*Pride*) in 1998 (Nuckolls, 2006). The dual nature of Tōjō's legacy emerged when his granddaughter, Yūko, an ultranationalist and apologist for Japanese militarism who sought to restore Tōjō's reputation, ran for election to the House of Councillors in July 2007. She was shunned by the ruling LDP and Prime Minister Abe Shinzō and ultimately unsuccessful but received some media attention outside of Japan because of her grandfather's reputation (NBC News, 2007).

Hirota has been described as 'an historical figure in search of his niche' (Farnsworth, 1974: 227). The IMTFE charged him with having sought 'overzealously to protect and enlarge Japan's position in China, and when diplomacy failed, … willingly endorsed military threats and aggression' (Farnsworth, 1974: 228). He was found guilty as a Class A war criminal and executed on 23 December alongside Japan's military leaders, becoming the only civilian to be executed. Although he may have felt that he did not stand shoulder to shoulder with Tōjō and Japan's military leaders, the ashes of the seven executed Class A war criminals executed the same day were conveyed to a shrine near Atami, where in 1959 a monument dedicated to 'seven patriots' was erected at an unveiling ceremony attended by Yoshida Shigeru (Shiroyama, 1977: 2).

Anchor Point

As mentioned in the previous chapter, Tsuda describes how Satō Eisaku provided political stability during a time of upheaval in the 1970s despite his relatively short post-premiership. Former prime ministers playing the role of an Anchor Point can also be seen during the tumultuous period explored in this chapter. Often referred to as the last of the *genrō*, Connors regards Saionji's domestic and international role as that of a figurehead, meaning 'a figure of critical importance in politics', rather than denoting a passive role (Connors, 1987: 63). During summer 1918, the putative benefits of establishing a third Saionji cabinet, which was dubbed the 'National Unity Cabinet' but never realized, were seen very much in terms of consistency and an Anchor Point (Connors, 1976: 30). Ultimately, during his long post-premiership, 'Saionji was a conduit between a variety of elites in all of which he had acceptability and credibility' (Connors, 1987: 213–14).

In a more specific example, Yamamoto's return to the role of prime minister in September 1923 almost a decade after his first premiership was in response to the national emergency of the Great Kantō earthquake and sudden death of Katō Tomosaburō in office. Yamamoto served until January 1924, when he again resigned over the Toranomon Incident of December

1923 when an assassination attempt was made on the Crown Prince Hirohito (Oka, 1986: 196).

Summary

It is worth making some initial observations at this early stage as regards the relevance and prominence of the categories of post-prime ministerial afterlives during this period of nascent and truncated democracy. Chapters 4 and 5 will revisit these observations and develop them in light of their temporal focus, ahead of a more detailed analysis in Chapter 6.

First and foremost, Still Ambitious is a heavily populated category with 13 of the 29 prime ministers who served during this period returning to the position of prime minister at least once. Many former prime ministers also served in ministerial roles or other positions of power and influence. The fact that various positions of power should be occupied, sometimes on multiple occasions, by the same people is not surprising when considered against the context of the period and the tight grip on power exerted by a small group of Meiji oligarchs and thereafter military leaders. This will contrast starkly with the postwar and post-Cold War periods explored in Chapters 4 and 5.

In contrast to a return to power, assassination represents an extreme example of extinguishing political careers during this period. This phenomenon would disappear with the establishment of a stable democracy after WW2 but still occasionally rears its head, along with other forms of political violence, as will be seen in the following chapters.

Political dabbling appears to be less of a stand-alone category and instead conflates with other categories, most notably First Citizens, as well as protégés and acolytes. On the one hand, this is because of the institution of the *genrō*, and later *jūshin*, which provided a recognized vehicle by which some former prime ministers could continue to exert influence. On the other hand, the close ties and lines of lineage among the Chōshū leaders with Yamagata Aritomo at their head enabled some former prime ministers to continue dabbling. Chapters 4 and 5 will continue to trace this trend ahead of more detailed consideration in Chapter 6.

The development of celebrity culture goes hand in hand with the development of modern media and communications in the late 19th and 20th centuries. As a result, some former prime ministers certainly had reputations at the time, for example Ōkuma and Hara. The institutionalization of an honours system as a trapping of a modern nation possibly played some role in elevating the status of former prime ministers after their resignation or posthumously. However, instrumentalizing celebrity as a political resource or the possibility of a celebrity career were not realistic options for a former prime minister at this time. However, from the viewpoint of today and with enough passing of time, the reputations of some prime ministers have been forged during this extended afterlife. Similarly, although Family Affairs as a category does not seem as relevant to this period as it will to the others that follow, with the passing of time a number of political dynasties can be observed.

Finally, the period under examination in this chapter was particularly dramatic with the emergence of Japan as a modern nation, the death of the Meiji emperor, the destruction of the Great Kantō earthquake, war and defeat. The stability that a former prime minister and experienced safe pair of hands could provide as an Anchor Point at difficult times was acknowledged at times during this period. The following empirical chapter will continue the stories of prime ministerial afterlives between two major watershed events: defeat and occupation in 1945 through to the end of the Cold War.

4

Former Japanese Prime Ministers, 1945 to 1989

Overview

This chapter will focus on the period from the end of World War Two (WW2) to the end of the Cold War and the 17 prime ministers who served during this time. These prime ministers, listed in Table 4.1, held office through a period of profound changes in Japanese society and politics. Defeat in WW2 and the Allied Powers' occupation (1945–52) marked a transition toward liberal democracy, the re-emergence of party politics and the establishment of a pacifist constitution. During the early postwar years, political parties rose and fell according to diverging political and ideological interests. Countering the popularity of left-wing movements, conservatives merged to form the Liberal Democratic Party (LDP, *Jiyū Minshutō*). This so-called '1955 system' stabilized as a two-party contest between the LDP and the Japan Socialist Party (JSP, *Nihon Shakaitō*) until the end of the century. As democratic norms were entrenched, Japanese leaders were increasingly beholden to popular sentiment. Thus, political crises such as the mass protests against the Japan–US Security Treaty (1960) and involvement in scandals like Lockheed Martin (1974) and Recruit (1989) forced the resignation of contemporary premiers Kishi, Tanaka and Takeshita, respectively.

Internationally, Japanese political leaders navigated the various dynamics of the Cold War. Japan regained its sovereignty in 1952 under a peace treaty signed with the Allied nations but not, crucially, with communist forces. As the Cold War heated up in East Asia, Japan entered a security alliance with the US which maintained American bases on Japanese territory. Within the capitalist camp, Japan enjoyed relatively few international disturbances through the 1960s even as its ally entered the war in Vietnam. However, the 1970s was a tumultuous decade; not only was a prime minister arrested on bribery charges (Tanaka), but Japan navigated ups and downs such as the end of the Bretton Woods, the reversion of Okinawa, normalization of

Table 4.1: Former Japanese prime ministers, 1945 to 1989

Name	Born	Party[1]	Tenure as PM	Days in office[2]	Former PMs alive	Age at leaving office	Died	Total post-PM years
Higagashikuni Naruhiko	1887	Independent	17 August 1945 to 9 October 1945	54	10	58	1990	44
Shidehara Kijūrō	1872	Independent	9 October 1945 to 22 May 1946	226	10	73	1951	5
Yoshida Shigeru	1878	Liberal; Democratic Liberal (from 1948 to 1950)[3]	May 22 1946 to 24 May 1947; 15 October 1948 to 10 December 1954	368; 1,682	11; 11	68; 76	1967	14
Katayama Tetsu	1887	JSP★	24 May 1947 to 10 March 1948	292	12	60	1978	30
Ashida Hitoshi	1887	Democratic[4]★	10 March 1948 to 15 October 1948	220	13	60	1959	11
Hatoyama Ichirō	1883	Democratic (until 1955) and LDP (after merger in 1955)	10 December 1954 to 23 December 1956	745	4	72	1959	2
Ishibashi Tanzan	1884	LDP	23 December 1956 to 25 February 1957	65	5	72	1973	16
Kishi Nobusuke	1896	LDP	25 February 1957 to 19 July 1960	1,241	6	63	1987	27
Ikeda Hayato	1899	LDP	19 July 1960 to 9 November 1964	1,575	5	64	1965	< 1

Table 4.1: Former Japanese prime ministers, 1945 to 1989 (continued)

Name	Born	Party[1]	Tenure as PM	Days in office[2]	Former PMs alive	Age at leaving office	Died	Total post-PM years
Satō Eisaku	1901	LDP	9 November 1964 to 7 July 1972	2,798	6	71	1975	3
Tanaka Kakuei	1918	LDP	7 July 1972 to 9 December 1974	886	5	56	1993	19
Miki Takeo	1907	LDP	9 December 1974 to 24 December 1976	747	5	69	1988	12
Fukuda Takeo	1905	LDP	24 December 1976 to 7 December 1978	714	5	73	1995	17
Ōhira Masayoshi	1910	LDP	7 December 1978 to 12 June 1980	554	5	70	1980	0
Suzuki Zenkō	1911	LDP	17 July 1980 to 27 November 1982	864	5	71	2004	22
Nakasone Yasuhiro	1918	LDP	November 27 1982 to 6 November 1987	1,806	6	69	2019	32
Takeshita Noboru	1924	LDP	6 November 1987 to 3 June 1989	576	6	65	2000	11

[1] Affiliation during tenure as prime minister.
[2] According to https://japan.kantei.go.jp/past_cabinet/index.html
[3] Yoshida's administrations were in coalition to greater or lesser degrees, except in 1953–1954 when his Liberal Party (*Jiyūtō*) was in minority government.
[4] Ashida's Democratic Party (*Minshutō*, 1947–50) and Hatoyama's Democratic Party (*Nihon Minshutō*, 1954–55) are separate political parties.
★ Indicates coalition government.

relations with Beijing and the dual oil crises. Especially the so-called Nixon Shocks of 1971 sowed doubt on the extent to which Japan could rely on the US. These doubts came to a head in the 1980s when Japan's economic boom led to a trade deficit and tension between the two countries.

Both the Shōwa era and the Cold War came to an end in 1989. The prime ministers of those 45 years contended with profoundly differing political, social and international contexts. A number of categories stand out in this era as the most prominent routes for former prime ministers to extend their influence. Compared to the frequency with which prewar prime ministers returned to the post as discussed in Chapter 3, postwar prime ministers were rarely able to do so, with Yoshida the sole exception this era. Instead, former prime ministers still ambitious for the premiership became powerful actors in backroom politics. Through widened democratization from the end of WW2, maintaining popularity was paramount for the LDP to retain their position in government. As a result, powerful but unpopular former premiers were inhibited from a return to the post; yet, their prominence as Political Dabblers in this period marks the limits of democratic norms since the establishment of the LDP. As we will see in this chapter and the next, the specific domestic and international currents of the times have shaped which categories of influence former prime ministers are able to mobilize, as well as how. While Acolytes and Protégés remained an important avenue of power, in the postwar democratic era, forging a political legacy as a 'family business' became equally significant. Each prime minister had different interests and ambitions, as well as personal legacies which drove their actions. Yet, as we will see in this chapter, those contexts also shaped *how* different prime ministers were able to act and continue to influence Japanese politics and foreign policy.

Still Ambitious

Some former prime ministers continued to demonstrate an ambition for political influence as a public official. For some, this meant holding on to elected or bureaucratic positions, though they may not seek the highest position as prime minister again. Shidehara Kijūrō exemplifies this subcategory. A career diplomat, he served as ambassador to the United States from 1919 to 1922 and was appointed foreign minister in 1924 under Katō Takaaki, his brother-in-law through their wives, a position he retained in Wakatsuki Reijirō and Hamaguchi Osachi's administrations. He was pro-US/UK and known for his opposition to the army, incurring considerable criticism as a result. As seen in the previous chapter, Shidehara served as caretaker prime minister after Hamaguchi. He retreated from politics after the second Wakatsuki cabinet was forced to resign in 1931 after failing to prevent the Imperial Army from escalating tensions in Manchuria.

However, he was convinced out of retirement by Yoshida Shigeru in the immediate aftermath of Japan's defeat. Shidehara stepped in as premier upon Higashikuni Naruhiko's resignation in October 1945, considering this duty as his 'last public service' (Amakawa, 2016: 11). One of his key achievements was to successfully negotiate the continuity of the imperial court with General Douglas MacArthur (Hattori, 2021a: 274–5).

Shidehara stepped down on 22 May 1946 as a result of Japan's first postwar elections the previous month, which installed Yoshida's first coalition government. Joining a political party for the first time, Shidehara stayed on in the cabinet as the leader of the conservative Progressive Party (*Shinpotō*) to see out the transition to the new constitution (Amakawa, 2016: 11). He was elected to the Lower House for the first time in the 1947 general election, though the same result brought down the first Yoshida government. He was re-elected for a final time in 1949, at the same time that Yoshida's Liberal Party (*Jiyūtō*) mandate was re-established. Shidehara had hoped – and perhaps expected – that Yoshida would appoint him to the cabinet, given Shidehara had mentored the younger Yoshida's rise through the Foreign Ministry. However, he was side-lined in favour of a younger generation of politicians and appointed instead as the Speaker of the House of Representatives, a position he would hold until his death in-post in 1951 (Shidehara Heiwa Zaidan, 1955: 747–8).

Despite the relegation to a largely ceremonial role, the appointment re-invigorated Shidehara's efforts to guide foreign policy, especially as Japan looked toward a peace treaty in the context of the emerging Cold War in East Asia. Shidehara had long insisted that foreign policy and domestic party politics ought to be kept separate. To him, the peace negotiations were the prime moment for Japanese parties to have a bi- or non-partisan foreign policy (*chōtōha gaikō*). As speaker, he brought rivalling Liberal and Democratic parties together to establish a joint foreign policy council (Hattori, 2021a: 313). In this period, the JSP and the Communist Party (JCP, *Kyōsantō*) sought a comprehensive peace treaty which included a settlement with Moscow and Beijing, but this was opposed by conservatives who favoured a treaty with US-led capitalist states linked to a security deal with the US. Shidehara sought to bridge the gap between the conservative and progressive parties by shuttling discussions between Yoshida, Tomabechi Gizō, chairman of the Democratic Party, and Asanuma Inejirō, General Secretary of the JSP (Igarashi, 1985: 324). Ultimately, Asanuma rejected his proposal and the progressives maintained their position on a comprehensive peace deal. Nevertheless, Shidehara's efforts did bear fruit; he is credited for uniting the Democratic and Liberal parties in peace treaty policy, overcoming their contentious differences over Japan's rearmament, before his sudden death in 1951 (Shidehara Heiwa Zaidan, 1955: 760–1).

Meanwhile, other former prime ministers were *personally* ambitious to regain the top role. By stark contrast to the prewar period (see Chapter 3), rarely have such efforts been successful in the decades following WW2. The notable exception was Yoshida Shigeru's comeback after a poorly regarded first term and a year and half out of government. Like his mentor Shidehara, Yoshida was also a career diplomat who was deeply critical of the militarists. He served as consul-general in Mukden (1925–28), clashing with the military authorities, before serving in Europe as ambassador to Italy (1931–32) and the Court of St James (1936–38). Yoshida was no stranger to informal politics: though he resigned his ministry position in 1931, he worked behind the scenes to resist the militarist government's move to war and thereafter to negotiate favourable terms for Japan's surrender (Finn, 1992: 19–21). From September 1945 after Japan's defeat, Yoshida served as foreign minister under Higashikuni and Shidehara, stepping up to prime minister in May 1946 as a result of Japan's first postwar elections.

Yoshida's Liberal Party lost its majority by a small margin in April 1947, leading to the short-lived Katayama and Ashida cabinets under a coalition of the JSP and Democrats. As Dower (1979: 314) has noted, it was only in his second term that the famous 'Yoshida era' of early postwar politics was inaugurated. When the Ashida cabinet was forced to resign as a result of the Shōwa Denkō scandal in October 1948, Yoshida considered himself entitled to form the next government as the leader of the opposition (Yoshida, 2007: 72). In his time outside of the prime minister's office, Yoshida had been courting parliamentarians disgruntled with Ashida to join his party (*The Japan Times*, 1948). While the transition was not smooth owing to resistance from the Occupation and within his own party, Yoshida's grouping absorbed defectors from the Democratic Party and formed the Democratic Liberal Party (*Minshu Jiyūtō*, which was re-styled as the Liberal Party again in 1950). By the time Ashida's cabinet collapsed, Yoshida was poised to step into the premiership as the leader of the largest party. Three months later in early 1949, Yoshida's party won an absolute majority in the Lower House, securing a crucial public mandate (Dower, 1979: 314). Yoshida went on to form five governments in total through 1954, shaping the core of Japan's postwar trajectory and earning him varying reputations as a 'strong-man' by detractors or otherwise praised as a 'Japanese Churchill'.

Most former prime ministers of the Shōwa era with ambitions for a return to the top job were unsuccessful. A wide cast of characters that include Kishi Nobusuke, Tanaka Kakuei, Miki Takeo and Fukuda Takeo are rumoured to have plotted a return to the premiership. For all four, their political durability made their potential declarations to run for LDP presidency a real and tangible possibility. Fukuda, for example, had stepped down in 1978 yet had hopes to reclaim the position, and despite his elderly age, at 84 the

Japanese press considered him a possible successor to Takeshita and Uno in 1989 (Hayao, 1993: 103).

Despite their achieving the highest public office once, many former prime ministers were ambitious for a return, many considering themselves to have unfinished business. This was clearly the case for Shidehara and Yoshida, who sought to affect Japan's foreign policy at a crucial moment in the country's history. As we will see further later, this was also true in Kishi's case, for whom the premiership was a means to pursue constitutional revision and rearmament. Ultimately, Yoshida was the only former prime minister who was able to make use of the unstable party landscape of the early postwar era and return to the highest office.

Exhausted Volcanoes

Compared to the previous era, only a small handful of former prime ministers were politically exhausted after their time in office, active in neither backroom politics nor on the national and international stage. In this period, Ōhira Masayoshi was the only prime minister to die in-post in June 1980.

A notable exception is Higashikuni Naruhiko, who lived 45 years as a former prime minister and a private citizen with little involvement in politics until his death at age 102 in 1990. Born into the imperial family and opposed to war, Higashikuni served as Japan's first postwar prime minister. In office for only 54 days, the main task for his administration was to sign the instruments of surrender and prepare for and oversee the transition to the US-led Occupation. After stepping down, Higashikuni was subject to the Occupation's purge from public office and was stripped of his royal status along with other members of the imperial branch families. As a private citizen, he founded a number of unsuccessful business ventures and in 1950 established a Buddhism-based eponymous religious organization. Originally named *Heiwa-Kyō* (Peace Teaching), the tenet of Higashikuni-Kyō was the abolition of war by transcending religious differences and facilitating inter-religious discourse (Akimoto, 2022: 37). The sect was ultimately disbanded as it violated new postwar laws controlling the registration of religious organizations. He continued to engage with the upper echelons of society as a close relative of the emperor and became honorary president of several cultural organizations including the International Martial Arts Federation. Over the years, he published his journal and memoirs of his time in politics, but he never resumed public office.

Most often, the short afterlives of former prime ministers contribute to this category, as was the case for Satō Eisaku. A protégé of Yoshida Shigeru, Satō was an elite bureaucrat before being elected to the Lower House in 1949 and appointed to Yoshida's cabinets in 1951 and 1954.

He served in Kishi's and Ikeda Hayato's cabinets and was subsequently appointed prime minister in late 1964 after Ikeda resigned due to ill health. Satō is remembered for his long tenure – he was the longest-serving prime minister in postwar Japan, only beaten by his great-nephew Abe Shinzō. In office during a turbulent period of both high-growth and international economic turmoil, his administration oversaw significant changes such as the reversion of Okinawa and Ogasawara islands from US control. Satō stepped down in July 1972. His final days in office were characterized by the Nixon Shocks and rivalry between LDP heavyweights Fukuda Takeo and Tanaka Kakuei, giving the impression that Satō's was a beleaguered administration.

As Taro Tsuda (2023) has shown, despite only surviving a further three years as former prime minister, Satō was deeply influential as a party elder and in diplomacy. Within the LDP, he acted as a 'peacemaker' between the warring Tanaka and Fukuda factions. He was structurally enabled to do so as an unpopular Tanaka government needed to reconcile with his rival to shore up public support (Tsuda, 2023: 14). Satō also leveraged ties made while prime minister. For one, he is said to have negotiated Japan's sovereignty over Okinawa islands personally with Richard Nixon in secret, in exchange for tacitly allowing the US military to transport nuclear weapons through US bases in Japan (Akimoto, 2022: 122). This personal connection was key to Satō's continued influence as a former prime minister. Invited to Nixon's second inauguration in 1973 as a friend of the president, Satō circulated among US policy makers on a trip that also included attending Lyndon Johnson's funeral. His presence as an elder statesman shored up Japan's alliance with the US when the latter was having doubts about the state of Japanese foreign policy under Tanaka. Henry Kissinger, for one, praised Satō as a 'sincere friend of the United States' in his 1979 memoir (quoted in Tsuda, 2023: 12).

Hatoyama Ichirō and Ikeda Hayato similarly had short post-prime ministerial lives but, unlike Satō, spent it outside of the political arena. Hatoyama carefully judged the right time to leave office and voluntarily resigned in 1956. Although he ran for and won his Lower House seat again in 1958, in effect he spent three quiet years retired from politics. Ikeda had little opportunity for influence as an elder. Having stepped down in late 1964 due to cancer, he succumbed to his illness in 1965.

To be an Exhausted Volcano is not a monolithic category. A former prime minister may not be active in the political world but may have a long and ambitious list of achievements. Others quietly retire, often fighting an illness though they may hold onto an elected office. Still for others, death cuts short what could have otherwise been a prolonged political career. The case of Satō presents a striking comparison to others in this category as he was active in informal politics until his fatal stroke in 1975.

Political Dabblers

Political dabbling took two forms in the era studied in this chapter. In the first decade after the war, Japanese leaders, including former prime ministers, were heavily involved in forming and dissolving political parties in the fledgling democracy.

One key area of contention was Yoshida's 'one-man' dominance in the early postwar era. Critique of Yoshida and his foreign policy was a major motivator for a wide cast of characters in this period, including Ashida Hitoshi both before and after his premiership. Broadly considered a liberal-leaning conservative, Ashida left the Foreign Ministry in 1932 in opposition to the Manchurian Incident (1931) and was first elected to the Lower House the same year. Concurrently serving as president and editor of *The Japan Times* (1933–39), he was a vocal critic of the militarist government's foreign policy (Akimoto, 2022: 62). Although Ashida had assisted in forming the Liberal Party after the war, he left the party in 1947 owing to frustrations with Yoshida's dominance. Ashida took over the premiership in 1948 from Katayama Tetsu in the Democrats' anti-Yoshida coalition government with the JSP. However, he was forced to resign in October when it came to light that members of his cabinet had received kickbacks from the chemicals producer Shōwa Denkō. In December, Ashida was himself arrested on corruption charges after the Diet (now under Yoshida's second administration) voted to lift his parliamentary immunity (Uji, 2001: 248).

Ashida announced his intention to run for re-election from his jail cell; released on bail, he won his campaign in January 1949. As a Diet member, he continued to voice criticism of Yoshida and the Liberal Party's foreign policy platform. Where Yoshida continued to emphasize economic reconstruction over re-armament, Ashida was increasingly concerned with communist forces and argued that Japan must be capable of militarily defending itself (*The Japan Times*, 1950). The anti-Yoshida movement gained momentum when the prime minister refused to step down in 1952 with the end of the US Occupation. In response, Ashida and his allies formed a centrist coalition Reform Party (*Kaishintō*) to directly oppose Yoshida's policies (Masuda, 2012: 569). As Yoshida's popularity waned, Ashida and future prime ministers Hatoyama Ichirō, Ishibashi Tanzan and Kishi Nobusuke formed a new party with defectors from Yoshida's camp (*The Japan Times*, 1954). In the end, Yoshida resigned from the premiership in December 1954 rather than be ousted from the job through a vote of no confidence (Shinoda, 2000: 66; Itoh, 2003: 119; Watanabe and Eldridge, 2016: 87). While Yoshida's tenure in the top job came to an end in this way, his influence cast a long shadow until his death in 1967, as we will discuss later.

To be sure, Ashida was not the only former prime minister in this period to have a hand in reshaping the party landscape. Shidehara Kijūrō allied with

Ashida in an effort to reconcile the conservative movement as discussed previously. However, when his efforts were side-lined, Shidehara re-joined Yoshida to form the Democratic Liberal Party in 1947 as its chief advisor (Hattori, 2021a: 281).

Neither were leftists immune to political instability. Katayama Tetsu, who was Japan's first postwar left-wing prime minister from 1947 to 1948, was unable to prevent the JSP from breaking off into the Right Socialist and Left Socialist parties in 1951. While the two factions reconciled in 1955 – and despite the strength of the labour movement in this period – ideological tensions continued. Katayama joined a defection from the JSP in 1959, helping to establish the more centrist Democratic Socialist Party (*Minshatō*, DSP) as its senior advisor.

The second pattern of political dabbling took shape as the electoral landscape settled into the so-called '1955 system'. The reunification of the JSP in 1955 catalysed the merger of the two conservative parties to form the LDP. The consolidation of the two left and right catch-all parties led to relative stability. In this era of LDP dominance, many former prime ministers engaged in political machinations, whether successfully or not, through intra-party factional politics. Because prime ministers relied on a coalition of factions to support their agenda, the power wielded by factional leaders was considerable, particularly in appointing members to influential positions in the party and government (Uchiyama, 2023: 84). A wide cast of (former) prime ministers held sway in backroom politics in this landscape, including Yoshida Shigeru, Kishi Nobusuke, Satō Eisaku, Tanaka Kakuei, Miki Takeo and Fukuda Takeo. By the turn of the 21st century, the next generation such as Nakasone Yasuhiro and Takeshita Noboru had continued to influence party politics as party elders.

The most emblematic period of backroom factional politics was the 1970s and 1980s, which were dominated by the fierce rivalry between LDP heavyweights Tanaka Kakuei and Fukuda Takeo. Tanaka, known familiarly as Kaku-san and in the media as the party's 'Shadow Shogun', was one of the few prime ministers without a university education, instead amassing a fortune in the construction industry through military contracts (Sterngold, 1993: 54). By contrast, Fukuda was born into an elite rural family, graduated from Tokyo Imperial University and rose through the ranks of the prewar Ministry of Finance. Both men were elected to public office after the war, Tanaka in 1947 and Fukuda in 1952; and both men were familiar with charges of corruption from early in their careers, Fukuda in 1950 and Tanaka in late 1947. The so-called Kaku–Fuku rivalry first sparked over the question of succession when Satō Eisaku stepped down in 1972. Though Satō was mentor to both men, his wish for Fukuda to succeed him was an 'open secret' (Hirasawa, 1972: 1; Fukuda, 1995: 193). However, Tanaka narrowly won the LDP presidency when future premier Nakasone Yasuhiro sided with Tanaka. His premiership, which was associated with the normalization of Japan's relations with communist China, came to an end in 1974 owing to declining popularity and accusations of financial impropriety.

The Tanaka–Fukuda rivalry resulted in tumultuous leadership changes. Despite his arrest in 1976 in connection to the Lockheed scandal, Tanaka wielded significant power within the LDP such that, by 1980, 'Tanaka's group had become the most important influence-and-patronage-dispensing center within the party, totally controlling who would be named prime minister' (Johnson, 1986: 2). The same year as his arrest, Tanaka was able to force Miki Takeo's resignation by campaigning with opposition parties against the prime minister in his home constituency (Babb, 2000: 100). While Fukuda narrowly won the LDP presidency and premiership in 1976, Tanaka was instrumental in ensuring the prime minister's defeat in 1978 by throwing his weight behind Ōhira Masayoshi. Fukuda, along with Miki, sought to undermine the Ōhira government in 1979 and successfully did so in 1980. When the incumbent Ōhira died suddenly, his successor, Suzuki Zenkō, was chosen as a compromise choice among the party elders (Fukuda, 1995: 258; Takeuchi, 2023: 663). In 1982, Tanaka-backed Nakasone won the party leadership despite Fukuda's efforts. So great was Tanaka's influence over the Nakasone government that it was dubbed the 'Tanakasone administration' (Babb, 2000: 102). Frustrated with this balance of power, the former prime ministers Fukuda, Miki and Suzuki sought to drive a wedge between Tanaka and Nakasone in 1984 but to no avail (Fukuda, 1995: 266–7).

However, the same 1984 contest marked the end of this era of factional politics. Tanaka suffered a paralysing stroke in 1985, though he retained his seat in the 1986 Lower House election. Politically, a younger generation of politicians were coming into power: the younger Nakasone was premier, Takeshita Noboru effectively usurped the Tanaka faction, and Fukuda and Suzuki had passed on their factions (Pharr and Kishima, 1987: 25; Babb, 2000: 3; Takeuchi, 2023: 683). The intensity of this era of factional intra-party conflict drew to a close with the electoral reforms of the mid-1990s (Hayasaka, 1994: 162). Nevertheless, former prime ministers like Nakasone, Takeshita and Suzuki continued to wield background-influence to varying degrees of success. While Suzuki was unable to overcome a crisis in his former faction, both Takeshita and Nakasone were powerful kingmakers within the LDP and influenced the next generation through the turn of the 21st century (Takeshita, 2001: 324; Hattori, 2023: 231).

Political dabbling in the second half of the 20th century primarily took two forms, according to Japan's changing political landscape. As the form of Japan's post-imperial democracy took shape, former prime ministers (as well as other political heavy weights) influenced the rise and fall of new political parties. In particular, the dominant figure of Yoshida Shigeru was a common foe against whose influence political alliances were struck. In the context of the LDP's long dominance from the 1950s, former prime ministers maintained significant influence as faction leaders in intra-party politics.

First Citizen

As outlined in Chapter 2, the category of First Citizen conveys a sense of dignity and non-partisanship to the former prime minister's activities. The role of *genrō* and *jūshin* who acted as extra-constitutional advisors to the emperor as discussed in the previous chapter was no longer apt in the context of postwar democracy. Yet, some former prime ministers are broadly considered to have acted in the interests of the nation and its people at a higher level than their personal or their party's narrow interests.

In the early postwar years, there were few influential former prime ministers because of the tumult of war and their association with militarism, much less those who could act as First Citizen (see Chapter 3, especially Exhausted Volcanoes). The closest to a postwar *genrō* and the First Citizen *ne plus ultra* was Yoshida Shigeru. Yoshida continued to hold his parliamentary seat after stepping down as prime minister in 1954 but was generally absent from the Diet. Instead, he hosted social events, received foreign dignitaries and counselled younger politicians from his home by the sea in Ōiso, Kanagawa prefecture (Kuwahara, 1992: 210–20; Hara, 2005: 228, 238). He played host to a wide range of foreign visitors, including Princess Alexandra of Kent and the Garden Club of America; Yoshida was deeply fond of gardening, and he was particularly proud of his rose garden (Asō, 1992: 506; Wada, 1992: 484–5; Yoshida, 1992: 256–8). His activities were far from frivolous or simply symbolic. From Ōiso he maintained a keen eye over Japanese foreign policy, with the Foreign Ministry unofficially allocating bureaucrats to keep Yoshida abreast of international affairs. According to Shimoda Takesō, as vice minister for the Foreign Ministry it was his role to regularly brief the former prime minister at his home (Mikanagi, 1992: 579; Shimota, 1992: 574–5).

Yoshida rarely left his residence. Yet on those occasions, he embarked on ceremonial and diplomatic engagements to various nations in North America, Europe, South America, southeast Asia and the south Pacific. Particularly fond of the West German chancellor Konrad Adenauer, in 1960 the two men reciprocated visits in Yoshida's Ōiso home and Adenauer's Lake Como vacation villa (*New York Times*, 1960; Yoshida, 1992: 20). According to Horie Shigeo, who was the incumbent head of the Bank of Tokyo and had accompanied Yoshida's excursion, the direct fruit of the Yoshida–Adenauer meeting was the 1962 loan from West German banks for Japanese infrastructure projects (*New York Times*, 1962; Horie, 1992: 518–19).

Not only did Yoshida harness his reputational standing to pursue Japan's strategic interests, he was also keen to influence foreign policy at the height of the Cold War. A central concern for Yoshida was the rising tensions between communist forces and the waning Western powers in southeast Asia. In the summer of 1962, Yoshida embarked on a world tour which included an invitation from the president of Brazil, meetings with John F. Kennedy in the US, Charles de Gaulle in France and Walter Hallstein, the first president of the European Economic Community, in Brussels (Wada, 1992: 485; Yoshida, 1992: 39–42, 44, 84). High on Yoshida's agenda on the eve of escalating tensions in Vietnam was convincing fellow leaders of the capitalist order of investing in southeast Asia to incorporate it into the liberal order. He argued:

> Such a coordinated international effort on the part of the free countries of the world to develop South-East Asia economically and to increase wealth and well-being of its peoples would not only open new and expanded markets to the free countries, but would act more powerfully than any other measure to combat the menace of communism. ... Even the Chinese living in the area would support such a scheme, since they would be free to make money, which they would not be permitted to do under the communist system. Through them, communication might very well be established with the people of mainland China. (Yoshida, 2007: 86)

Thus, diplomacy was a key activity in this category of continued post-prime ministerial influence in this period. In this sense, Fukuda Takeo is another example of a former prime minister who sought power on a broader non-partisan international scale. Fukuda had placed a particular emphasis on diplomatic relations during his premiership (see Edström, 1999a). Fukuda was ousted from office by Ōhira Masayoshi in 1978, but the subsequent administration of Suzuki Zenkō did not freeze him out. In fact, in 1981 the administration dispatched Fukuda to the United States when trade tensions between the two countries were increasing. There, he gave a speech to the influential Trilateral Commission and met with then-President Ronald Reagan. Acting as a go-between of Reagan and Suzuki, National Security Advisor Richard Allen called Fukuda 'an old friend of the United States' and that Suzuki had been 'wise to send him on this important mission' (Allen, 1981).

In 1983, Fukuda established the InterAction Council, an independent international forum for former heads of state located in Vienna, Austria. The aim of the organization is to promote international cooperation in the fields of peace and security, world economic revitalization and universal ethical standards, by mobilizing the collective experiences and networks of elder statesmen. To this end, the council distributes policy recommendations to international leaders on pressing global issues (InterAction Council, 2024).

While its direct influence is unclear, the Council has received some critical responses from high-level political figures such as the South Korean prime minister Kim Dae-jung (though before his tenure as head of state) and the Dutch Jurist Theo van Boven, who served as director of the UN Division for Human Rights (see Kim, 1993 and van Boven, 1998).

Of course, Yoshida and Fukuda were not the only former prime ministers of this period to engage in formal or marginal diplomatic efforts. By their very status, many have had opportunities to engage with international power brokers and political elites. Ashida Hitoshi toured France, England and Israel in 1958, and was hosted in the last by David Ben-Gurion (Ashida, 1986: 90–1). Kishi Nobusuke held meetings with Richard Nixon on the reversion of Okinawa while in the US for Dwight Eisenhower's funeral in 1969, while his brother Satō Eisaku attended Nixon's second inauguration in 1973 (*The Japan Times*, 1969; Tsuda, 2023: 12). Nakasone Yasuhiro was dispatched to Moscow to meet Mikhail Gorbachev in 1988 and 1989, then in 1992 to meet Boris Yeltsin in an attempt to resolve Japan's peace treaty issue (Hattori, 2023: 239). Takeshita Noboru represented Japan in 1996 when he travelled to France to attend the state funeral of François Mitterand.

Marginal diplomacy can enable a former prime minister to act in line with the principles of first citizenship or to shore up their reputation. Yet, whether they are *remembered* as such is dependent on their positive or negative public image. Here, post-office honours are an important element of the former prime minister's public image, especially if these are conferred while he is still alive. Yoshida was one of only three living prime ministers (along with Satō and Nakasone) who were awarded the Grand Cordon of the Order of the Chrysanthemum (*Daikun'i Kikka Saijushō*), the highest honour conferred to Japanese citizens during their lifetime. He had also been shortlisted for the Nobel Peace Prize in the mid-1960s. Not only was his nomination supported by domestic elites (including Satō, who would be the first and only Japanese recipient in 1974), the Foreign Ministry initiated a sustained campaign to raise support from political elites abroad (Yoshitake, 2017: 64). While Yoshida's death in 1967 put an end to the campaign, the seriousness of his candidacy demonstrates both significant political acumen and reputational influence as a First Citizen.

The role of a *genrō* was abolished with the democratization of Japanese politics after WW2. Yet as political elders, former prime ministers were primed to fill a similar role as a First Citizen, a non-partisan advisor and power broker in his own right. While many prime ministers of the mid to late 20th century have sought the mantle, none have enjoyed the political heft and reputation of Yoshida Shigeru. This may, in part, be due to the turbulent historical moment he was in power as the country rebuilt after war and defeat. By comparison, quasi-First Citizens like Fukuda and Nakasone were in office during a relatively stable period of Japanese history.

Embracers of a Cause

For many former prime ministers, the purpose of maintaining political, social and cultural influence was a means to pursue a specific cause or a series of interrelated issues. The causes could be 'moral' in that they relate to the personal or political beliefs of the former premier. Such was the case for Katayama. Raised Christian, his faith was the bedrock of his socialist and pacifist values. Prior to entering politics as a member of the prewar Social Democratic Party (*Shakai Minshūtō*), he was a lawyer who advocated for workers' and tenant farmers' rights, as well as women's suffrage. Though he was elected Japan's first socialist prime minister in 1947, hardships of early postwar shortages led to declining popularity, and he ultimately resigned in favour of Ashida in 1948 (Fukunaga, 2016: 53–4).

Katayama was active in both formal and informal politics as a Diet member until his retirement in 1963, seeking to advance the core causes of postwar Japan's socialist movement. Not long after stepping down, Katayama was invited to the Moral Re-Armament (MRA) movement's World Assembly held in Caux, Switzerland, in 1949. Founded in the 1930s by the evangelical Protestant minister Frank Buchanan, in the years following WW2 it served as a non-denominational forum for the pursuit of a broadly defined peace (see Hofmann, 2021). For Katayama, the assembly in Caux and the following tour of Germany, France and the UK served as a meeting place with other political leaders and an opportunity to learn from labour movements abroad (Katayama, 1967: 311).

Katayama sought to protect Japan's postwar pacifism against attacks from the political right. He was a staunch defender of the 1947 constitution, penning the 1954 monograph *Heiwa Kenpō o Mamoru* (Defending the Peace Constitution) and helping to establish the Council for Protecting the Constitution (*Kenpō-yōgo Kokumin Rengō*), an alliance of progressive political parties and civic organizations (Katayama, 1967: 303). He was also an avid anti-nuclear activist, sponsoring the first World Conference Against Atomic and Hydrogen Bombs held in Hiroshima in 1955 (Wittner, 1997: 9). Part and parcel of his pacifist activism was to seek reconciliation with Moscow and Beijing, travelling to the former in 1957, and twice to the latter in 1955 and 1959. In China, he met with Mao Zedong and Zhou Enlai. In the Soviet Union he met with Nikita Khrushchev and – demonstrating his religious leanings as a member of the Temperance Union – recommended the virtues of sobriety to the Russian leader (Katayama, 1967: 318–19).

That the socialist Katayama sought normalization with the communist world is perhaps unsurprising. He was not alone, however, joined by the liberal–conservative Ishibashi Tanzan who advocated reconciliation and warned against the use of armed force in the budding Cold War. Ishibashi was a prominent journalist before WW2, opposing militarism, colonialism and the government's financial policies such as lifting the gold embargo. Though he served in Yoshida's first administration, he was purged by the Occupation between 1947 and 1951 citing the broadsheet *Tōyō Keizai Shinpō*'s pro-Axis editorial stance during the war (Radtke, 2003; Inoki, 2016: 88–93). In 1956 he became the first elected president of the newly formed LDP, narrowly beating out Kishi Nobusuke. However, he served only 65 days as prime minister before resigning due to illness in February 1958 (see Table 4.1).

Ishibashi was critical of a foreign policy that focussed diplomatic relations solely with the United States. According to him, a unilateral alliance was a security risk as it could further antagonize communist forces in East Asia, and instead he called for a 'Quadrilateral Peace Alliance' which included Beijing and Moscow (Inoki, 2016: 94). He rallied support at home and abroad for his cause. During a visit to Beijing in September 1959, Ishibashi and then-Chinese Communist Party (CCP) premier Zhou Enlai released the famous joint communiqué outlining principles of establishing Sino-Japanese relations, which expressed that 'both sides believed that the peoples of China and Japan should hold hands and contribute to peace in the Far East and the world' (Akimoto, 2022: 94). Domestically, he was highly critical of the Kishi cabinet's staunch anti-communist stance. In May 1960, Ishibashi and his faction boycotted the vote to extend the Japan–US Security Treaty and called for Kishi's resignation in the wake of the mass protests and violent counter-protests which ensued (Tanaka, 2004: 155).

While his foreign policy interventions caused a stir within the LDP, Ishibashi had allies across political, cultural and business elite circles. Notable allies such as the politician Matsumura Kenzō and businessman Takasaki Tatsunosuke credited Ishibashi and followed suit with their own visits to Beijing through the 1960s (Nolte, 1987: 329; Kapur, 2018: 71). On the eve of his Beijing trip to normalize relations in September 1972, the incumbent prime minister Tanaka visited 87-year-old Ishibashi in hospital to ask for his elder's blessing ('*Ishibashi-sensei, Chūgoku ni ittekimasu*') (Tanaka, 2004: 159). And on the occasion of Ishibashi's death in 1973, Zhou sent his condolences and gave credit for the achievement of Sino-Japanese friendship (Suzumura, 2014: 109).

Ishibashi's stance on relations with communist powers and rearmament showed a serious cleavage within the LDP, not only with right-wing former prime minister Kishi Nobusuke but also with moderate and liberal-leaning conservatives like Ashida Hitoshi who were pro-rearmament. For both moderate and more radical conservatives, anti-communism (from both domestic and foreign forces) was a core concern. Ashida, who was forced to resign as prime minister in 1948, steered his parties toward a unilateral peace treaty with only the liberal camp as the Cold War intensified. To his mind, the conflict over the Korean peninsula was an indication that communist forces sought to expand militarily across East Asia. Japan, he argued, therefore required the capacity to defend itself against the eventuality of a full-scale invasion (Masuda, 2016: 67; see also Ashida, 1956).

Ashida advocated anti-communist rearmament until his death in 1959. He headed the LDP's Foreign Affairs Research Council and was deeply critical when the Hatoyama government moved to normalize relations with the Soviet Union in 1956. Outside of parliament, Ashida spread his views in lectures to the officers of the now-established Self-Defense Forces on diplomacy in the nuclear age (Ashida, 1986: 27). Ashida was a *liberal* Cold Warrior; yet his anti-communism allied him to bedfellows such as the radical right-wing nationalist Akao Bin, whose work he helped to fund. Inspired by a meeting with Akao, in 1952 Ashida and a group of political and business elites founded the New Armament Promotion Association (*Shin Gunbi Sokushin Renmei*) and its affiliate Student Defense Research Association (*Gakusei Kokubu Kenkyū Kyōkai*) (Yoshida, 2022: 44–46; Kusunoki, 2016: 66).

Another former prime minister who supported an anti-communist rearmament, one who has perhaps more organically aligned to Akao, was Kishi Nobusuke. Kishi's influence across wartime and prewar Japanese politics earned him the moniker 'Monster of the Shōwa Era'. Having overseen Japan's colonial project in Manchuria from 1936 to 1940, Kishi was arrested after the war as a suspected war criminal, but he was de-purged and elected to the Diet in 1953 with the help of his brother Satō (Kitaoka, 2016: 105; see also Levidis, 2020). Taking over from Ishibashi Tanzan's short-lived premiership in 1957, the Kishi government controversially re-signed Japan's security alliance with the US in 1960, against mass popular protests and opposition from the JSP and even members of his own party. Kishi was forced to resign when protests and violent counter-protests led to the highly publicized death of university student Kanba Michiko (Shimizu, 1960; Kapur, 2018).

Kishi sought to reverse many of the Occupation-era anti-militarist and pro-democracy reforms. For example, he considered limits to police powers 'a residue of the Occupation' and introduced measures to extend police duties while prime minister (Yasui, 2016: 92). Vehemently anti-communist, he spread his pro-Taiwan message through the LDP and caused difficulties as Tanaka Kakuei sought normalization with Beijing in 1972 (Hayasaka, 1994: 30). In a 1965 article penned for *Foreign Affairs*, he critiqued the LDP for its inability to overcome internal factionalism and come together to revise the constitution. He argued that:

> This issue [of revising the constitution's limitations on Japan's military] should be taken up not only as a means of uniting the conservative forces, but also as a means of eradicating completely the consequences of Japan's defeat and of the American Occupation. It is necessary to enable Japan finally to move out of the postwar era and for the Japanese

> people to regain their self-confidence and pride as Japanese. The true rehabilitation of Japan will begin at this point. Japan cannot be said to have found itself as a nation just because everyone has a TV set, plenty to eat and a higher income. (Kishi, 1965)

For Kishi, an alliance with the US was simply a pragmatic necessity during the Cold War. His ultimate goal was a 'true independence' free of Japan's reliance on US armed forces; this required, to his mind, revising the constitution to allow rearmament and the right to belligerence (Delury, 2015: 448–9). To this end, in 1969 he helped establish the National Citizens' Council to Enact an Independent Constitution (*Jishu Kenpō-seitei Kokumin Kaigi*, now known as *Atarashii Kenpō o Tsukuru Kokumin Kaigi*). According to Yasui Kōichirō, Kishi seriously contemplated making a play for the top job because of his frustration with the successive administrations of Ikeda Hayato and Satō Eisaku – his own brother – for their lack of interest in revising the pacifist constitution. Kishi was convinced that the issue had to be led from the top-down, and that perhaps his return as prime minister could do this (2016: 146).

Causes have also been advanced in less direct manners, such as in the cases of Yoshida Shigeru and Nakasone Yasuhiro whose involvement in educational and research projects were ideologically coloured. Yoshida was a central force in the restitution of Kōgakkan University in the late 1950s after it had been threatened with closure by the US Occupation. The university, which is the main teaching centre for Shinto priests, was necessary to restore traditional religious and cultural mores, Yoshida argued (Yoshida, 1992: 218). Some three decades later, Nakasone similarly argued that a reform in education and research were necessary. Following Kishi, Nakasone was a right-wing proponent for revising the postwar constitution which codified Japan's pacifism. Critiquing left-wing influence in postwar education as a hindrance to constitutional revision, in 1988 Nakasone founded the thinktank International Institute for Global Peace (Nakasone, 2002: ix). Renamed the Nakasone Peace Institute in 2018, it conducts research on national security and economic strategy and publishes the English-language journal *Asia-Pacific Review*, overseen by notable academics like Kitaoka Shinichi.

A cause taken up by a former prime minister may not be strictly (or only) ideological, as in the case of Takeshita Noboru's involvement with global climate change activism. Rising through the ranks under the patronage of Satō Eisaku and Tanaka Kakuei, the main achievements during Takeshita's premiership was to implement a consumption tax and the *Furusato Sōsei* regional revitalization programme. However, Takeshita was implicated in the Recruit insider trading scandal and was forced to resign in June 1989. Owing to the tax raise and the suicide of his personal secretary for connections with the Recruit Scandal, by the time of his resignation Takeshita held the dubious record of the being the least popular prime minister to date (Shapiro and Hiatt, 1989).

Like his mentor Tanaka Kakuei, it was after his premiership – and its scandal-laden end – that Takeshita gained influence in political circles. Climate change advocacy was not without its political benefits. As Yves Tiberghien and Miranda Schreurs argue, 'for Takeshita, who had been tainted by political scandal, it was a way to reinvent his own image as a green and clean politician and to make the LDP a more modern party' (2010: 150–1). This is not to say his activism was purely cynical, and environmentalism was clearly a cause he cared for: the 1989 Tokyo Conference on the Global Environment and Human Response toward Sustainable Development was initially proposed by Takeshita in 1988 after discussions with leaders at the Toronto G7 summit. In his words, 'politicians who do not know and act for environmental issues are those who lack intelligence, education, and courage' (quoted in Ohta, 2000: 100).

In the early 1990s, he helped establish the Global Environmental Action (GEA) for which he served as the first chairman. Takeshita was an advocate for differentiated financial responsibility, proposing that developed nations should compensate for the environmental degradation caused in the course of industrialization (*The Japan Times*, 1992). In April 1992, the GEA hosted the 'Eminent Persons' Meeting on Financing Global Environment and Development' of 29 political and business leaders. The meeting served as a jumping-off point for the UN Earth Summit in Rio de Janeiro later that year, to which Takeshita led a group of cross-party delegates. At Rio, the UN Conference on Environment and Development (UNCED) adopted Takeshita's proposal that industrialized nations should provide environmental development assistance. Japan, for its part, pledged between 900 billion and one trillion yen over five years. Takeshita was also influential domestically by putting climate change on the agenda of his ally Hashimoto Ryūtarō (who served as prime minister between 1996 and 1998).

The causes taken up by former prime ministers are shaped by the international political context. Throughout the Cold War the former premier's attitude toward the communist camp was a watershed: on the one hand were those who sought rapprochement with Beijing and Moscow such as Katayama and Ishibashi. For them, combatting the tensions in East Asia required building bridges between the two ideological sides. On the other hand, the cold warriors Ashida and Kishi considered re-armament a necessity in order to protect Japan against communist powers. For this, the postwar pacifist constitution required revising. As the rivalry between the two superpowers waned at the end of the 1980s, Takeshita's interest in environmentalism reflected both the increasing urgency of climate change and the liberal universalism of the era. Yet the cause of re-armament did not end with the Cold War, instead the mantle was taken up by the next generations of conservative prime ministers.

Seekers of Vindication

In postwar Japan, it has been exceedingly rare that prime ministers are able to step down even nominally on their own terms. Whether through their own making or because of contemporary political circumstances, many – if not most – prime ministers of this period left office with poor or weakened reputations. As a result, some sought to revise popular narratives of their personal and political histories and correct (perceived) wrongs.

Scandals brought the terms of some prime ministers like Kishi Nobusuke, Ashida Hitoshi, Tanaka Kakuei and Takeshita Noboru, to premature ends. Tanaka is a preeminent example of a former prime minister whose post-office reputation was mired with a legacy of political bribery scandals. Tanaka's connection to pork-barrel politics is well established. He was arrested on bribery charges for the first time only a year into his first term as a Diet member, when in 1948 the Shōwa Denkō scandal led to the resignation of Ashida Hitoshi, as discussed previously (Johnson, 1986: 6). A shrewd political operative nicknamed the 'Computerized Bulldozer', he rose through the LDP ranks to the premiership supported by a powerful electoral network in his home prefecture of Niigata. Tanaka resigned under suspicion of corruption in 1974; then, in July 1976 he was among a number of high-profile political elites arrested on charges of taking bribes from US aircraft manufacturer Lockheed. Tanaka became the first former prime minister to be convicted of corruption in a case that shocked the nation (*The Japan Times*, 1983).

Tanaka denied the allegations throughout the nearly seven-year trial, refusing to step down from his Diet seat. According to Chalmers Johnson, Tanaka had every reason to expect the incumbent prime minister, Miki, to instruct the justice minister to drop the case against him as such a practice was common in postwar Japanese politics (1986: 7). Miki, however, had been selected as premier for his reputation of 'clean' politics; his refusal to save Tanaka from embarrassment led to a movement by Tanaka's allies to unseat the prime minister (Babb, 2000:100). The LDP performed poorly in the subsequent general election in December 1976, leading to Miki's resignation. Tanaka was re-elected as an independent, vowing to 'retrieve [his] honor by having the truth of the Lockheed affairs clarified as soon as possible' (*The Japan Times*, 1976).

Even after his conviction in 1983, Tanaka believed he had not acted out of the ordinary remit of Japanese backroom politics and continued to appeal the decision until his death in 1993. Against renewed calls for his resignation and censure in the Diet, Tanaka ran in that year's snap elections, which came to be called the 'Tanaka Verdict Election'. The LDP performed poorly again, threatening Nakasone's administration, yet Tanaka won more votes in his district than he had as prime minister. Though Nakasone vowed publicly to distance himself, Tanaka's faction was better represented in the second Nakasone cabinet than any other. Thus, though he was never successful in overturning his conviction, until his health declined in the mid-1980s 'Tanaka remained the single most powerful politician in the country' (Johnson, 1986: 19; Tsuda, 2024: 471).

Nakasone, meanwhile, sought vindication not only *for* his reputation but *against* perceived wrongs. First elected in 1947 for the Democratic Party, he served in prominent positions in the administrations of Kishi, Satō, Tanaka, Miki and Suzuki. Nakasone is best remembered for being one of the more charismatic and dynamic premiers, and his major achievements include bolstering the relationship with the US through his friendship with Ronald Reagan (the 'Ron-Yasu' relationship). Domestically, he attempted to enact a series of bold reforms, some more successful than others. While he managed to privatize the railways during his time in office, his education and administrative reforms took longer. He is also associated with trying to settle postwar accounts in East Asia, but he contributed to the emergence of the history problem in Japan–China and Japan–Korea relations with his controversial visit to Yasukuni Shrine in 1985. He resigned in November 1987 having reached the end of the maximum term he could serve as prime minister.

While Nakasone continued as a powerful political figure as an LDP elder, he also worked to extend his considerable publication record. This included his memoirs, reflections on Japan's political history, current domestic and international affairs, and the nature of leadership (Nakasone, 1992, 1996). Most prominently, he was an active agent in constructing a heroic narrative of his life and career. In his telling, a heady mix of prewar education and culture and his personal character traits were the sources of his political success (Nakasone, 2010: 89; Nakasone, 2011).

He was concerned not only with glorifying his personal history but also with avenging himself against perceived injustices, especially after he was forced into retirement at age 85. In 2003, then-prime minister Koizumi Junichirō set an upper age limit for candidates standing from the LDP in an attempt to revive the party's image ahead of the general election. Nakasone took umbrage at Koizumi, angrily accusing his successor of age discrimination and calling the move tantamount to 'political terrorism' (Nakasone, 2006: x). Notably, his political cachet only grew after retirement (Hattori, 2023: 239). Yet, Nakasone continued his attacks in interviews and print media. Indeed, the Japanese title for his memoir, *Meditations: A Defendant in the Court of History*, demonstrates his sense of grievance (it was later published in English with the subtitle *On the Nature of Leadership*). In it, Nakasone begins with a piercing criticism of the prime minister, accusing Koizumi's government of being a 'show-window cabinet: no big guns, but good to look at' (2006: xi).

In this way, putting pen to paper has been a typical method of both rehabilitating one's image as well as exacting revenge. Many others, like Shidehara, Yoshida, Katayama, Ashida, Hatoyama, Ishibashi, Kishi and Miki were keen to record their legacy through memoirs. Notably, former prime ministers of the elder generation were keen to revise or justify their actions as a public figure during the war. On the one hand, as a liberal, Shidehara Kijūrō took to recording his prewar and war-time recollections to 'correct' the record and justify his actions (Hattori, 2021a: 314). On the other hand, for a reactionary like Kishi Nobusuke, colonial projects like the construction of the puppet state Manchukuo were not only justifiable but *just*. Thus, for Kishi seeking vindication was not an apologia for his imperial activities, as it was for Shidehara. Rather, it was to carry over the imperial ideology of Japan's exceptionalism (Delury, 2015: 449).

Vindication sought by former prime ministers can be against two objects: on one hand, they seek reputational restitution in some way. This may be against accusations – and convictions – of corruption as in the case of Tanaka; or, especially for former prime ministers in the earlier postwar era, against any legacy of their involvement in prewar Japanese politics. On the other hand, personal grudges against perceived wrongs can be a target of vindication. This is clear in the case of Nakasone, who became a vocal critic of prime minister Koizumi because of his forced retirement from public office, albeit not from political influence.

Acolytes and Protégés

As we have seen, leveraging one's factional members is a central mechanism through which former prime ministers have maintained political influence. While acolytes and protégés are often part of the former leader's faction, they are differentiated by the *personal* relationship fostered between the mentor and mentee. In the postwar period, as we will see in this chapter and the next, the junior up-and-coming politicians have served as a right-hand-man (*sokkin*) or engaged in the same cause as the former premier. In turn, they became the heir apparent and anointed as a future leader of the faction, party and even nation. For the former prime minister, manoeuvring their protégés into positions of power was not only a way to consolidate their legacy but also to maintain influence and progress particular ideological projects. Such was the case for Yoshida Shigeru (Ikeda Hayato and Satō Eisaku), Kishi Nobusuke (Shiina Etsusaburō, Abe Shintarō and Fukuda Takeo), Tanaka (Hata Tsutomu, Takeshita Noboru and Ishiba Shigeru), Miki Takeo (Kaifu Toshiki) and Takeshita Noboru (Hata Tsutomu, Hashimoto Ryūtarō and Obuchi Keizō).

The pre-eminent example of an elder statesman's influence over Japanese politics through a direct and personal relationship can be seen in Ikeda and Satō's veneration of Yoshida. Considered 'honours students' of the so-called 'Yoshida School' (*Yoshida Gakkō*), they are known primarily for carrying out the foreign policy course set up by their elder (Nakamura, 2016: 124; Hattori, 2021b: 52). In particular, this involved the priorities of navigating the security alliance with the United States in order to maintain a limited military and focussing instead on economic growth. The two men – who had known each other since their high school entrance exams in 1918 – were both held in high regard by Yoshida and their careers followed the elder's ebbs and flows. Both served ministerial positions in his cabinet; Ikeda was appointed Liberal Party secretary in 1954 at the peak of the anti-Yoshida movement, using his authority to expel chief detractors like Kishi and Ishibashi; when Yoshida resigned and left the party, Satō followed suit. Yoshida's followers split between Ikeda and Satō in the newly formed LDP. The Ikeda faction was so powerful it was dubbed the 'party within the party' (*tōnaitō*). Thus, though out of power, Yoshida and his protégés continued to hold significant sway within conservative politics. So great was Yoshida's influence that while Ikeda was the ostensible head of a kingmaking faction, even political rivals like Kishi would travel to Ōiso to court Yoshida's favour (Yasui, 2016: 99–100).

Yoshida was an active Political Dabbler for the purpose of manoeuvring his acolytes into positions of power. Despite his deeply held critiques of Kishi, there were strong suspicions that the two men had made an agreement in the late 1950s: in exchange for setting up Ikeda as the next prime minister after Kishi, Yoshida would support Kishi's efforts to address inequality of military capabilities and responsibilities with the US ahead of renewing the security treaty (Yasui, 2016: 103). According to witnesses, when Kishi's cabinet was forced to resign in the wake of protests against the Japan–US Security Treaty in 1960 (the so-called Anpo protests), the two men held a secret meeting in the onsen town of Hakone to hash out the succession. The result was Kishi backing Ikeda to be the next LDP president and thus prime minister ahead of his brother Satō (Yasui, 2016: 125–7). Yoshida had not abandoned Satō, however. When Ikeda stepped down due to his ill health in 1964, he named Satō as his successor on advice of party elders and Yoshida's recommendation (Nakamura, 2016: 137). Satō became prime minister on 9 November of that year, and he reappointed every member of Ikeda's cabinet. Though he passed away in 1967, between Ikeda and Satō's premiership, Yoshida's influence carried on for 12 years to 1972. Indeed, it is during this period in particular that Yoshida's activities are most First Citizen-like, or dispatched as an Anchor Point to calm tumult as will be discussed later.

Kishi, who was the other of the two major LDP power brokers at this time, was no stranger to political dabbling, as we have seen previously. Among his close followers were Abe Shintarō (his son-in-law), Shiina

Etsusaburō and Fukuda Takeo. Shiina had been his contemporary in the Japanese imperial puppet state of Manchukuo and one of the reform-minded group of bureaucrats (*kakushin-ha*) led by Kishi. Inspired by pan-Asianist ideology, these bureaucrats had strong connections with the imperial army and sought to implement a statist planned economy in the colony. Shiina was a long-time supporter of Kishi, advocating for his release from Sugamo prison after the war; as prime minister, Kishi appointed Shiina to be Chief Cabinet Secretary as his right-hand man (Levidis, 2023: 2). Shiina went on to head the Ministry of International Trade and Industry (MITI) during the high-growth era. Though he did not agree with all of Kishi's key policy positions (especially with Kishi's advocacy of remilitarization), he continued to be a trusted envoy and intermediary for the former prime minister as we will discuss later (Kanda, 2016: 195).

Kishi's most successful protégé was the prime minister Fukuda Takeo. Although he formally retired to Gotemba, Shizuoka prefecture, in 1979, with Fukuda effectively taking over his faction, Kishi extended his influence over the LDP until his death in 1987 (Hayasaka, 1994: 132). According to Fukuda, he was proud to have been relied upon by Kishi and sought to extend his mentor's initiatives such as those in population control and development (Fukuda, 1995: 328–9). Indeed, Fukuda took over Kishi's chairmanship of the Diet group Parliamentarians on Population and Development, which later expanded into the Asian Population and Development Association (APDA). Fukuda also served as an important linchpin of the Kishi-Abe familial legacy, as will be discussed further in the next section.

Hierarchy is a hallmark of social relations in wider Japanese society, and the political sphere is no exception. The relationship between a political elder – especially one with enough power to serve as prime minister – and his acolyte is mutually beneficial. On one hand, it is clear that having a former prime minister as a political patron can enable the protégé to move through to the highest echelons of power. This was the case for Yoshida's and Kishi's chosen tutees, but it was also true of Miki Takeo with Kaifu Toshiki and Tanaka with Takeshita Noboru, Hata Tsutomu and Obuchi Keizō, all of whom served as prime minister. It was also a benefit to the elder former prime minister. Yoshida was elevated to the status of a First Citizen during Ikeda's and Satō's administrations, while Kishi ensured political succession through Fukuda.

While we have presented lines of influence through these hierarchical relationships for the sake of clarity, loyalties may not always be as clear-cut in reality. While Satō is broadly considered Yoshida's mentee, his relationship to his brother Kishi also impacted his political trajectory, as we will see in the next section. Similarly, Kaifu was part of Miki's political lineage, but he also had a relationship with Takeshita, who was his senior (*senpai*) from their time at Waseda University. Personal loyalties were thus cross-cutting and deeply related to the Political Dabbling and Family Affair categories.

Family Affair

As is clear from the discussion thus far, politics in Japan has been highly elitist and hierarchical through the modern period. As discussed in Chapter 3, in prewar and wartime Japan the governing class was oligarchical and the political circle was made up of the uppermost echelons of society, which included the military, royalty and business titans. Many former prime ministers of the postwar era were themselves products of powerful political and business dynasties. At the same time, there is a sharp contrast between the imperial and postwar eras, namely the number of political progeny who went on to hold elected office. Where previously political offspring could carry on the family legacy through the peerage or the military, such paths were no longer available with postwar democratization.

Out of the 17 prime ministers reviewed in this chapter, 12 have had members of their direct family (children, siblings or children-in-law) become public officials. It is simpler and quicker to name those who did not: Higashikuni, Shidehara, Katayama and Ashida. Though never elected, Ishibashi's son-in-law Chiba Kō was a diplomat, and Ikeda's son-in-law Ikeda Yukihiko served as foreign minister as an alumnus of the Foreign Ministry. Even Ōhira is represented in this category through his son-in-law who won the vacated seat when the prime minister died in-post. Most famous are those where former prime ministers' immediate family members and progeny have risen to the highest echelons of power. The brothers Kishi Nobusuke and Satō Eisaku both became prime minister, Fukuda Takeo's son Yasuo and Hatoyama Ichirō's grandson Yukio both became prime minister, while Tanaka Kakuei's daughter Makiko became the first female foreign minister.

Emblematic of politics as a family business is Nakasone Yasuhiro's line: the former prime minister's son, Hirofumi, apprenticed as his father's secretary and before being elected to the Upper House representing Gunma and served as foreign minister. In turn *his* son, Yasutaka, served as his aide before standing for election for the Lower House in 2017, also representing Gunma (1st District), a seat which he continues to hold after the 2024 general election.

Some former prime ministers directly dabbled to ensure their family line maintained political power. Kishi was an interventionist promoter of his family line, and in discussions with the party elder Yoshida Shigeru, he advocated for his brother Satō Eisaku to succeed his premiership (though, ultimately, Satō took over only after Ikeda) (Yasui, 2016: 125). The following generation followed in the two brothers' footsteps. Satō's son Shinji, who was serving in the Upper House, ran from his father's seat in the Lower House in 1979 after the former prime minister's death, and he went on to serve in the Takeshita Noboru and Hashimoto Ryūtarō cabinets. Kishi also actively manoeuvred his son-in-law Abe Shintarō through the ranks. After failing to win his first re-election campaign in 1963, Abe returned to the Diet in 1967 with help from Kishi and Satō (Nakagawa, 2022: 107). In 1986, a year before Kishi's death, Fukuda Takeo passed on his mentor's faction to Abe. Though he ultimately lost out to Takeshita Noboru, Abe was a top candidate to succeed Nakasone Yasuhiro's premiership. It was his son Shinzō – Kishi's grandson – who returned the lineage to the premiership and in doing so, broke his great-uncle Satō's record for the longest tenure in office. The Kishi name also remained in the uppermost echelons of influence with Shinzō's brother Kishi Nobuo, who served as defence minister in Suga Yoshihide's cabinet (2020–21). In 2023, his son Nobuchiyo won in a by-election in Yamaguchi, called in the wake of Nobuo's resignation due to illness, thereby continuing the Kishi/Abe family lineage in the prefecture (*The Japan Times*, 2023a).

Other former prime ministers had little active hand in the political career of their progeny. This is the case for Hatoyama Ichirō, who hailed from one of Japan's most well-known political families, often referred to as the 'Kennedys of Japan'. Hatoyama was himself a second-generation politician (*nisei*): his father served as leader of the Lower House in the prewar Diet, his mother was a prominent educator, and his biological and adoptive siblings were involved in politics directly or through marriage. After wresting control of the Liberal Party from Yoshida, Hatoyama accomplished the rare feat of stepping down from the premiership on his own terms in 1956 with his legacy assured (Itoh, 2003: 138). However, he was unable to convince his son Iichirō to run for office – the latter instead spent three decades at the Ministry of Finance. Though Iichirō did eventually run for office and served as finance minister, this was many years after Ichirō's death.

Instead, Iichirō's children – the former prime minister's grandchildren – proved more politically ambitious and leveraged their famous family's legacy. Kunio, who had worked as Tanaka Kakuei's secretary, ran from his grandfather's Tokyo district in 1976. His elder brother, Yukio, entered politics in 1986, running from Hokkaido. Yukio's district was largely made up of land historically owned by the Hatoyama family (Itoh, 2003: 164). In six generations the Hatoyama family have produced eight parliamentarians. The October 2024 general elections saw Hatoyama Kiichirō – Ichirō's great grandson and Yukio's son – stand for election for the Democratic Party For the People (DPFP) from the Hatoyama family's traditional Tokyo district (*Nikkan Sports*, 2024). While he failed to gain the constituency seat, he won the proportional representation seat. The Hatoyama political dynasty also continues with Hatoyama Yukio's nephew Jirō who was elected to his father Kunio's seat (Fukuoka 6th district) in 2016.

For children and offspring of the former prime minister, leveraging the family's name and connection can also help ensure his legacy. When Tanaka Kakuei suffered a paralyzing stroke in 1985, his daughter Makiko was central to preserving her father's continued political influence (Babb, 2000: 103). She was the unofficial first lady during Tanaka's premiership, and he lamented that she was not born male since he considered it impossible for a woman to succeed in politics. Carrying on the family name was a priority; thus when Makiko married her husband, Naoki, he changed his surname to Tanaka (Nakagawa, 2022: 117). Though Naoki's father, Suzuki Naoto, was also a parliamentarian and he later ran for office from his father's district, the national recognition of the Tanaka name was arguably more valuable (Smith, 2018: 134).

Despite her father's concerns, in 1993 Tanaka Makiko was elected to the Diet from her father's Niigata prefecture district not long before his death in 1994. Her rise was meteoric, and she became the first woman to serve as foreign minister and for a brief period she was touted as a potential future prime minister. Characteristically outspoken, Makiko's appeal derived from similarity to her father, 'but with the rough edges worn down' (Babb, 2000: 112). She continued to buttress her father's memory, penning numerous memoirs centred on her relationship with Kakuei (Tanaka, 1989, 2005, 2017, 2019). She and her husband resided in Kakuei's Tokyo residence known as Mejiro Palace, which long symbolized his profound influence over Japanese politics in the public imagination. Makiko and the Palace graced headlines again in January 2024 when the residence was razed by a fire started accidentally by Makiko lighting an altar incense (*Yomiuri Shimbun*, 2024a).

Tanaka Makiko and Miki Takeo's daughter Takahashi Kiseko are rare exceptions of *daughters* who were able to leverage their famous father's legacy for their own political career. Most often, women have played supporting roles to their male family members who carry on the family business. This was the case for Kishi's daughter Yōko, who as the wife of LDP heavyweight Abe Shintarō and mother of Prime Minister Abe Shinzō was known as the 'godmother' of Japanese politics (*Jiji Press*, 2024a). Similarly, Yoshida Shigeru's daughter Kazuko was politically minded in her own right, acting as her father's secretary and as adviser on his diplomatic missions, including to sign the San Francisco Peace Treaty in 1951. Her son Asō Tarō, Yoshida's grandson, entered politics and went on to serve as prime minister (Nakagawa, 2022: 42).

Former prime ministers are sometimes interventionist in ensuring their legacy through their family line. Like Hatoyama or Fukuda, they encouraged or expected their children to pursue elected office whether successfully or not. Typically, male heirs apprenticed as the elders' personal secretaries until they took over a district seat associated with the family name. Former prime ministers with no male heir-apparent enabled their son-in-law to run for office. Interventionists like Kishi politically dabbled while Tanaka's son-in-law took his wife's surname for a mutually beneficial arrangement. Daughters' roles varied; until the turn of the 21st century, they were overlooked as their fathers' heirs. Instead, they enabled political (and business) dynasties to extend their influence, a structure which works to sustain the elitist nature of Japanese politics.

Celebrity

Many, if not most, former prime ministers have sought to ensure their reputations extended past their time in office. Chapter 3 noted that this category has only become salient over recent decades with the proliferation of popular digital media. Nakasone Yasuhiro was the principal example of those select few who actively courted fame among the wider public. From his time as premier, Nakasone had garnered a reputation as interventionist and cultivated a 'presidential' or strong-man style of political leadership (Akimoto, 2022: 167). His immense publishing activities were no small part of his continued influence, especially after his forced retirement from elected office in 2003. Not only did he pen his visions for Japanese politics and foreign policy, he was also a vociferous commentator in popular publications such as news editorials and magazine articles (see Nakasone, 2008, for example).

Crucially, he did not shy away from the camera. As prime minister, he was more sensitive to media perceptions than his predecessors (Hattori, 2023: 160). After his retirement, he frequently appeared on television with politicians across the political spectrum such as the former LDP prime ministers Miyazawa Kiichi and Mori Yoshirō as well as Doi Takako, the former leader of the JSP (Hattori, 2023: 239). Moreover, he hosted his own talk show *Nakasone-Sō* (Nakasone Villas), which ran annually in December from 2004 to 2014, reflecting on the events of the year past with guests including the right-wing author and former Tokyo governor Ishihara Shintarō. In characteristic form, the show was produced because Nakasone 'had more he wanted to say' despite having stepped down as a parliamentarian (Nakasone, 2015: 14).

Alongside Yoshida Shigeru and Satō Eisaku, Nakasone became the third living recipient of Japan's top honours in 1997 for serving 50 years in national politics. Whether actively pursued or not, Nakasone and his predecessors' reputations continued to be *celebritized* in popular media. While biographies of former prime ministers are a dime a dozen, some are also subjects of semi-fictionalized novels, films, mangas and even videogames. A famous example is *Shōsetu Yoshida Gakkō* (The Yoshida School: A Novel), a long-running fictionalization of Japan's political drama by Togawa Isamu, published between 1971 and 1981, and later adapted to film and manga.

Few former prime ministers in the postwar era courted fame as a form of influence. Ashida Hitoshi and Ishibashi Tanzan, for example, were famous prior to their political careers as journalists, but it was not until Nakasone that celebrity-influence was actively harnessed, continuing his media-consciousness. While other former prime ministers were mythologized as larger-than-life by various popular media, as television media came to the fore Nakasone opened a new era of political influence.

Anchor Point

The former prime minister's reputation as a stabilizing figure can be harnessed by both himself and the government of the day. As Tsuda (2023) demonstrated in the case of Satō Eisaku's short post-premier life, these figures provide a point of stability in moments of crisis or upheaval in Japan's domestic or international politics. Shidehara Kijūrō's premiership in the immediate aftermath of defeat was emblematic in this regard, as he was seen as a safe pair of hands among both the Japanese political elites and American occupiers until a general election could be called. As noted in earlier discussions, in his post-premiership Shidehara sought to bring rivalling parties together to unify Japan's response to the growing Cold War in East Asia.

The cleavages of the Cold War formed the structural backdrop for many former prime ministers to act as an Anchor Point, as was the case for Satō who shepherded the Japan–US alliance through the international turbulence of the early 1970s (Tsuda, 2023: 12). Satō was not the first prime minister to help stabilize Japanese relations with allies; both Yoshida and Kishi played key roles in Cold War-era diplomacy as ex-leaders. In the case of Yoshida, he helped smooth over relations with Taipei as Japan increased dealings with Beijing. As seen throughout this period, the question of 'two Chinas' was a point of contention both between the LDP and the JSP but also within the governing party itself. While the Japanese government had formally recognized the government in Taiwan, relations with the communist mainland increased throughout the 1960s (Mendel, 1964: 1076; see also Hosoya, 1984: 256). Part and parcel of these shifts were Katayama Tetsu and Ishibashi Tanzan's activities with communist powers as discussed previously. When France normalized its relations with Beijing in 1964, the Ikeda government indicated that Japan could follow suit given the right circumstances, which sparked outrage from Taipei. Thus, at age 85, Yoshida travelled to Taiwan to smooth over ties with the Nationalist government. Billed as a 'private trip', Yoshida met with President Chiang Kai-shek to deliver a letter from Prime Minister Ikeda indicating Japan's continued support of Taiwan's claims (*New York Times*, 1964a; *New York Times*, 1964b). Although its political sensibilities would soon follow economic ties toward Beijing, Yoshida's known position as pro-Taiwan enabled Japan's ruling party to navigate relations across the Taiwan Strait.

Similar to this was Kishi Nobusuke's role. His personal tie to President Park Chung Hee was deployed in moments of crisis between Japan and

South Korea after normalization of relations in 1965. Kishi had long been a supporter of normalized relations between the two countries and considered Park's militarist regime a bulwark against communism in East Asia (Lee, 2011: 438). The strength of diplomatic relations was tried numerous times throughout the following years and Kishi and his acolytes were dispatched to Seoul on a number of occasions throughout the 1970s. In 1973, Kishi visited Seoul to smooth over relations between Park and then-premier Tanaka in the aftermath of then-opposition leader (and future president) Kim Dae-jung's kidnapping in Tokyo by South Korean intelligence. Similarly, in 1974 Kishi's protégé Shiina Etsusaburo was dispatched to mend relations when a Japanese-born ethnic Korean man attempted to assassinate Park and fatally shot his wife (Delury, 2015: 453–4).

At times Japan and the former prime minister face a wider international tumult. Such was the case for Nakasone Yasuhiro who was an important (unofficial) envoy to Iraq during the Persian Gulf War. Nakasone was one of several former leaders who met with Saddam Hussein in November 1990 to secure the release of hostages held by Iraq. Nakasone sought to capitalize on a previous relationship with Hussein, who he had met as MITI minister to negotiate a loan agreement for oil. As a result of the meetings, several dozen Japanese hostages were released. Writing to the American president, he urged Washington to continue dialogue with Baghdad (Nakasone, 1996: 596). Yet, as Hattori Ryūji points out, this was not only a public service on Nakasone's part. He had previously resigned from the LDP and as faction leader in relation to the 1989 Recruit scandal. Nakasone capitalized on his enhanced reputation from the hostage crisis and successfully staged a return to the party in 1991 (Hattori, 2023: 231–2). Thus, despite the image of a First Citizen/Anchor Point as a politically neutral public figure, their actions and power are shot through with both personal ambitions and ideological leanings.

Like the First Citizen, the Anchor Point relies on heavy political cachet. The former prime ministers who were able to act as a steady hand already wielded influence a cut above other former premiers. At the same time, it required some luck: a particular crisis required the personal character or advantageous relations of the particular former prime minister. For those former prime ministers who could fulfil these criteria, however, successfully shepherding Japan through a crisis could help to elevate their reputations and garner them even greater influence.

Summary

This chapter has unpacked the informal politics of former prime ministers who were in power between 1945 and 1989. This was a period of dramatic social and political changes both domestically and internationally. The different historical contexts had a bearing on how former leaders continued their political influence. In the first decade after WW2, the country's new democratic system was taking shape. This period was dominated by Yoshida Shigeru's two terms in office. Former prime ministers of the era either had little effect in influencing party politics (Higashikuni, Shidehara) or else made dethroning Yoshida a central focus of their political machinations (Katayama, Ashida).

The political system settled from the mid-1950s with the end of the Occupation, Yoshida's ousting and the (re)establishments of the LDP and the JSP. At the same time, the budding Cold War served as a structural backdrop to many former prime ministers' activities. On the one hand were those who sought reconciliation with communist forces, such as Katayama (the sole left-wing prime minister of this era) and Ishibashi. On the other were Ashida and Kishi, for whom rearmament was a necessary deterrent against international communism. It is worth noting the differences between these former prime ministers' embrace of *causes* and Yoshida's informal diplomacy as *first citizenry* or acting as an *Anchor Point*. The 1960s and 1970s saw a long period of Yoshida's protégés in power who carried on his policy directions; Yoshida's actions thus accorded with the nation's direction. Unlike those who actively sought to change Japan's foreign policy course – whether normalization with communist powers or aggressive remilitarization – Yoshida's actions could be considered politically *neutral* because they aligned with the status quo. As will be noted further in Chapters 5 and 6, these three categories have become increasingly blurred moving forward through the postwar era.

Though Satō was an acolyte of Yoshida's, his brother Kishi also supported his move to the top through both backroom and factional politicking. This marked a new era of political dynasties in postwar Japan. Given the older age that Japanese politicians tended to step into the prime minister's office, often their offspring or sons-in-law were a ripe age to continue the family business (Kishi, Satō, Tanaka, Miki, Fukuda, and Nakasone). In Takeshita's case, his Shimane seat was taken over by his much younger brother. Among these, the Hatoyama, Kishi-Satō and Fukuda families went on to produce two or more prime ministers.

The decade between the end of Satō's administration and the beginning of Nakasone's marked a period of intense intra-party rivalry, nearly toppling the LDP's dominance at times. The rotating cast of prime ministers in this period produced elder statesmen who sought to retain their political influence even after stepping down. Many, like Tanaka, Miki and Fukuda continued to vie for a return to the top job. The primary mechanism was through controlling – or appointing successors for – their respective factions. But they also retained power through other means, such as staying active on the international stage (Fukuda) or establishing their political lineages through acolytes and family (Miki, Tanaka and Suzuki).

The death of Emperor Hirohito in 1989 marked a turning point – the prime ministers who served beyond this point will be discussed in the next chapter. Suffice to say here that new challenges in Japanese and international politics impacted former prime ministers as well. Former leaders were engaged in diplomatic missions in a new international order after the end of the Cold War (Nakasone) and emergent issues such as climate change (Takeshita). Nakasone was the last of an older guard. Having remained an elected official for another decade and a half after stepping down, he was finally forced to step down in 2003 when the LDP under Koizumi Junichirō introduced a retirement age of 73 – though, as we saw previously, this did not preclude him from indirect political meddling.

We see in this chapter that the categories of political influence overlap, their boundaries often contingent on the historical or political context. By far, political dabbling was the most popular mechanism of retaining influence, especially through factional and backroom politics. Often, these were not *solely* for a will to power, but in order to advance particular causes or promote one's protégés. As compared to Chapter 3, the postwar democratic system eliminated various official and unofficial mechanisms for political dabbling. Yet, as will be discussed further in Chapters 5 and 6, we see that despite structural transformation to a liberal democratic electoral system and norms, this undemocratic political practice remains deeply important in Japanese former prime ministers' influence specifically and in Japanese politics more broadly.

5

Former Japanese Prime Ministers, 1989 to 2024

Overview

The period from 1989 to 2024 encompassed some seismic changes in the international system – from the end of the Cold War, the War on Terror, financial crises, through to conflict between Russia and Ukraine, and in the Middle East. East Asia was impacted not only by global changes but also regional concerns such as the Asian Financial Crisis, the 'rise of China' and the threat of North Korea's missile development. These international and regional shifts inevitably impacted upon Japan and led to changes in foreign policy, but a series of domestic economic and political 'shocks' in addition to natural disasters (most notably the Great Hanshin earthquake of 1995 and the 2011 triple disaster/Great East Japan earthquake) also produced considerable upheaval and transformation after 1989.

The collapse of Japan's bubble economy marked the beginning of this period, leading to long-term stagnation during the 'lost decade(s)' with successive governments implementing various types of economic reform plans, from Hashimoto's administrative reforms, through Koizumi's structural reforms, to Abenomics from 2012. Political reforms were also a central feature during this time as the perceived faults of the '1955 system' came to outweigh the benefits. Problems associated with a one-party dominant system, a flawed electoral system, political scandals and corruption, and a dominant bureaucracy were tackled through a set of rolling reforms most closely associated with prime ministers Hosokawa (electoral reform), Hashimoto (administrative reform), Koizumi (postal reform and the attempt to get rid of Liberal Democratic Party [LDP] factions) and both Abe administrations (economic revitalization and changes to security policy). The period ended very much as it began in terms of the political environment – from 2023 to 2024 the LDP was embroiled in scandal, experiencing internal conflict, changing its leadership with increasing regularity and losing the trust of the people. Its position was considerably weakened in the October 2024 election, while opposition parties such as the Constitutional Democratic Party of Japan (CDP, *Rikken Minshutō*), Japan Innovation Party (*Ishin no Kai*) and the Democratic Party for the People (DPFP, *Kokumin Minshutō*) fared relatively well. A period of coalition governments and power-sharing agreements was on the cards.

Table 5.1 lists the former prime ministers dealt with in this chapter and points to several distinctive features in Japanese party politics during this period. These, in turn, underscore the changing nature and instability of the political system and the challenges facing prime ministers during their time in office. First, is the frequency of turnover of prime ministers, and the particularly short-lived nature of some prime ministerial tenures, with the exception of Koizumi Junichirō and Abe's second term. This was especially the case between 2006 and 2012, which gave rise to the concept of 'revolving door' politics. Second, is the (albeit brief) alternation of power for the first time since 1955 between the LDP and various opposition parties (which also changed over time as old parties splintered and merged with new ones, often in the run-up to an election). Third (indicated with *), is the emergence since 1989 of a series of coalition governments (for example, between the LDP and Komeito, or Japan New Party [*Nihon Shintō*] – a coalition of eight parties) and therefore a change to the hitherto one-party dominant system. Finally, given the relative youth of this group of post-prime ministers (as compared with those between 1945 and 1989, see Chapter 4), many of them enjoyed a longer period of time in which to find new roles and causes.

Still Ambitious

This category ranks alongside that of the Political Dabbler as the most highly populated for the former prime ministers of the post-1989 period and includes those who sought to return to political office at the national level, though not necessarily pitching for the top role. In order of strength of ambition, this includes Abe Shinzō after his first term, Asō Tarō, Hashimoto Ryūtarō and Noda Yoshihiko as the most ambitious, with others such as Kaifu Toshiki, Hosokawa Morihiro and Hata Tsutomu, at the lower end of the scale. With the exception of Asō (68 years old), most of them were in their 50s to mid-60s when they stood down as prime minister with much career time ahead of them.

Abe represents the most ambitious former prime minister in this period. He hailed from one of Japan's most prominent political families – his father was Abe Shintarō, his grandfathers were Abe Kan and Kishi Nobusuke (who he revered as his main role model), and his great-uncle was Satō Eisaku (see Chapter 4). Abe took a traditional route into politics, becoming secretary to his father on his appointment as foreign minister in 1982, and he was elected to his father's seat in Yamaguchi in 1993 at the age of 39. He swiftly rose up the ranks of the LDP and took over as prime minister from Koizumi in September 2006 having served in important positions as LDP secretary-general and deputy chief cabinet secretary. Initially he seemed to continue his predecessor's high approval ratings. However, over a ten-month period his popularity collapsed and the LDP lost heavily in the House of Councillors election of July 2007. Rather than taking responsibility immediately, Abe sought to remain in power, but ill-health prompted his resignation on 12 September, and he was hospitalized with an intestinal disorder the following day. Nonetheless, once recovered, Abe continued in politics, though he initially maintained a low profile as a back-bencher.

With the LDP in opposition from 2009 to 2012, Abe's attention turned to the question of his own political ambitions and beliefs. Reflecting on his short stint as prime minister, he put his mind to how he could get back into power to implement his 'vision of a strong, independent nation' (Harris, 2020: 157) – a vision that grew in large part from the ideas of his role-model and grandfather Kishi Nobusuke (Abe, 2006). In practical terms, he underwent some media re-training, began to rebuild his image (with appearances on popular TV programmes and effective use of social media), explored how to better instrumentalize the institutions of government and researched economic policy making (see Burrett, 2017). By 2012 he had re-emerged with a set of bold new initiatives designed to revitalize Japan or 'bring Japan back' (Abe, 2013). This included his new economic policy (coined 'Abenomics'), a doggedly historical revisionist stance and the pursuit of a 'proactive pacifism' (see Dobson, 2017).

The handling of foreign policy matters by the Democratic Party of Japan (DPJ, *Minshutō*) (for example, the ongoing Okinawa base issue under Hatoyama and the 2010 China fishing boat collision under Kan and Noda) gave Abe the ammunition to attack the opposition for what he saw as the governing party's failure to protect Japan's national interests, a sentiment shared among the public (Harris, 2020: 165). The perceived failure to deal effectively with the aftermath of the Fukushima disaster later brought the DPJ to its knees. Abe and his allies gradually began to rebuild support within the party for his possible return to the leadership position, with the strong encouragement of Suga Yoshihide, who would later become his chief cabinet secretary (Harris, 2020: 180). When LDP president Tanigaki Sadakazu resigned in September 2012, Abe was well positioned to return to the leadership role, winning among four other candidates including future prime minister Ishiba Shigeru. By December, he was elected prime minister and set about his project of 'bringing Japan back'. Abe's own 'restoration' demonstrated his determination to pursue the goals of his grandfather Kishi to end the postwar structure and regain Japan's autonomy (see Pyle, 2018), objectives which he was able to realize

Table 5.1: Former Japanese prime ministers, 1989 to 2024

Name	Born	Party[1]	Tenure as PM	Days in office[2]	Former PMs alive	Age at leaving office	Died	Total post-PM years
Uno Sōsuke	1922	LDP	3 June to 10 August 1989	69	5	67	1998	9
Kaifu Toshiki	1931	LDP	28 February 1989 to 5 November 1991	818	6	60	2022	31
Miyazawa Kiichi	1919	LDP★	5 November 1991 to 9 August 1993	644	7	74	2007	14
Hosokawa Morihiro	1938	Nihon Shintō★	9 August 1993 to 28 April 1994	263	7	56	–	30+
Hata Tsutomu	1935	Shinseitō★	28 April to 30 June 1994	64	8	59	2017	23
Murayama Tomiichi	1924	JSP★ (DSP from 1996)	30 June 1994 to 7 November 1996	561	8	72	–	32+
Hashimoto Ryūtarō	1937	LDP★	11 January 1996 to 30 July 1998	932	8	61	2006	8
Obuchi Keizō	1937	LDP★	30 July 1998 to 5 April 2000	616	9	63	2000	0
Mori Yoshirō	1937	LDP★	April 5 2000 to April 26 2001	387	8	64	–	23+
Koizumi Junichirō	1942	LDP★	26 April 2001 to 26 September 2006	1980	8	64	–	18+
Abe Shinzō	1954	LDP★	26 September 2006 to 26 September 2007; 26 December 2012 to 16 September 2020	366; 2822	7; 10	53; 66	2022	5; 2

Table 5.1: Former Japanese prime ministers, 1989 to 2024 (continued)

Name	Born	Party[1]	Tenure as PM	Days in office[2]	Former PMs alive	Age at leaving office	Died	Total post-PM years
Fukuda Yasuo	1936	LDP★	26 September 2007 to 24 September 2008	365	8	72	–	16+
Asō Tarō	1940	LDP★	24 September 2008 to 16 September 2009	358	9	68	–	15+
Hatoyama Yukio	1947	DPJ	16 September 2009 to 8 June 2010	266	10	63	–	14+
Kan Naoto	1946	DPJ	8 June 2010 to 2 September 2011	452	11	65	–	13+
Noda Yoshihiko	1957	DPJ	2 September 2011 to 26 December 2012	482	12	55	–	12+
Suga Yoshihide	1948	LDP★	16 September 2020 to 4 October 2021	384	11	73	–	3+
Kishida Fumio	1957	LDP★	4 October 2021 to 1 October 2024	1094	9	67	–	0+

[1] Affiliation during tenure as prime minister.
[2] According to https://japan.kantei.go.jp/past_cabinet/index.html
★ Indicates coalition government.

partially over the next decade. The commitment to revitalizing Japan's fortunes continued even after Abe stood down from his premiership in 2021. While he was not appointed to any official government positions thereafter, he did remain active in politics, in particular as head of the largest faction in the LDP, the *Seiwakai*, and through his frequent attempts to steer policy (see Political Dabblers discussed later).

Asō Tarō also stands out in this category as a former prime minister who continued to pursue his political ambitions after a brief time in office, later returning to the top echelons of the LDP. Coming from a family of entrepreneurs, Asō could also claim a strong political heritage – his grandfather was Yoshida Shigeru and his father-in-law was Prime Minister Suzuki Zenkō, who supported Asō when he entered politics in 1979. His first attempt at the LDP presidency was in 2001, when he lost to Koizumi Junichirō. Koizumi appointed him as minister for internal affairs and communication from 2003 to 2005, then minister for foreign affairs from 2005 (to 2007). He made his second bid to become LDP president when Koizumi's term of office ended, running against Tanigaki Sadakazu and Abe Shinzō. A victorious Abe retained Asō as minister for foreign affairs, before switching him to the post of secretary-general of the LDP in 2007. When Abe stood down, Asō once again ran for the LDP presidency but once again lost out, this time to Fukuda Yasuo. With the revolving door of Japanese politics in full swing, however, Asō did not have to wait long for another attempt at LDP presidency, a position he achieved on 24 September 2008, becoming the country's 59th prime minister.

Domestically, his time in power was focused on economic policy, having to navigate the 2007 global financial and economic crisis. Asō was in power for just less than a year, having failed to revive the party's fortunes. The landslide defeat in the House of Representatives election of 30 August 2009 saw the LDP out of power for the first time since 1955. Asō was identified as a significant contributing factor to the party's election disaster (*Japan Times*, 2009b), and he was replaced as LDP president by Tanigaki Sadakazu in September 2009.

Asō did not disappear into the shadows after this defeat, however, and undertook a number of informal diplomatic roles. In May 2011, he was appointed by the DPJ as an anime envoy to China – demonstrating both his love of the medium but also the importance of soft power and Asō's initiatives in this area during his time as foreign minister (he established the International Manga Award and International Cosplay Summit). His interests in sport (he was a member of the shooting team at the Montreal Olympics in 1976) were also in evidence when, as chairman of the bipartisan sports-related lawmakers' group, he sponsored a bill through the Diet in June 2011 to improve Japan's sporting facilities. The bill constituted the first major revision to the Sports Promotion Act since its introduction prior to the

1964 Tokyo Olympics, and it was seen to be part of Japan's bid to secure the hosting of the 2020 Olympics.

After three years of DPJ government, Asō's hopes to return to the higher echelons of power came to fruition with Abe Shinzō's triumphant comeback in 2012. Reflecting Asō's veteran status in the party, he was appointed deputy prime minister, finance minister and minister in charge of financial services, posts that he retained throughout Abe's time in office and continued under Prime Minister Suga. During this time he was tasked with implementing Abenomics, increased the sales tax (twice, in 2014 and 2019) and steered the economy through the COVID-19 crisis (*Mainichi Shimbun*, 2021c). Yet, despite his length of time in these offices (he was the longest-serving postwar finance minister), Asō is perhaps more well known for his frequent gaffes and being embroiled in scandals than for any substantive policy achievements. His various transgressions include sexist comments (one about Foreign Minister Kamikawa Yōko) and alleged involvement in a Finance Ministry scandal over the falsification of documents (which also implicated Prime Minister Abe and his wife, Akie) (*BBC News*, 2018). Nonetheless, he managed to retain high level positions in the party. Under Prime Minister Kishida, Asō was appointed vice president of the LDP. While the role might suggest less power than he previously held, it nonetheless kept him at the top of the LDP executive. In addition, he wielded considerable influence through his position as faction leader, in particular during the kickback scandal that rocked the LDP from late 2023, and as kingmaker during the 2024 LDP leadership election (see Political Dabblers, discussed later). When Ishiba Shigeru formed his new cabinet in October 2024, Asō was replaced as vice president by rival kingmaker Suga, and he accepted the role of LDP 'top advisor' instead.

Hashimoto Ryūtarō was another heavyweight in the LDP who demonstrated a desire to return to high office after his time as prime minister. He was first elected to the House of Representatives in 1963 at the age of 26 and rose through the ranks, securing ministerial positions under Ōhira, Nakasone, Kaifu and Murayama. When Kōno Yōhei chose not to stand for re-election as LDP president, Hashimoto was chosen over Koizumi Junichirō in September 1995 and appointed prime minister in January 1996 after Murayama's resignation. The LDP's success in the general election in October 1996 secured its return to single-party rule (with Kōmeitō in loose alliance) after a brief period out of office from 1993. Domestically, Hashimoto's focus was on revitalizing Japan's economy through the so-called 'big bang' reforms and the reorganization of ministries that would be implemented in 2001. However, austerity measures and a deteriorating economy led to poor results for the LDP in the Upper House election of July 1998, for which Hashimoto took responsibility and resigned as prime minister. He, nonetheless, took on some high-profile roles over the next few years. He was made 'Chief

Foreign Policy Advisor' to Obuchi in 1998, and by 2001 he had returned to the cabinet as Director of Okinawa Development Agency and Minister in Charge of Administrative Reform under Mori. After the administrative reforms of early 2001, his role changed to minister in charge of Okinawa and Hokkaido development and minister in charge of regulatory reform. When Prime Minister Mori resigned due to disastrously low polling rates, Hashimoto put his hat into the LDP leadership ring in an attempt at a prime ministerial comeback, but he lost to Koizumi.

Hashimoto's opposition to Koizumi's postal reform programme meant that he was not appointed to ministerial or high-ranking roles thereafter, but he was made special envoy on a number of occasions in light of his foreign policy expertise, thereby playing a quasi-elder statesmen role. He also inherited the Obuchi faction, the largest faction at the time, indicating his continued stature in the party. His final few years in politics were marred by ill health and his implication in a money politics scandal (an unrecorded 100 million yen donation from the Japan Dental Association). In 2005 he announced he would not stand at the next election, and his seat (in the Chūgoku regional bloc) was won by his son Gaku in September of that year (see the section on Family Affair). Hashimoto died in 2006.

Given the relatively infrequent alternation of power in Japanese politics, former prime ministers whose parties have lost power invariably have to bide their time for an opportunity to return to government. Noda Yoshihiko is one such example. He was the third and final DPJ prime minister in the 2009–12 'interregnum', having taken over from Kan Naoto in September 2011. During his time as prime minister he was faced with the legacy of the 2011 Fukushima disaster, a ratcheting up of tension with China over the disputed Senkaku islands and domestic opposition to his pledge to increase Japan's consumption tax. Although he won the September 2012 DPJ leadership election, he dissolved the Diet in November, and amidst falling popularity (due largely to the consumption tax hike), the party lost to the LDP under Abe Shinzō in the December general election.

After defeat, Noda resigned as DPJ leader, but he remained in politics – at just 55 he was the second youngest former prime minister in this period, and he was still ambitious. He continued to be active in his local constituency and was a member of the Diet Special Committee on Political Reform as well as the Budget Committee (reflecting his expertise as former finance minister, and ironically scrutinizing his own budget in 2013). He was also involved in foreign affairs-related activities, such as the Japan–UK summit meeting in April 2013.

Between 2012 and 2020 he acted as chief advisor for various opposition parties as they merged and evolved, including the DPJ, the newly formed *Minshintō* (a merger between the DPJ and the Japan Innovation Party) and by 2020 the CDP. He once again retained his seat in the 2021 general election and continued to publish his 'kawaraban' newsletters, with regular commentary on the need for political reform, good economic policy and careful diplomacy (Noda, 2024). He became well known for distributing leaflets in person at train station entrances and for actively supporting candidates in local elections with his soapbox speeches. In the Diet, Noda also maintained a high profile, delivering a well-received eulogy for Abe (*Yomiuri Shimbun*, 2022) and posing some tough questions to Prime Minister Kishida in the Ethics Committee session in February 2024 about the kickback scandal (*Yomiuri Shimbun*, 2024).

Noda's return to the heart of Japanese politics came in 2024, reflecting his personal ambition and desire for political change. Noda was suggested as a possible candidate for CDP leadership in August 2024 in response to Renhō's third-place fail in the Tokyo gubernatorial election in July and internal disquiet about CDP's leader Izumi Kenta's abilities raised by veteran party disrupter Ozawa Ichirō. Noda himself initially expressed caution about taking on the leadership role, fearing that he would lose supporters because of his failure to hold on to office in 2012 (*Jiji Press*, 2024b). By late August 2024, however, he made the decision to stand for leadership, citing precisely his experience in government as one of his strengths. Noda's decisive victory meant that the party was in a stronger position to challenge the LDP in the October 2024 general election. While falling short of the numbers needed to oust the LDP, the CDP increased its number of seats by 50 up to 148 seats, putting it in a strong position for the forthcoming Upper House elections in 2025.

As we have seen with Noda's return to opposition party leadership, part of the work to get back into power involves the reorganization and renewal of opposition parties in the hope of offering electors new choices. A number of former prime ministers in this period have therefore demonstrated their ambitions not by seeking a return to the top job or resuming ministerial-level positions but by seeking leadership of newly formed parties in a time of flux. Kaifu, Hosokowa and Hata are relevant in this regard.

Kaifu Toshiki had been elected president of the LDP in August 1989. He was a low-profile candidate with a clean image, though regarded by some as former prime minister Takeshita Noboru's puppet (see Hayakawa, 1994). His fresh image contributed to the success of the LDP in the Lower House election February 1990, and he was enthusiastic about political reform in light of the spate of scandals that had brought down his predecessors. However, his handling of Japan's financial and human contribution to the Persian Gulf War resulted in international criticism of his country's low profile stance. He also faced challenges on the domestic front. Seen as risk-averse and unable to capitalize on the resources available to him, he was unable to overcome resistance to reform from within the LDP and staunch opposition to the introduction of a new electoral system (see Edstrom, 1999b and Gaunder, 2007).

After resigning in November 1991, Kaifu nonetheless remained in politics and continued to be a vocal advocate of economic and political reform, even attempting a return to the top position against the LDP. This came after Prime Minister Hata's resignation as leader of a minority government in 1994, when the LDP forged an unlikely coalition with their long-term opponents in the Social Democratic Party of Japan (SDP, *Shakai Minshutō*), nominating SDP leader Murayama as coalition head. Kaifu saw the LDP/SDP 'alliance' as a betrayal of the country, and, in a sudden bolt from the LDP, was nominated to lead the anti-LDP coalition group (Kaifu, 2010: 165). In the ensuing run-off election, Kaifu lost to Murayama (261 to 214 votes). Undeterred, in December of that year, Kaifu formed and initially led the pro-reform *Shinshintō* (New Frontier Party), but the party ultimately failed in its bid to oust the LDP in the 1996 general election and was dissolved in 1997. He then became chief advisor for a series of new but short-lived parties that characterized the political vicissitudes of the 1990s and early 2000s, but ultimately returned to the LDP in November 2003 (*The Japan Times*, 2003). In the landslide DPJ election victory of 30 August 2009, Kaifu lost his Lower House seat to DPJ candidate Okamoto Mitsunori thereby becoming one of the few former prime ministers to experience electoral defeat – the first for 46 years since Katayama Tetsu and Ishibashi Tanzan in 1963.

Like Kaifu, Hosokowa's election as prime minister was greeted with hopes for a fresh approach to Japanese politics. Appointed in August 1993 as the first non-LDP prime minister since 1955, Hosokawa led a rainbow coalition of anti-LDP parties including his own *Nihon Shintō* (Japan New Party), which he had founded in May 1992. Grandson of Konoe Fumimaro (Chapter 3). Hosokowa had served in the House of Councillors in the 1970s and then as governor of Kumamoto until 1991. Hugely popular, his administration commanded approval ratings of over 80 per cent initially. He led some radical changes by officially describing Japan's actions in World War Two (WW2) as an act of aggression. He also instituted electoral reform that would come to fruition after he left office and commissioned an investigation into Japan's strategic stance after the end of the Cold War. However, his prime ministerial career was cut short when he suddenly announced his resignation and stepped down on 28 April 1994 over personal financial impropriety (*Time*, 1994). After resigning, Hosokawa declared that he had no intention of returning to the political world citing exhaustion (Uji, 2001: 354). However, he continued as a Diet member, joining the *Shinshintō* (along with Kaifu and Hata) before leaving in June 1997. He formed the 'From Five' group (joined by Hata Tsutomu) in 1997, which merged with the Good Governance Party (*Minseitō*) before finally joining the DPJ in 1998. He announced his retirement at the end of April 1998 citing the fact that 'his duty in realizing an expanded DPJ is completed' (*The Japan Times*, 1998b). Thereafter, he briefly undertook some work in the media, but then withdrew from the political and media spheres, taking up ceramic arts and becoming somewhat of a minor celebrity (see Celebrity category, discussed later). He briefly came out of retirement to run for Tokyo governorship in 2014, campaigning for non-nuclear energy and supported by former Prime Minister Koizumi.

Hosokawa's successor, Hata Tsutomu, was placed in the vulnerable position of being in charge of a minority government as internal divisions within the anti-LDP coalition started to emerge. The SDP announced its intention to break away on the day he was chosen as prime minister, soon followed by the New Party Sakigake (*Shintō Sakigake*, New Harbinger Party). Serving only 64 days (the shortest postwar administration), Hata's main legislative achievement was to pass the 1994 budget before resigning on 30 June 1994 to avoid a no-confidence motion from the LDP. After his resignation and similar to Kaifu and Hosokawa, Hata was also active in the party-political manoeuvrings of the time, declaring his commitment to 'real political reform' (*The Japan Times*, 1998a). He participated in the creation of *Shinshintō*, serving initially as its deputy leader. He left in 1996 to form the Sun Party (*Taiyōtō*) but then formed a new political grouping ('From Five') with former Prime Minister Hosokawa (*The Japan Times*, 1998a). In June 1998, he joined with Kan Naoto and Hatoyama Yukio to found the Democratic Party of Japan and served as its secretary-general and later senior adviser. Hata announced his retirement from politics on 28 September 2010 and died in 2017. His son, Yūichirō (see Family Affair, discussed later) continued to represent Nagano Prefecture as a member of the DPJ (and later CDP) in the House of Councillors until his own death in 2020 due to COVID-19.

Kaifu, Hosokawa and Hata are at the lower end of the Still Ambitious category when compared with the likes of Abe and Asō, but they nonetheless played active roles in the frequent shape-shifting of political parties that characterized the mid-1990s. Although each of them enjoyed only brief stints as prime minister, they remained committed to their respective beliefs in the need for reform of Japan's political system and pursued their ambitions for change by helping to establish new political parties that they hoped would in turn challenge a return to the LDP status quo.

Exhausted Volcanoes

At the opposite end of the spectrum to those in the Still Ambitious category are Exhausted Volcanoes who, in this period, fall into one of two sub-categories: those former prime ministers who die in office (or shortly after), or those who disengage from political life. The former case applies to Obuchi Keizō and Abe after stepping down in 2020, while the latter applies to Uno Sōsuke. Koizumi Junichirō is also included here due to his relative lack of activity and ambition during his time as a 'back bencher' – particularly when contrasted with his very energetic time in office.

Obuchi Keizō won his father's Gunma seat in 1963, becoming one of the youngest ever members of the House of Representatives at the age of 26. He held some of the top posts, including Director General of the Prime Minister's Office in Ōhira's administration, chief cabinet secretary under Takeshita and foreign minister under Hashimoto in 1997. He was appointed leader of the Takeshita faction in 1992, but this led to a split with former LDP secretary-general and strongman Ozawa Ichirō and his followers, after which the Obuchi faction emerged with depleted numbers.

Obuchi was elected as president of the LDP in July 1998, and therefore prime minister, after Hashimoto's resignation. Initially regarded as something of a non-entity – famously dismissed as having 'all the pizazz of a cold pizza' by John F. Neuffer in the *New York Times* (see Kristof, 1999), he nonetheless achieved some policy successes during his 20-month period in office (part of the time in coalition with the Liberal Party and Kōmei Party). In particular, he tackled an economy in recession, updated the Japan–US defence guidelines, built constructive relations with South Korea by acknowledging the difficult past between the two countries and took a tough line on intrusion by North Korean spy ships into Japanese territorial waters. He also passed controversial domestic legislation on the national flag and anthem (MOFA 1999, see also Aspinall and Cave, 2008). His time in office was cut short when he suffered a stroke and fell into a coma on 2 April 2000. The cabinet resigned on 4 April and Obuchi died on 14 May in Juntendo Hospital, Tokyo. Alongside Ōhira, he was one of the few Japanese prime ministers to die of natural causes while in office. His daughter, Obuchi Yūko, inherited his seat in the Lower House election of 25 June 2000 and served in the cabinet of Asō Tarō as Minister of State for Social Affairs and Gender Equality, the youngest postwar minister to serve (see Family Affair, discussed later).

As noted in Chapter 3, assassinations represent the most extreme example of this category. Political violence is not unheard of in postwar Japan – the fatal stabbing of Asanuma Inejirō, leader of Japan's Socialist Party, in 1960 springs to mind. Abe's assassination in July 2022 took place while he was giving a campaign speech to support LDP councillor Satō Kei in the run up to the House of Councillors election. The first assassination of a former prime minister since Saitō and Takahashi in 1936 (see Chapter 3), Abe was targeted because of his links with the controversial Unification Church,[1] a religious organization with which the LDP had close ties. Abe had stayed active in politics since his resignation in September 2020, and he remained an influential figure in the party (see Political Dabblers, discussed later) – indeed, he was tipped to become Japan's most powerful kingmaker since Tanaka Kakuei and Shin Kanemaru until his untimely demise (Takeuchi, 2021).

An example of a former prime minister who continued in politics while very much taking a back seat is Uno Sōsuke. First elected to the House of

Representatives in 1960, he held a number of ministerial-level positions, including director general of the Defence Agency in the second Tanaka administration (1974), science and technology minister (1976–77), head of the Administrative Management Agency (1979–80) and MITI minister in the first Nakasone administration (1983). Uno benefitted from the patronage of Prime Minister Takeshita who appointed him as foreign minister and then supported him to become LDP president, and therefore prime minister, in June 1989.

Hayasaka (1994) outlines the machinations that took place in the background surrounding Uno's election. Ultimately, Uno was regarded as a compromise and unblemished figure after the controversy of the Recruit Scandal, and his administration promised a clean break from the previous corruption. But Uno was himself forced to resign just over two months after taking office. A combination of the introduction of the consumption tax under Takeshita, antipathy towards the scandal-tainted LDP and Uno's own sex scandal led to a poor showing in the House of Councillors election of July 1989. The LDP lost its majority and Uno publicly took full responsibility for the defeat and resigned on 10 August 1989 (Hayasaka, 1994: 38).

Although he continued in politics for a further seven years, Uno held no ministerial positions and did not undertake the sort of informal, albeit ceremonial, roles typical of other former prime ministers. He stood down before the 1996 general election and retired to pursue his interests in painting, music and writing poetry (*The Independent*, 1998). Uno died on 19 May 1998 of lung cancer aged 75 in his hometown of Moriyama, Shiga Prefecture.

While Uno's quiet withdrawal from the front line of politics might be understandable given the shame of the scandal, former Prime Minister Koizumi's placement in this category might seem counterintuitive. One of the most instantly recognizable Japanese politicians and also one of the longest-serving prime ministers (before Abe Shinzō), Koizumi was elected at the age of 30 to the House of Representatives and served as Minister of Health under Takeshita, Minister of Posts and Telecommunications under Miyazawa, and Minister of Health again under Hashimoto. He hailed from a political family, his father having served as director of the Defense Agency (before its upgrade to the Ministry of Defense in 2007) and his grandfather as minister of communications, but he was seen as something of a maverick in Japanese politics. Koizumi's victory in the LDP presidential election and his subsequent appointment as prime minister in April 2001 was something of a surprise. He had already stood and lost in 1995 and 1998, but on his third attempt he enjoyed a comprehensive victory over Kamei Shizuka, Asō and Hashimoto. Kabashima and Steel (2007) demonstrate how Koizumi secured his victory by taking advantage of his public face in the media and changes in the procedures to appeal directly to rank and file members of the LDP. In the words of Karel van Wolferen, 'Koizumi's becoming prime minister was a great surprise to Koizumi himself' (*The Japan Times*, 2007). During almost five and a half years in power, Koizumi's premiership saw considerable change in Japan's domestic and international politics – postal privatization, declaring war on the LDP's factions, visits to Yasukuni Shrine, the War on Terror and so on. Koizumi resigned as he had reached the full term that an LDP president could serve, although there was some discussion of extending the term.

Given his relative popularity, and his skills in handling the Japanese media (Kabashima and Steel, 2010: 79–84), it was unlikely that media attention would wane after he stepped down from the office of prime minister on 26 September 2006 to make way for his anointed successor, Abe Shinzō. Yet, he only continued to serve as a Diet member for a brief time, announcing on 25 September 2008 his intention to step down at the end of his term in the House of Representatives (*The Japan Times*, 2008b). This would happen in the August 2009 election when he did not contest his district in Kanagawa prefecture but saw his 28-year-old son, Shinjirō, secure victory.

During his three years as a Diet member, his influence waned surprisingly quickly. As a backbencher, he adopted a low profile, except for the occasional snipe at Prime Minister Asō from the sidelines (*The Japan Times*, 2009a). In addition, the fact that Kabaya Ryōichi, the candidate backed by Koizumi, was defeated in the Yokosuka mayoral election of June 2009 suggested that Koizumi's support could no longer guarantee electoral success. When he resigned, Koizumi indicated his intention to continue his political activities through advisory positions on such issues as environmental protection, economic development and food safety (*The Japan Times*, 2008b). He went on to embrace the cause of non-nuclear energy in the wake of the Fukushima triple disaster (see Embracers of a Cause, discussed later) and attracted some attention in his voice-over role for Ultraman King (see Celebrity, discussed later). Despite his departure from the political scene, he, nonetheless, retained his popular appeal, regularly ranking highly in evaluations of former prime ministers and named as the prime minister people would most like to see return to power (Green and Szechenyi, 2009; Maeda, 2024).

Political Dabblers

The previous chapters have demonstrated the extent to which former prime ministers have continued to wield influence in their parties through informal structures and mechanisms. The former prime ministers in this period are no exception, and a number stand out for their considerable sway in factional politics within the LDP and in their kingmaking roles. Abe, Asō, Mori and Suga are of particular note, and represent the most active and high-profile in this group, but others such as Hashimoto and Miyazawa engaged in lower-level dabbling by virtue of their positions as faction leaders.

After Abe's resignation on 28 August 2020 on health grounds, he took some time to recuperate but retained his Diet seat. As Harris argues, Abe remained 'determined to continue his life's work of remaking the LDP', using 'his faction, the party's right wing and its allies in the press, and his bully pulpit' to try and achieve his goals (2022: 88). Abe was not appointed to any cabinet roles, but it was his behind-the-scenes influence during this period that stands out. This was in evidence when Suga, Abe's chief cabinet secretary for many years, took on the premiership. Seen as a continuity candidate, Suga retained many of the ministers from Abe's fourth cabinet and advanced Abe's policies on security and the economy.

When Prime Minister Suga stood down in 2021 (partly because Abe and Asō withdrew their backing), Abe backed Takaichi Sanae in the LDP presidential election, acting as 'master strategist' and galvanizing support for her from across the party (Harris, 2022: 90). Though ultimately losing to Kishida Fumio, Takaichi's appointment to one of the top party roles (as head of the LDP's Policy Affairs Research Council) 'stirred claims that it is as if Abe conducted the personnel choices' (*Mainichi Shimbun*, 2021d). Kishida was careful, however, to manage Abe's influence, ensuring that his cabinet appointments maintained a balanced factional representation. Furthermore, Kishida's decision to make Abe-rival Hayashi Yoshimasa foreign minister in November 2021, was seen as a turning point in Kishida's relationship with Abe, indicating Kishida's desire to move away from Abe's influence (*Nikkei Asia*, 2021).

Abe, nonetheless, continued to vocalize his positions on foreign and domestic politics and economic policies (Harris, 2022: 93), and he remained a powerful figure in the party and country until his assassination. As Tsuda notes, Abe's new role as head of the largest LDP faction, *Seiwa Seisaku Kenkyūkai (Seiwakai)* from November 2021 meant that he 'remained arguably the top power broker in Japanese politics' (2023: 1). Replacing Hosoda Hiroyuki, the faction had previously been headed by Abe's father, Shintarō, and produced prime ministers Mori, Koizumi and Fukuda Yasuo. Under Abe, the faction grew from a membership of 89 to 97, rivalling the size of the Tanaka faction in its heyday.

Abe's legacy remains as controversial as was his time in (and out of) office, tarnished by links with the Unification Church and the kickback scandal which began with revelations about Abe's own faction. The leadership succession process for the *Seiwa-kai* after Abe's assassination was also messy, with divisions of opinion between younger and older generations threatening a potential factional split and weakening of its overall power (Pollmann, 2022). Continuing with his own political dabbling (to be discussed later), former Prime Minister Mori attempted to guide the selection of the faction leader, becoming the de facto 'faction owner' (*Asahi Shimbun*, 2023c). Ultimately, the issue of who would inherit Abe's faction became redundant once the faction was dissolved. Abe's influence continued, however, in the form of protégé Takaichi Sanae. She presented herself as Abe's true successor in the LDP leadership election in 2024 (see Acolytes and Protégés, discussed later), but other Abe favourites also invoke his policies and visions (for example, Kobayashi Takayuki who was one of 'Abe's children' – the influx of new Diet members in 2012).

Another LDP heavyweight with considerable back-room influence is Asō. His long political career and key appointments have been noted in the Still Ambitious category, but his role as Political Dabbler merits attention, in particular his position as head of his own faction (*Shikōkai*, formerly *Ikōkai*). He took formal control of the faction in 2006, and it grew to become the second largest, behind the Abe faction, with 55 members. In the 2012 LDP presidential election, Asō cooperated with the Kōmura faction to back Abe Shinzō. Asō then supported Suga in the 2020 LDP presidential election, alongside the Hosoda faction (*Nikkei Shimbun*, 2020). In the 2021 presidential election, Asō initially backed Kōno Tarō, but other faction members (notably LDP secretary-general Amari Akira) supported Kishida so the faction agreed to allow a dual candidacy (*Yomiuri Shimbun*, 2021).

During the early years of Kishida's prime ministership, the powerful triumvirate of Kishida, Asō and Motegi Toshimitsu directed policy and strategy, but relations between Kishida and Asō became fractious over Kishida's stance on the need to dissolve party factions in light of the money politics scandal that dominated the agenda in late 2023 and 2024. While other factions were disbanded, Asō and Motegi insisted on keeping their factions intact. Ironically, Prime Minister Kishida appeared to have to rely even more on Asō's influence in replacing LDP ministers and executives who were sacked or resigned having been implicated in the scandal. The re-staffing meant that the Asō faction became the top provider of new ministers in the Cabinet, followed by the Motegi and Kishida factions (*Kyodo News*, 2024).

Asō's influence in the party continued in the 'contest for kingmaker' in the 2024 LDP presidential election. Asō represented the mainstream factions and was initially expected to support Kishida (before the latter announced that he would not be seeking re-election), Motegi or Kōno (who had been supported by Suga in the 2021 election). When Kōno announced his candidacy, it was with Asō's support, though members of the Asō faction were not obliged to follow suit. Kōno's poor showing in the first round of voting meant that Asō had to support one of the two top vote-getters in the run-off: Ishiba Shigeru or Takaichi Sanae. Given Asō's rivalry with Ishiba, it was Takaichi Sanae who received the support of the Asō faction, while former prime ministers Suga and Kishida supported the successful Ishiba (*Nikkei Asia*, 2024). While Asō accepted the honorary role of top advisor (a post that had been unfilled for 30 years since Nakasone), the loss of his vice-president role to Suga could be seen as somewhat of a snub, and he rather conspicuously absented himself from the commemorative photo of the new LDP executive line-up (*Nikkei Shimbun*, 2024). With the exception of Asō's brother-in-law Suzuki Shunichi (son-in-law of Suzuki Zenkō), who was appointed as head of the LDP Executive Council, no other Asō faction members were appointed to key LDP positions or to the Ishiba cabinet.

Mori Yoshirō's ambitions after his brief stint as prime minister were slightly different to Abe and Asō in that he did not seek a return to top government positions, but he did retain power within the party and also went on to pursue his interests in national sports associations and events (see Embracers of a Cause). Since being elected to the House of Representatives in 1969 he had held various important party and government posts during his career, including assistant chief cabinet secretary under Fukuda, education minister under Nakasone, MITI minister under Miyazawa, construction minister under Murayama and LDP general-secretary under Hashimoto and Obuchi. After Obuchi's sudden death, Mori took over as prime minister on 5 April 2000 in a process that was compared to the secrecy of the Kremlin (Uji, 2001: 370), but Mori was one of Japan's most unpopular prime ministers with single-figure approval ratings. While he hosted the G8 Kyūshū-Okinawa Summit and oversaw the reorganization of ministries during his time in office, he is perhaps remembered more for his gaffes. He resigned on 26 April 2001 to avoid a poor outcome for the LDP in the forthcoming election for the House of Councillors, but he continued to serve as a member of the House of Representatives.

His seniority and longevity in the party gave him considerable influence after his resignation as prime minister, primarily as faction head. He had already taken over leadership of the Mitsuzuka faction (formerly Fukuda/Abe) in 1998, then the second largest faction after the Hashimoto faction. After temporarily handing the faction leadership to Koizumi during his time as prime minister, Mori resumed the role in 2001 and continued until 2006. He was influential in steering the party towards the election of Asō Tarō as Fukuda's successor (Edström, 2009: 32). Even after transferring faction leadership to Machimura Nobutaka in 2006, he, nonetheless, maintained some influence in his capacity as the faction's chief advisor, and he provided support to younger faction members (*The Japan Times*, 2021). Furthermore, when he officially withdrew from the faction in 2010 over internal squabbles, he continued to be consulted on key decisions about the running of the faction. A decade after he stood down as a Diet member in 2012, Mori continued to attempt to hold sway in the party. For example, he lobbied Prime Minister Kishida to appoint Obuchi Yūko as chair of the LDP's Election Strategy Committee in 2023 (*The Japan Times*, 2023c), and, as noted previously, he played a role in deciding the leadership of the *Seiwakai* after Abe's assassination. In the 2024 presidential election he indicated his support for Takaichi Sanae (she had formerly been a member of the Mori faction).

While Abe, Asō and Mori were able to capitalize upon the nature of the faction system in the LDP, Suga offers an example of a non-faction-based kingmaker whose popularity and power was enhanced when the true extent of the kickback scandal in 2023–24 became clear and factions were being dissolved. After stepping down in September 2021 over his handling of the COVID-19 pandemic and the decision to go ahead with the Tokyo Olympics, Suga Yoshihide reverted to type as a low-key but influential back-room operator. Re-elected to his Kanagawa Second District seat in the October 2021 general election, he actively pursued some of the initiatives that had been implemented during his time as prime minister, most notably around energy projects and carbon neutrality established through the Green Initiative fund (see Suga, 2024).

Having been Abe's chief cabinet secretary (CCS) for over eight years (the longest serving CCS), Suga had a reputation as an iron-willed politician. The son of a farmer from Akita, Suga deviated from the traditional image of Japanese politicians, lacking the family, education and political background of so many of his peers. As prime minister he benefited more from popular support than a strong internal LDP power base (he was not a member of a faction, having left the *Kōchikai* in 2009), so that once the public lost trust in him in the face of a surge of COVID-19 cases, he could not rely on the party to buttress his position (*Mainichi Shimbun*, 2020). On the other hand, his lack of factional affiliation gave him considerable credibility when the slush-fund scandal broke in 2023, and he was a vocal advocate for the abolition of factions. In the run-up to the LDP leadership election in autumn 2024, he criticized the failure of the LDP to respond quickly to calls for political reform, and he called for Kishida's resignation in June 2024 (*Asahi Shimbun*, 2024b). His vocal and frequent commentaries on the state of the LDP and potential leaders put him back in the political spotlight, with some media seeing him as potentially trying to make a comeback, some as a kingmaker (Kamata, 2023; *Sankei Shimbun*, 2024). Suga chose to support Koizumi Shinjirō in the first round of the leadership election and then backed Ishiba Shigeru over Takaichi Sanae. He was rewarded for his efforts by being appointed as LDP vice-president, thereby replacing Asō Tarō and returning to the top echelons of the LDP.

Other former prime ministers have played a more low-key role in intra-party matters than those discussed previously. Former prime ministers Miyazawa and Hashimoto were both faction leaders, which afforded them a certain degree of influence within the party, but their power was somewhat circumscribed by structural changes and intra-party rivalries. Miyazawa led his faction (*Kōchikai*) from 1987 to 1998, a tumultuous time in the party's history when it was embroiled in a series of scandals and lost power in 1993 (under Miyazawa himself). The new electoral system introduced in 1994 was partly designed to weaken the role of factions (by reducing the need for

LDP politicians to compete with each other in single-seat constituencies) and to establish a state subsidy system for political parties, thereby eroding the direct funding link between faction leaders and members. As Zakowski points out, the changing environment had a particularly acute effect on the *Kōchikai* where internal tensions had been growing between the former bureaucrats' camp (which included Miyazawa) and the professional politicians' camp, culminating in the '*KK senso*' in 1995 between Katō Kōichi and Kōno Yōhei. Miyazawa's main achievement was to maintain unity in the faction – a sign of the loyalty afforded him by his faction members. But when he stood down as faction leader and appointed Katō as his successor, Kōno left the faction in 1998, thereby splitting and weakening the faction as a whole (2011: 197).

Hashimoto was head of his faction (*Heisei Kenkyūkai*, formerly the Tanaka/Takeshita faction) from 2001 to 2004, coinciding with Koizumi's time as prime minister. Given the rivalry between the two politicians, as well as Koizumi's attempt to rid the LDP of factions, the extent to which Hashimoto could influence party politics was limited. As such, it is notable that Koizumi did not follow tradition in terms of ensuring a balanced distribution of cabinet posts across all factions – the Hashimoto faction was awarded no ministerial posts and just five vice-ministerial appointments (Lincoln, 2002: 70).

First Citizens

Chapter 3 noted ways in which former prime ministers in the late 19th and early 20th centuries acted in the nation's interests by guiding and advising the emperor (in their role as *genrō* and *jūshin*), while Chapter 4 identified elder statesmen like Yoshida, Fukuda and Nakasone who were active in representing Japan's interests on the national and international stage in various ways. In the post-1989 period, Murayama Tomiichi, Fukuda Yasuo and Hatoyama Yukio stand out as former prime ministers who are the closest to fitting the First Citizen profile, though they all tended to focus their activities on a set of interrelated issues rather than demonstrating a general sense of duty. Murayama pursued the broad issue of reconciliation (with North Korea, and also through the Asian Women's Fund), while Fukuda was active in maintaining close links with the People's Republic of China (PRC) at times when tension between the two governments was high. Hatoyama has devoted much of his post-premiership to friendship-building initiatives in the region. Given the specificity of the initiatives that each have pursued, they are perhaps placed at the lower end of the First Citizen category ('quasi' or 'aspiring' First Citizens), or at the higher end of the Embracers of a Cause category. In addition, Hatoyama's activities might partly be viewed as an attempt to seek vindication for his perceived failure in office to address the Okinawa military base issue.

Murayama was first elected to the House of Representatives in 1972 and took over the leadership of the Japan Socialist Party (JSP, *Nihon Shakaitō*) in 1993. In June 1994 he became only the second post-WW2 socialist prime minister (after Katayama) through a marriage of convenience between the LDP, JSP and New Party Sakigake (which had broken away from the LDP the previous year). Murayama was heavily tested during his time in office, having made a surprising and damaging U-turn on the JSP's longstanding position on the Self-Defence Forces and the Japan–US Security Treaty, and having to deal with crises such as the long-running *jūsen* (housing loan companies) issue of non-performing loans, the Kobe earthquake of January 1995 and the sarin gas attack of March 1995– his handling of which was severely criticized. A more positive legacy was the Murayama Statement (Murayama *danwa*) issued on 15 August 1995 to mark the 50th anniversary of the end of the war. The statement, though highly controversial within the ruling coalition, not least within LDP ranks, nonetheless later provided a benchmark against which successive prime ministers would be measured when issuing apologies (Sakata and Murayama, 2009). Nonetheless, his failure to deal effectively with the various crises led to his sudden resignation as prime minister on 5 January 1996. Although he was subsequently reappointed as leader of the JSP (later renamed the Social Democratic Party of Japan, SDP), he stepped down in September 1996 to be succeeded by Doi Takako.

Murayama bowed out of party-political matters, retiring in June 2000, but assumed a highly visible role in attempts to re-open normalization talks with North Korea from 1999 to 2000. The decision to do so could possibly be read as a form of vindication and a means of completing unfinished business from his time as prime minister when there had been an attempt to open talks in October 1994 and March 1995. Taking the opportunity presented by the thaw in US–North Korean relations and the agreement surrounding US inspections of North Korean nuclear facilities, Murayama sought to organize and lead a non-partisan delegation to North Korea. The visit was delayed several times during 1999 due to spikes in bilateral tensions but was eventually realized in December. The visit culminated in an agreement to re-commence normalization talks by the end of the year. To support this process, the non-governmental National Organization for the Promotion of Normalization between Japan and North Korea was established in July 2000 headed by Murayama. However, three rounds of negotiations during 2000 failed to bring about the hoped-for result, getting bogged down in apology and compensation issues on the one hand (the North Koreans rejected a statement along the lines of the 1995 Murayama Statement as inadequate) and the *rachi jiken* issue (abduction of Japanese citizens by North Korean agents) on the other hand (*The Japan Times*, 2000).

Murayama's other main post-premiership role was as president of the Asian Women's Fund (AWF) from September 2000 until it was disbanded on 31 March 2007. The AWF was established in 1995 during his time as prime minister and distributed 1.7 billion yen in compensation to former victims of Japan's wartime military sexual slavery system. In addition, it distributed letters of apology from the prime minister and private donors, and promoted regional educational and cultural activities as a means of atonement. However, from its inception, the AWF was the target of criticism from many who rejected its private nature and restitution in place of explicit state compensation alone. Lack of consistent leadership, poor administration, confusion over the admission of responsibility and mismanagement of former comfort women's expectations also contributed to the project's limited success (Kumagai, 2014: 121–28). Nonetheless, Murayama remained a keen advocate for resolution of the comfort women issue. He was critical of Prime Minister Abe Shinzō's much-anticipated statement made on the 70th anniversary of the end of WW2 (*The Japan Times*, 2015a) but welcomed the Japan–South Korea agreement on the comfort women in December 2015 (*The Japan Times*, 2015b).

Murayama's other post-premiership activities further underscored his role as advocate for Northeast Asian reconciliation. In 2005 he joined other former prime ministers in urging then Prime Minister Koizumi to '"use extreme caution" when deciding whether or not to visit the Yasukuni shrine' (*The Japan Times*, 2005). He visited China and South Korea on several occasions to attend friendship association events or meet with survivors of the comfort women system. His visit to South Korea in February 2014 was regarded as an attempt to reignite high-level diplomacy (Panda, 2014). He also served as chair of the Japan–Vietnam Peace and Friendship Promotion Council and an honorary advisor to the Japan–China Friendship Association. This latter role saw him coordinate with the sister organization in China (the China–Japan Friendship Association) to facilitate governmental talks (*The Japan Times*, 2013).

Fukuda is the only prime minister in this period to have had a father who had also served in that role – Fukuda Takeo, 1976 to 1978. Fukuda won the LDP presidential election on 23 September 2007 after Abe's resignation, having proved to be a consensus candidate. Although regarded by some as a caretaker prime minister, his domestic policies while in power included attempts to tackle pension problems, health care reform and an economic stimulus package. On the international level, he hosted a rare double of summits as chair of the Fourth Tokyo International Conference on African Development (TICAD-IV) and the G8 Hokkaido Tōyako Summit in May and July 2008. At the former, Fukuda pledged to double Japan's official development assistance contributions to Africa by 2012; while at the latter, he promoted Japan's Cool Earth initiative (Dobson, 2012b). He also continued his father's policies of engaging the Asian region and pursuing an 'omni-directional' foreign policy. In particular, he presided over the signing of the May 2008 Joint Statement on the China–Japan Mutually Beneficial Relationship Based on Common Strategic Interests, the groundwork for which had been put in place by Abe. However, Fukuda was constrained during his time in power as a result of opposition control of the House of Councillors that resulted in deadlock in the Diet and the blocking of many of the LDP's legislative efforts. He resigned unexpectedly on 1 September 2008 declaring that '[t]his is the perfect timing to not cause people too much trouble' (cited in the *New York Times*, 2008). However, the media's reaction was critical, reflecting a general feeling that Fukuda had been irresponsible in resigning (*The Japan Times*, 2008a). Fukuda retained his Diet seat in the 2009 election amid fears that he might lose out to the new DPJ candidate Miyake Yukiko. He continued in politics until the end of 2012, indicating in September his intention not to stand in the next election.

During his final years as a Diet member, Fukuda followed in his father's footsteps by taking on a range of foreign affairs-related roles, clearly something he relished (Interview with Fukuda Yasuo, 27 June 2012). He acted as a special envoy during Asō's premiership, visiting the United Arab Emirates and Oman, and accompanying the emperor on his visit to the US and Canada. He also attended the TICAD-IV interim meeting in Botswana in March 2009 and in the same year visited Kenya. Both visits linked back to his chairing of TICAD-IV and the G8 in 2008.

Fukuda's appointments to the directorship or boards of various international and regional non-governmental organizations attested not only to his desire to continue with his long-held interests but to explore new leadership opportunities and take on an elder statesman role. For example, he took on a number of formal and informal roles that enabled him to express his ideas on nuclear non-proliferation through the InterAction Council from 2009, economic integration and development through his directorship of the Boao Forum from 2010, sustainable development and human security issues through the Asian Population and Development Association from 2012, and East Asian reconciliation in general through the Northeast Asia Trilateral Forum (NATF) and the Genron-NPO Tokyo-Beijing Forum. His activities attracted a certain amount of positive attention, not least his Boao Forum directorship and his attendance at the NATF meetings.

Of particular note was Fukuda's informal role in facilitating a thaw in the tension between China and Japan that had been mounting over the Senkaku/Diaoyu island issue since 2012. Fukuda was generally considered to be one of China's 'old friends' (*lao pengyou*), making regular visits to China or meeting the leadership at regional fora. In April 2010, for example, he met then Vice-President Xi Jinping at the Boao Forum and in August 2010 attended the opening ceremony of the Japan Pavilion at the Shanghai World Expo. He also made a keynote speech at the Tokyo–Beijing Forum and attended regularly from 2012, becoming a 'top advisor' at this annual event that seeks to promote cooperative relations. When the Senkaku/Diaoyu island issue began to resurface in 2012, a meeting between Fukuda and Chinese Premier Wen Jiabao at the InterAction Council in May provided an opportunity for the Chinese side, in reference to Ishihara Shintarō's plans to purchase some of the islands, to ask that Japan take steps 'to prudently deal with troublesome issues' (*China Daily*, 2012). It is unclear whether the Chinese expected Fukuda to pass the message back directly to the Noda administration, but for the Chinese side this was at least a useful and high-profile meeting to send a signal to the Japanese government.

Fukuda continued his normal round of attendance at various forums during the rest of 2012 and 2013 and made speeches urging caution on the part of both the Chinese and Japanese governments as bilateral tensions failed to ease. In 2014, his role in Sino-Japanese rapprochement was stepped up. In April, Fukuda met Hu Deping (son of Hu Yaobang, former secretary-general of the Chinese Communist Party) during his visit to Tokyo, while in July, he made a secret visit to Beijing to discuss the possibility of a thaw in relations. Fukuda claimed that the visit was arranged independently, but National Security Advisor Yachi Shōtarō's attendance at the meeting suggests this was not the case (*Asahi Shimbun*, 2014). In his capacity as Boao Forum chair, Fukuda made a further visit to Beijing on 29 October and met Xi Jinping again, paving the way for the November meeting between Abe and Xi. Fukuda's dual roles as 'China friend' (informal) and chair of the Boao Forum (formal) enabled the Abe government to check the signals coming from the Chinese leadership and test the water for a possible rapprochement from a relatively safe distance. Similarly, for the Chinese government, Fukuda was a useful conduit for communication with the Abe administration in the form of someone who was trusted and of high symbolic value.

Another former prime minister who has been active in regional trust and friendship-building projects is Hatoyama Yukio. Son of Finance Minister Hatoyama Iichirō and grandchild of Prime Minister Hatoyama Ichirō (Chapter 4), Yukio hails from a powerful political dynasty. He was first elected as an LDP Diet member in 1986 but left to form New Party Sakigake in 1993 and served under the Hosokawa administration as assistant chief cabinet secretary. He joined the DPJ in 1997 sharing the leadership with Kan Naoto until becoming its sole leader in 1999. He was forced to resign in 2002 but returned as leader in 2009 just ahead of the general election of that year. Despite winning a landslide victory in the House of Representatives election of 30 July 2009 and ousting the LDP for the first time since 1955, Hatoyama's tenure as prime minister lasted only eight months.

Although Hatoyama came to power on a wave of enthusiasm promising a more balanced foreign policy that engaged with the East Asian region, reining in the power of bureaucrats and undertaking social welfare reform, his honeymoon period was brief. A number of issues, and the Hatoyama administration's inability to deal with them, led to his resignation on 2 June 2010. First and foremost was the broken election promise to seek the relocation of Futenma base out of Okinawa Prefecture (see O'Shea, 2014). This led to the splintering of the coalition that was necessary to pass legislation through the House of Councillors. Second, Hatoyama and Ozawa Ichirō (former president of the DPJ and party elder) were embroiled in long-running political funding scandals. The result was plummeting opinion poll results that forced Hatoyama to step down.

Reminiscent of Yoshida and Nakasone, Hatoyama actively engaged in informal diplomacy after his resignation. He acted as special envoy for the Kan government, undertook meetings with numerous foreign representatives (often at his country house in Karuizawa), led trade missions, and promoted cultural exchange and environmental cooperation, among many other endeavours. But it has mainly been the topic of reconciliation in East Asia that has been the constant thread through his post-prime ministerial life. This was symbolized in March 2013 when he established the East Asian Community Institute in a bid to pursue his long-held vision of building trust and friendship in the region. Also dubbed the 'World Yūai (fraternity) Forum', the organization is intended to embody Hatoyama's political philosophy of *yūai* (fraternity) and to bring about the East Asian Community he called for in 2009.[2] The Institute has a centre in Naha, Okinawa, as a sign of Hatoyama's continued commitment to the (ongoing) US military base issues and to 'building Okinawa's future' (East Asia Community Institute, 2024). Hatoyama was also closely involved in the family's (short-lived) Hatoyama Yūai Juku (Hatoyama Friendship Academy) which opened in 2008 and was run by Inoue Kazuko, elder sister of Yukio and Kunio. The school's mission was to 'foster talented individuals' to contribute to world peace (Hatoyama Yūai-Juku, 2024).

Hatoyama briefly indicated a desire to return to politics, establishing the *Kyōwatō* (Republican Party) in 2020, with the intention of running for a Diet seat in the next election. But he stood down as head of the party in October 2022 and instead took the helm of the newly established Kyōwa Research Centre. Self-proclaimed as Japan's 'first policy think tank', its remit is to provide 'policy advice and legislative support' to Diet members (Kyōwa Research Centre, 2024). Hatoyama uses the Centre as a vehicle to promote his vision for Japan, East Asia and indeed the world. He maintains a very active schedule, regularly visiting China (meeting Xi Jinping at a conference marking the 70th anniversary of the Five Principles of Peaceful Co-existence in June 2024, for example), hosting foreign visitors, and commissioning research projects on international and domestic issues (for example, on Myanmar, Ukraine, the environment and Japanese democracy). He hosts and attends numerous events, and publishes regularly, including a 2017 book (*Escaping Great Japan-ism*). Throughout his work, the recurring theme is the need to work towards peaceful resolution of issues. The fact that he has not deviated from the vision he enunciated during his time as prime minister underscores his firm belief in the cause of fraternity, but this can also be seen as an attempt to seek vindication and restore his damaged reputation.

As previously discussed, and as noted in Chapter 4, diplomacy features significantly in the activities of those aspiring First Citizens or elder statesmen. It has also been a recurring theme in the afterlives of many other former prime ministers in this period, albeit in a more ad hoc way. In the aftermath of the War on Terror, for example, Hashimoto was dispatched as special envoy to Egypt and the United Arab Emirates, and Mori visited India to meet Prime Minister Vajpayee (*The Japan Times*, 2001). In 2013, Mori met President Putin in Moscow ahead of Prime Minister Abe's April visit. Mori had developed a cordial relationship with Putin over the years, and he was seen as a friend to Russia due to his father's close links with the town of Shelekhov (Irkutsk) developed when he was mayor of Neagari (Richards, 2014). Suga took on some informal diplomacy activity in his roles as chairman of the Japan–India Association, meeting Prime Minister Modi in July 2023 (*The Print*, 2023) and Chairman of the Japan–Korea Parliamentary Friendship League (meeting President Yoon) in the same year. He was also special envoy and Advisor to the Japan–Vietnam Parliamentary Friendship Alliance (visiting Hanoi in July 2024) (*VoV World*, 2023; *Vietnam Plus*, 2024). While these activities may seem marginal or symbolic, they, nonetheless, indicate the ongoing utility of a former prime minister to the government of the day in addressing specific issues or keeping the (informal) diplomatic wheels turning with friendship and courtesy visits.

Embracers of a Cause

While the former prime ministers described in the First Citizen category discussed previously were active across a range of issues, those who fall into the Embracers of a Cause category do so by virtue of the specific nature of the chosen cause, often one that resonates personally. Koizumi sits squarely in this category, doggedly promoting non-nuclear energy in Japan after the Fukushima disaster. Mori, in addition to his political dabbling noted previously, also embraced his long-held cause of sports and sporting events.

After a fairly low-key period in the immediate aftermath of his prime minister-ship (see Exhausted Volcanoes), Koizumi took up the cause of renewable energy and became an energetic anti-nuclear power campaigner, regularly giving speeches and interviews, attending conferences and undertaking fact-finding missions (*Financial Times*, 2018). He teamed up with other former prime ministers in the wake of the triple disaster on the issue of nuclear energy, a topic on which they had changed their positions from support to opposition. In 2014 he supported former Prime Minister

Hosokawa's bid for governor of Tokyo and became a vocal advocate for zero nuclear power to counter Prime Minister Abe's promotion of nuclear power (*Jiji Press*, 2014). In 2021 he joined forces with former Prime Minister Kan to criticize Prime Minister Suga's position on reducing net carbon emissions (which they saw as a pretence to restart nuclear reactors), calling instead for greater use of renewables (*Kyodo News*, 2021). On the tenth anniversary of the disaster, Koizumi along with Kan, Hatoyama, Murayama and Hosokawa signed the '3.11 Declarations' at the Global Conference of a Nuclear Free, Renewable Energy Future (*Mainichi Shimbun*, 2021b; see also Nuke0 Re100, 2021). In 2022 Koizumi criticized the Kishida government's energy policy and joined up with former Prime Minister Kan again to denounce Europe's plan to label nuclear as sustainable energy (*Japan Forward*, 2022; Foreign Correspondents' Club of Japan, 2022). The fact that his son Shinjirō was appointed as environment minister in 2019 may have been a means by which Koizumi could have influenced thinking – Shinjirō said that he would look at how nuclear power plants could be scrapped, not retained (*Kyodo News*, 2019). The impact of Koizumi's campaigning is difficult to gauge, but he tapped into public sentiment at the time. While successive LDP governments persisted in their support for nuclear power, public opinion shifted against nuclear power and (as of March 2024) only 12 of 54 reactors have been restarted since Fukushima (*Asahi Shimbun*, 2024a).

In a very different sphere, Mori's long-held love of, and support for, sports (rugby in particular) continued into his post-prime ministerial activities, constituting a significant element of this aspect of his career. He was chairman of the Japan Sports Association from 2005 to 2011, and he was also made president of the Japan Rugby Football Union in 2005. He campaigned for Japan's bid for the 2011 Rugby World Cup (ultimately losing to New Zealand), and he later helped to secure Japan's 2019 bid and was made vice-chair of the Rugby World Cup Organizing Committee. Combining his political clout with his commitment to sports, he was a member of the bipartisan sports-related lawmakers' group (chaired by former Prime Minister Asō), which sought to improve Japan's sports facilities with a view to bidding for the 2020 Olympics. The successful Tokyo Olympics bid saw him instated as head of the organizing committee from 2014. He was forced to resign in February 2021 following sexist comments, a further blow to the 'cursed' Olympics which had been delayed by the COVID-19 pandemic and afflicted by other scandals (*Mainichi Shimbun*, 2021a).

Seekers of Vindication

Hatoyama and Kan Naoto's post-prime ministerial activities indicate some blurring around the edges of our suggested categories, which will be discussed further in Chapter 6. As noted in First Citizens earlier in the chapter, Hatoyama's activities ranging from informal diplomacy through to his grassroots work position him as an aspiring First Citizen. But his close involvement in the work of his two think tanks devoted to building trust and friendship in the region can also be seen as an attempt to restore the damage to his reputation during his time in office, specifically his failure to achieve his goals of US military base relocation and of creating 'a sea of fraternity' in East Asia.

Kan Naoto's devotion to the cause of non-nuclear energy in the wake of the Fukushima disaster could place him in the Embracer of a Cause category, but the frequency and vehemence with which he has sought to present his view of his government's actions and decisions made in the immediate aftermath of the disaster better describes him as a Seeker of Vindication. A former civil society activist, Kan Naoto was elected to the House of Representatives for the first time in 1980 with the *Shaminren* (short for *Shakai Minshu-rengō* or Socialist Democratic Federation) before moving to New Party Sakigake. In 1996 he served as health minister in the Hashimoto coalition and exposed the HIV-contaminated blood scandal. He became co-leader of the DPJ with Hatoyama Yukio and set about reforming the party in 1998. He lost the leadership to Hatoyama in 1999 but regained it at the end of 2002 and merged with Ozawa Ichirō's Liberal Party in September 2003, scoring electoral gains in the Lower House election of November that year. In 2004, he resigned over unpaid pension contributions. When the DPJ won the 2009 election, he was appointed finance minister and became prime minister in 2010 when Hatoyama stood down.

During his time in office, Kan faced internal power struggles and made an ill-fated decision to raise consumption tax. His biggest challenge, however, was dealing with the aftermath of the triple disaster of March 2011. He started to face criticism almost immediately after the disaster relating to many aspects of the government's response, for example, for failing to consult with senior members of his party, for failing to take swift action after the disaster and for poor communication. As Kingston points out, Kan became 'a lightning rod for widespread frustration and dissatisfaction. His ineffectual leadership skills and inability to formulate coherent policies and means to achieve them earned him widespread obloquy' (2012: 7). After returning from explaining the government's response to the crisis to the other G8 leaders in Deauville in May, Kan was faced with a no-confidence vote. Although he survived the vote, he offered his resignation for later in the year once the crisis had stabilized and the Fukushima Daiichi nuclear power plant had been brought to a cold shutdown. He resigned on 26 August 2011. Kan continued in politics, although in the 2012 and 2014 elections he lost his district seat, to be retained instead through the proportional representation bloc. In 2017, he joined the CDP, and he regained his district seat in the 2017 general election. In 2023, he announced that he would not run for re-election again, though he hinted at the possibility of involvement in local or prefectural politics (*TBS Newsdig*, 2023).

Kan's post-prime ministerial activities have been dominated by his experiences of handling the disaster, and he believes it is his role 'to realize a nuclear-free Japan and a nuclear-free planet' (Kan, 2017: 166). He returned to his activist roots, embracing the non-nuclear cause with a passion and joined up with former prime ministers, including Koizumi (discussed previously), and global anti-unclear civil society to amplify the message. He also acted as adviser to the DPJ's Energy and Environment Research Committee and set up the Committee for the Consideration of a Roadmap for a Non Nuclear Japan (Kan, 2017: 162–3). He has written extensively, and given numerous speeches and interviews, explaining the details of the Fukushima disaster, the government's and his own response. He is defiant in his justification of his actions and decisions in the immediate aftermath of the disaster, particularly in light of the lack of communication from the Tokyo Electric Power Company (TEPCO) who operated the Fukushima Daiichi Nuclear Plant and who failed to inform the government of the extent of the damage (Kingston, 2012: 6; Kan, 2017). In his memoirs published in 2024, Kan is highly critical of the role of then-opposition leader Abe Shinzō in spreading false information about a decision to delay the injection of seawater at the nuclear plant, which, Kan argues, led to the LDP bringing its no-confidence motion against him (2024: 209–10). Indeed Kan filed a lawsuit (which he lost) against Abe in 2015 seeking an apology and damages for defamation of character (*Sankei*, 2015). The Independent Investigation Commission on the Fukushima Nuclear Accident published in 2012 was damning about the government's overall response, and critical of Prime Minister Kan's micromanagement (2012: 105), but Kan's own view was that '[i]t is for history to evaluate what took place, but as Prime Minister I just did what I could' (McNeill, 2012).

Acolytes and Protégés

A number of prime ministers in this period benefited from the guidance of their predecessors, in particular Kaifu Toshiki (mentored by Miki Takeo), Hata Tsutomu, Hashimoto Ryūtarō and Obuchi Keizō (mentored by Takeshita Noboru). In addition, Miyazawa Kiichi was a Yoshida disciple (Edström, 1999b: 151), apprenticed by Ikeda in the Finance Ministry, and close to Ōhira Masayoshi (Mikuriya and Nakamura, 2017). Yet the number of former prime ministers in this period who have gone on to nurture successors in their own right is relatively low. This is possibly due to the changes in the internal structure of the LDP, for example, a weakening of the power of factions in the 1990s and the increase in the number of politicians who did not align themselves with a particular faction or faction boss. In addition, the rapid turnover of prime ministers often left reputations in question and power bases reduced. It is notable that only Abe and Koizumi nurtured acolytes and protégés in the way that previous prime ministers had done, and neither of them was able to replicate the success of the earlier generation in producing prime ministers in their own image.

In the absence of children or close family members who could succeed him, Abe nurtured a number of protégés who he hoped would eventually be able to continue his mission to revitalize Japan. During his second time in prime ministerial office he supported the rise of Inada Tomomi, who he appointed as minister of defence in 2017, despite her relative lack of ministerial experience. While seen as a reward for her loyalty to Abe and an indication that he saw her as a possible successor, her appointment was, however, short-lived. Her inexperience in Diet questioning, a visit to the controversial Yasukuni Shrine and a scandal over a cover-up of Japan's Self-Defense Forces activity in South Sudan ultimately led to her resignation in 2018, thereby dashing her hopes of running for the leadership position in 2021 (Fahey, 2017).

Instead, another of Abe's protégés, Takaichi Sanae, ran in the race against Kishida Fumio, Kōno Tarō and others to succeed Prime Minister Suga. Takaichi was widely seen to be Abe's logical successor given her hawkish conservative views and close alliance with Abe. During the leadership campaign she pledged a series of economic and strategic policy changes mirroring those of Abe (for example, 'Sanaenomics' as a continuation of Abenomics and the introduction of pre-emptive strike capability). While not an Abe faction member herself, securing the backing of the largest faction meant that had she been successful Abe would have continued to enjoy considerable influence in the party (*Asahi Shimbun*, 2021). However, she came third in the first round of the vote so did not go forward to the run-off, in which Kishida defeated Kōno.

Takaichi ran again for the leadership position in 2024. In the first (almost) factionless leadership election since the slush fund scandal, Takaichi could not rely on the formal support of the Abe faction, which had been dissolved in January 2024, but she did gain the support of some former members of the faction. Casting herself as Abe's successor, she articulated her vision of 'national greatness conservatism', building on aspects of Abe's project to boost Japan's economy and restore Japan's reputation. As Harris notes, she is 'an uncompromising believer in this vision for Japan, perhaps to an even greater extent than Abe' (2024). Lacking the pragmatism that Abe could demonstrate, Takaichi caused some jitters during the election campaign with her comments on interest rates (*Asahi Shimbun*, 2024f) and her staunch opposition to the introduction of a bill which would allow optional separate surnames for married couples (*Mainichi Shimbun*, 2024). While Takaichi won the first round of the election, she was narrowly defeated by Ishiba Shigeru in the run-off. She subsequently declined the position of chair of the LDP Executive Council in Ishiba's government.

Koizumi is another former prime minister who identified potential successors. For example, he supported Koike Yuriko in the LDP presidential election of 22 September 2009 to decide Fukuda Yasuo's successor, describing her as the 'successor to his reform policy'. However, Koike performed poorly coming third with only 46 votes, in contrast to Asō Tarō's convincing victory. His obvious protégé is son Shinjirō (see Family Affair), who he declared as his chosen successor (Smith, 2018: 164–5). That said, in the run-up to the September 2024 presidential election, Koizumi senior publicly encouraged his son to wait until he is in his 50s (*The Japan Times*, 2024a).

Family Affair

Hereditary politicians continue to feature in this period, with a number of second generation (Miyazawa, Hata, Hashimoto, Obuchi and Fukuda) and third generation (Koizumi, Abe, Asō and Kishida) politicians becoming prime ministers. In this period, Hatoyama Yukio became the first prime minister who was the *fourth* generation of a political family. In some cases, although the former prime minister did not have a politician parent, they hailed from prominent political families: Hosokawa's grandfather was the former prime minister Konoe Fumimaro, and Mori's line governed the historical Kaga clan.

As noted in Chapter 4, 12 of the 17 prime ministers between 1945 and 1989 had children, siblings or children-in-law who became Diet members. This number dropped in the post-1989 period with just Miyazawa, Hata, Hashimoto, Obuchi, Koizumi and Fukuda passing their seats directly onto family members (usually children or nephews). The drop corresponds with Smith's observation about the number of legacy candidates within the LDP overall, which fell from 47 per cent in 1993 to 28 per cent in 2012 and 2014. Among new recruits in the LDP, the number of legacy candidates dropped from 43 per cent before the electoral reform of 1994 to an average of just 14 per cent after the reform (2018: 160–1). This can be partly explained by a change in political culture and election strategy in the post-reform period. Smith notes that a number of political parties, including the LDP, introduced an open recruitment system to encourage a more diverse party image, and in turn this 'undermine[d] the inevitability of a legacy candidate' (2018: 151). The DPJ went as far as to ban the practice of heredity in its 2012 manifesto, but the LDP did not follow suit. Legacy candidates continue to enjoy the advantages of a ready-made support group, a funding stream and name recognition, and Smith notes in particular that 'many of the older generation of the LDP incumbents and their offspring still want to practice politics like a family vocation' (2018: 178).

The most high-profile and (relatively) successful political offspring are Obuchi Yūko and Koizumi Shinjirō. Obuchi Keizō's daughter Yūko worked as his aide in 1999 and was elected to his seat in the Lower House in the 2000 general election. As noted in Chapter 4, it remains rare in Japan for daughters to follow in their father's political footsteps, and the majority of kin secretaries have tended to be male (Smith, 2018: 177). After her father's sudden death, she benefited from the support of prime ministers Asō (who appointed her minister of state for social affairs and gender equality in 2008, making her the youngest cabinet member since 1945), Abe and Mori. Tipped at one point to be the first female prime minister, she was, however, implicated in a funding scandal and resigned from her position as minister for trade, economics and industry in 2014. She has since served on various LDP committees, and in 2023 Kishida appointed her as chair of the LDP's Election Strategy Committee, a post she held until newly elected Prime Minister Ishiba replaced her with Koizumi Shinjirō in October 2024. Ishiba appointed her instead as head of the LDP Organization and Campaign Headquarters, and she was re-elected in the October general election, winning a robust 62 per cent share of the vote in her district.

Koizumi's son Shinjirō was his father's private secretary from 2007 to 2008, and he was elected to his father's seat in August 2009. He was made minister for environment in 2019 but otherwise has a fairly thin political résumé. After Abe's resignation in 2020, Shinjirō considered running as party leader but endorsed Kōno Tarō instead. In 2024, he announced his candidacy for the LDP leadership after Kishida indicated he would not seek re-election. Running against eight other candidates, Koizumi gained the support of former Prime Minister Suga and other independents (*Asahi Shimbun*, 2024d) and early public opinion polls placed him second after Ishiba Shigeru (*Asahi Shimbun*, 2024e). Part of his appeal was considered to be due to his relative youth, but it was mainly the family name and reputation of his father that seemed to draw the crowds. In a 2024 favourability survey of Japanese leaders, Koizumi Junichirō ranked top indicating the esteem with which he is still held by the public, no doubt boosting Shinjirō's own ratings (Maeda, 2024). Shinjirō did not succeed in his bid, coming third in the leadership race after Ishiba and Takaichi, with critics citing his youth, lack of experience and poor preparation during the campaign for the loss. Nonetheless, Ishiba rewarded him with the important role of head of election strategy, becoming the 'face' of the LDP in the run up to the October election. While Koizumi retained his seat in the election, he resigned his election strategy role to take responsibility for the party's losses. Nonetheless, with youth (and the Koizumi brand) in his favour, he has the potential to run again for the LDP presidency in future years.

Another rising star is Fukuda Yasuo's son Tatsuo who has represented Gunma 4th district since 2012. He was made head of the Executive Council, one of the LDP's top posts in 2021, but was replaced in 2022. He retained his seat in the 2024 election (despite having been implicated in the slush fund scandal) and was appointed Acting Secretary General in Ishiba's cabinet in September 2024. Fukuda is keen to see a generational change in the party and has called for party reform (*Asahi Shimbun*, 2024c).

In a number of other cases, the budding political careers of offspring have been cut short due to failure to get elected, scandal, criminality or their own demise. Hashimoto Ryūtarō's seat (Chūgoku proportional representation block) was won by his son Gaku in September 2005. From 2012 he represented Okayama 4th district and served on various Special Committees including Okinawa and Northern Territories, Anti-Piracy Measures and Prevention of International Terrorism, and Internal Affairs and Communication. From 2019 to 2020 he was vice-minister of health, labour and welfare. His political career stalled, however, when he failed to retain his seat in the 2024 general election, losing to CDP candidate Yunoki Michiyoshi. Kan's eldest son Gentarō tried for election in 2003 but did not succeed. Mori's son Yūki was elected to Ishikawa Prefectural Assembly in 2006, and was serving a second term, but resigned after a drunk-driving offence in 2010. Kishida's son Shōtarō was fired as his executive secretary in June 2023 for misuse of resources. After Hata's retirement in 2010, his son Yūichirō continued to represent Nagano Prefecture as a member of the DPJ (and later CDP) in the House of Councillors until his own death in 2020 from COVID-19. While not in politics, Suga's son Seigo, an executive in the Tohoku Shinsha Film Corporation, embroiled his father in an influence-peddling scandal when it was discovered that Seigo had entertained bureaucrats from the Ministry of Internal Affairs and Communications (*NHK*, 2021).

For those former prime ministers or politicians who either have no offspring, or offspring who do not follow in their parent's political footpaths, the question of legacy is sometimes resolved by passing the seat onto a family member or another designated successor. This was the case with Uno's son-in-law, Uno Osamu, who was elected three times in the local assembly in Shiga (from 1991), and then twice to the House of Representatives. Miyazawa's nephew Yōichi was elected to his uncle's Hiroshima seat between 2000 and 2009, losing it to the DPJ in 2009. He has served as a member of the House of Councillors since 2010. Asō's children have also eschewed politics, but the family 'business' is represented by his brother-in-law Suzuki Shunichi. Suzuki is son of former Prime Minister Suzuki Zenkō and was first elected in 1990. He took over from Asō as Finance Minister in October 2024, and retained his seat in the 2024 general election (*Mainichi Shimbun*, 2021c).

Given Abe's assassination, and in the absence of children or other family members, there was no apparent successor. Abe's seat remained in LDP hands in the 2023 by-election, with Yoshida Shinji, a three-term member of Shimonoseki city council. Backed by Abe's wife Akie, Yoshida pledged to 'carry the soul of Abe-sensei' (*Asahi Shimbun*, 2023a; *Asahi Shimbun*, 2023b). The reduction of districts in Yamaguchi in 2023 meant that Yoshida would not fight the 2024 general election in a single-seat constituency. Instead, Foreign Minister Hayashi was selected as the candidate for the new Yamaguchi 3rd district, and Yoshida sought (and won) election in the Chūgoku regional bloc instead. The choice of Hayashi (a former Kishida faction member and Abe rival) was seen as an indication of the Abe family's waning influence in the area (*The Japan Times*, 2023b). As noted previously, Abe's ideological mantle has been picked up by protégé Takaichi Sanae, a candidate for the LDP leadership contests in 2021 and 2024 whose policy pitch had strong echoes of Abe's mission to revive Japan through a strong economy (see Acolytes and Protégés).

Celebrity

As was the case in the earlier periods, former prime ministers have engaged in various activities that brought them into the public spotlight, though for different reasons. Nakasone stood out in particular in Chapter 4 as an able communicator who actively engaged with the press and television. The media landscape changed rapidly in the post-1989 period with the introduction of new political TV programmes and the use of social media. Prime ministers (and former prime ministers) began to recognize the utility of building and maintaining an online presence to showcase their views and enhance their public image (Krauss and Nyblade, 2005: 361; see also Fahey, 2021).[3] The more adept instrumentalization of the media began with Hosokawa who recognized the benefits of leveraging television to increase his popularity (Krauss and Pekkanen, 2011: 229). Koizumi went further by introducing his weekly email magazine (including his own column called 'Lionheart'), which proved very popular, gaining over 2 million subscribers (Kantei, 2005). Many former prime ministers have continued to make active use of their social media accounts on Facebook, Twitter and YouTube, and maintain personal websites with regular updates and musings. They also make appearances on the now numerous political TV/internet programmes and contribute to newspapers or current affairs magazines, some having their own series (for example, *Mori no Seidan*, an irregular series in current affairs journal *Shokun* which ran from the end of his prime ministership through to the start of Koizumi's). If not seeking celebrity status through these activities, they at least maintain a relatively high public profile and contribute to debates on current issues, perhaps as a means to retain some influence and relevance in political circles, or as a form of political dabbling from the sidelines.

Away from media and politics, other former prime ministers have carved out very different niches for themselves. Hosokawa became well known for his love of ceramics and art. After retirement, he set up his studio at his private residence at Futōan villa in Yugawara, Kanagawa. He studied ceramics initially and broadened his repertoire to calligraphy, painting, lacquer work and bamboo crafts (Hosokawa, 2008). He has been publicly exhibiting his work since the late 1990s in Japan and internationally, including a charity exhibition for Ukraine at the Pola Museum Annex in 2022, and at Ogata Paris 2023 (*The Japan Times*, 2022), and he has published a number of books including his diaries (Hosokawa, 2008, 2010, 2011).

Other former prime ministers have dabbled in popular culture. Ever the populist, Koizumi provided the voice for the character of Ultraman King in the film *Mega Monster Battle Ultra Galaxy: The Movie* with the encouragement of his son (Reuters, 2009). Others have depicted him in other scenarios – for example, as a mahjong-playing prime minister pitted against other world leaders in the manga and later anime *Mudazumo naki Kaikaku* (given the title *Legend of Koizumi* in English) or as the object of fun by comedy team *The Newspaper* in their regular imitations of the former prime minister in a country thought to be lacking in political satire (*The Japan Times*, 2004). Hatoyama had a fleeting encounter with the theatre, playing a fictional female president of the US in retirement in a stage musical in Tokyo (*Waist Size Story*, a parody of *West Side Story*) (*Wall Street Journal*, 2015). On a more serious topic, he appeared in conversation with director Ōta Takafumi in the 2024 documentary film *Okinawa Kyōsōkyoku* (Okinawa Rhapsody) on the topic of the Okinawa base issue, a long-held cause on his part.

Murayama sought to leverage his status and capital to focus public attention on a chosen cause when he made his film acting debut at the age of 79 appearing in Takahashi Iwao's *8-gatsu no Kariyushi* (Happiness in August) in 2003. Despite refusing various approaches to appear in films, Murayama eventually agreed to appear in this film set in Okinawa citing its anti-war message but also because the 1995 Okinawa Rape Incident took place during his time as prime minister (*Okinawa Taimusu*, 2003). Murayama had to learn the Okinawan dialect to play an elderly wheelchair-bound man who lost both legs in the Battle of Okinawa and is tasked with explaining some of the young protagonist's supernatural experiences. This stands in stark contrast to the celebrity activities of Koizumi and Hatoyama mentioned previously that appear to be celebrity for celebrity's sake and serve no discernible cause or end.

Anchor Point

As the previous two chapters showed, former prime ministers such as Saionji, Yamamoto, Satō, Kishi and Nakasone acted as Anchor Points at times of national crisis. Japan experienced no shortage of crises after 1989: natural disasters in 1995, 2005 and 2011, financial crises (the bursting of the bubble economy in the late 1980s and the Asian financial crash of 1998) and the COVID-19 pandemic in 2020. However, it is difficult to identify former prime ministers in this period who stand out as individuals on whom the nation's hopes rested. Instead, the role of 'consoler in chief' can be seen to have been taken on by Emperor Akihito and Empress Michiko whose 'human touch' helped to give people strength and succour at times of distress (*BBC News*, 2019; Kingston, 2019). Akihito's televised address to the nation in the wake of the 2011 disaster, for example, can be likened to the positive effect of Queen Elizabeth II's address to the British TV audience during the COVID-19 pandemic – indeed, both seemed to fill the vacuum left by the political leadership of the time.

Former Prime Minister Miyazawa Kiichi represents the only contender as Anchor Point in this period, when he returned to a ministerial role after his rather ignominious end as prime minister. Despite an initial reluctance to do so, he accepted the role of finance minister in 1998 at the request of Prime Minister Obuchi (with input from former prime minister and faction boss Takeshita) and calmed foreign government fears of the escalating Asian financial crisis in so doing (*The Japan Times*, 1998c). Prior to this he had acted as chairman of an LDP special committee set up in November 1997 specifically to tackle the financial crisis (Suginohara, 2004: 6).

In one sense, Miyazawa's appointment to Obuchi's 'Cabinet for Economic Revival' (Obuchi, 1998) was surprising and met with some concern – his first stint as finance minister in the 1980s ended with him having to stand down due to a money scandal, and his prime ministerial experience ended badly due to his failure to enact the political reforms needed to put Japan back on track. He was therefore seen more as a very able back-room operator, and it was certainly not his time as prime minister that brought him back to a top job. With Japan facing the worst economic crisis in decades, it was his long experience in government, his economic acumen and renowned ability to negotiate that meant that he was regarded as a safe pair of hands – an Anchor Point – to guide the Japanese economy through the crisis and help rebuild the regional economy. Indeed, Prime Minister Obuchi appointed him precisely to 'gain credibility from foreign markets' and to signal the government's commitment to addressing the financial crisis (Suginohara, 2004: 11).

Miyazawa was the first former prime minister to become finance minister since Takahashi Korekiyo (see Chapter 3) and the first to return to cabinet since Shidehara in the Yoshida cabinet (see Chapter 4). He remained in position under Mori Yoshirō's prime ministership. Miyazawa enunciated his ideas about how to deal with the crisis in his December 1998 speech in which he called for Japan to play a leading role in the creation of a 'New International Finance Architecture' (Miyazawa, 1998). While opinions remain divided about the success or otherwise of Japan's response to the Asian

Financial Crisis, Miyazawa's implementation of his eponymous initiative in 1998, which paved the way for the Chiang Mai Initiative two years later (a system of bilateral currency swaps between Japan and the countries of East Asia), certainly helped to calm the nerves of at least the US and the IMF (see Hughes, 2000; Amyx, 2002).

Summary

This chapter has shown that the period from 1989 to 2024 was no less tumultuous for Japanese politics than the previous two periods covered in Chapters 3 and 4. The ousting of the LDP for two, albeit brief, interludes rocked the relative political stability of the 1955 system and opened up opportunities for new opposition parties and non-LDP prime ministers to emerge on the scene. Wholescale political reform in the 1990s had implications for the electoral system, which in turn impacted on internal party structures, not least the role of factions, and funding mechanisms. At the same time, prime ministers were severely tested by a series of crises and disasters – natural and man-made, national and international – which shone a light on their leadership skills and, in turn, contributed to a high turnover of prime ministers. In some cases, even a brief time in prime ministerial office impacted post-prime ministerial ambitions and careers, political or otherwise. The relative youth of the prime ministers in this period meant that their afterlives were, with some exceptions, longer than those of their predecessors opening up space and time for a variety of post-prime ministerial incarnations.

The categories of Still Ambitious and Political Dabblers are the most highly populated in this period, echoing the findings of the previous chapters. While only Abe managed to make a comeback, other former prime ministers returned to ministerial positions and fulfilled their ambitions to remain central to Japanese political life. Others were able to influence politics through the informal means open to them – mainly through their leadership of factions or in 'advisory' capacities. But even when factions were under threat – for example during Koizumi's time in office, or more recently with the dissolution of factions as a result of the kickback scandal, former prime ministers have still managed to influence party and public opinion. The most powerful example of this was the jockeying for position between former prime ministers Suga, Asō and indeed Kishida in the October 2024 LDP presidential election, all of whom used their considerable political capital to attempt to sway the vote their way (with Asō losing out in this particular case). Ambition and political dabbling is not the preserve of the LDP – Noda's return to the leadership of the CDP over a decade on from his tenancy as prime minister is an, albeit rare, example.

Family Affair is another well-populated category but raises questions about the nature of dynastic politics in Japan and the quality and fitness to serve of legacy candidates. The 'revolving door' of Japanese prime ministers in the 1990s and again in the 2000s can partly be attributed to weak leadership of prime ministers who may have been 'less qualified to handle the difficult policy issues facing them once in office' (Smith, 2018: 28). While legacy candidates had the advantages of financial support and ready-made political connections, they were not necessarily the best candidates for the job and did not match their predecessors in terms of longevity in office. Nonetheless, dynastic politics continues in Japan in the 21st century, with generational change moving up the agenda.

The Celebrity category sheds light on the ways in which the changing role of the media in Japan has impacted on the lives and afterlives of prime ministers – the majority of whom became increasingly adept at engaging with, and leveraging, traditional and new media to maintain their public profiles. While not seeking out celebrity per se, some of their activities (not least those of Koizumi, Murayama and Hatoyama) certainly brought them back into the public eye from time to time.

The categories of First Citizen, Embracers of a Cause and Seekers of Vindication tended to overlap somewhat, suggesting the need for greater nuancing of these categories in the Japanese case, to be discussed in Chapter 6. The less well-represented categories are Acolytes and Protégés and Anchor Point. In both cases, there are fewer examples than in previous chapters of prime ministers who have, on the one hand, inspired and nurtured successors in the way their predecessors did, or, on the other, have had the gravitas and cachet to act as the nation's safe pair of hands. Chapter 6 will explore the reasons for the changing nature of categories over time and suggest how we might modify our understanding of Japan's former prime ministers based on the empirical evidence provided in Chapters 3, 4 and 5.

Notes

[1] Founded in 1954 in South Korea, the Unification Church (original name: Holy Spirit Association for the Unification of World Christianity) was granted religious organization status in Japan in 1964 and developed close links with members of the LDP, including the Kishi/Abe family.

[2] Hatoyama Ichirō founded the NPO 'Yūai' in 1953, and since 2019 it has been a public interest incorporated foundation. Hatoyama Yukio is still involved in Yūai activities as Chairman. See https://www.yuai-love.com

[3] Note that online campaigning was prohibited until the 2013 amendment to the Public Offices Election Law, but individual politicians began to make use of social media from the 1990s.

6

Analysis and Conclusions

Overview

As mentioned at the outset of this book, there is no formal or single template for what leaders do after stepping down. Their afterlives can vary across several roles and activities, which will often overlap with each other. These roles and activities can be consistent with their time in power or take an unexpected turn. The evidence presented in Chapters 3, 4 and 5 demonstrates all these aspects in the case of Japanese prime ministers and their post-premierships. This diverse patchwork picture of their afterlives is very much a function of the informal nature of their existence once out of power. It also fits the definitions of informal politics cited in Chapter 2. In this light, the empirical chapters have demonstrated former prime ministers engaging in a range of public and private activities with a strong focus on the interpersonal that exist outside of official structures. These activities may on occasions skirt the edges of what can be considered legitimate, but they are rarely illegal and often have personal or public ends at their heart. Ultimately, former Japanese prime ministers and their afterlives remind us of the importance of incorporating informal actors and spaces in our understanding of politics.

In light of the empirical evidence presented across the activities of Japan's 64 former prime ministers, this concluding chapter returns to the questions outlined in Chapter 1 as regards the relevance or fit of the existing categories in the case of Japan and their relative importance. In other words, how similar and different are Japan and its ex-prime ministers from other, particularly Western and democratic, countries that originally engendered most of these categories? Do relevance, similarities and differences change over the three time periods explored in each of the three empirical chapters? Moreover, does the Japanese case suggest any modifications to our understanding of former prime ministers and how might they inform future research directions?

Still Ambitious

Chapters 3, 4 and 5 demonstrate that several official political positions are open to former Japanese prime ministers, making this one of the most heavily populated categories across three historical periods. On the one hand, some of these positions are specific to a given time. For example, president of the Privy Council was only an available opportunity from its creation in 1888 through to its abolition in 1947. Similarly, Asō Tarō's appointment as an anime envoy to China in 2011 was dependent on Japan's rising soft power and unlikely to have happened at any other time prior to that. On the other hand, several positions are more generic across time and space, whether they be continuing to serve in the Diet, or assuming a bureaucratic role or a diplomatic appointment. The return to a ministerial position in a successor's cabinet is equally not uncommon and sometimes more desirable for the less ambitious ex-leader regardless of historical period.

As regards a return to the top job, the difference over time is immediately salient. During the Meiji and early Shōwa periods, 13 of the 29 prime ministers returned to serve a second term, if not third, or even fourth in the case of Japan's first prime minister, Itō Hirobumi. In the postwar period, only one prime minister, Yoshida Shigeru, out of the 17 under examination achieved the same feat. Since the end of the Cold War, similarly only one of the 18 serving prime ministers achieved a return to the *kantei*, Abe Shinzō. However, this is clearly an unequal comparison. The high number of returning prime ministers during the Meiji and early Shōwa periods can be explained by the narrow clique of oligarchs who led Japan and alternated their positions among themselves with little, if any, reference to the electorate. Although it could be argued that the postwar political class in Japan was still narrowly defined, with the postwar democratization of Japan it became harder for a prime minister to return to his former role. In the words of Hayasaka:

> In order for the prime minister who once went out of power to come back, it requires much greater power and energy compared to the energy exhausted when he first brought the entire country under his control ... In addition, he must have genius partners who could create situations, and the luck of time and good fortune. There must be all these three factors present in order for the resumption to become possible. (1994: 102)

As Chapters 4 and 5 highlight, this has not deterred some ex-prime ministers from staging, or at least contemplating, a return. For the most part, they were unsuccessful. Yoshida and Abe are the two exceptions that prove this rule, both known for their ambition and zeal and both able to benefit from an unstable political context that enabled their returns to power. Not only did Yoshida take advantage of the unsettled party politics of the early postwar years when he returned to the premiership in 1948, his success also came at the heel of two consecutive governments which had come to be considered especially inept. Similarly for Abe, the Democratic Party of Japan's (DPJ, *Minshutō*) failures in government, especially in the aftermath of the triple disaster of 2011, provided the broader political circumstance that enabled his restoration to power and ushered in a decade of relative stability.

Given the sense of despondence and lack of purpose described by many former leaders when stepping down from the highest office, it is no surprise that they seek to continue their political engagement in some official form. A parliamentary system, compared to a presidential one, offers opportunities such as staying on in an elected seat or within party politics. In Japan, it may be argued that the relatively long lifespan of politicians, the revolving-door nature of the premiership and the recent trend towards younger prime ministers (and therefore younger former prime ministers) contributes further. The result is that, since the end of World War Two (WW2), a greater proportion of former prime ministers has enjoyed longer post-premier lifespans, fostering a greater opportunity to continue political activities. The case of Higashikuni Naruhiko seems to be an exception that proves the rule. With the longest post-premier life by some margin, Higashikuni was an active civilian and pursued business and religious ventures to varying degrees of success. Instead, it is clear that very few former prime ministers in Japan regard their premiership as the ultimate culmination of their political careers. As the extant literature explored in Chapter 2 demonstrates, the desire to return to a position of power having experienced its loss is one of the traits of a political animal that transcends both time and space. Japan is no exception. However, its political history highlights in stark contrast the impact of democratization in limiting the choices available to a former prime minister.

Exhausted Volcanoes

If the preceding three chapters demonstrate that former Japanese prime ministers tend to be heavily involved in official political activities after stepping down from office, very few retire completely from the political arena to live out their days in relative quietude. Some, like Hatoyama Ichirō and Uno Sōsuke, retained their Diet seats but maintained a relatively low profile for the most part. Others, like Konoe Fumimaro and Tōjō Hideki, may have wanted to live out a quiet retirement, but war and eventual defeat denied them the possibility. Koizumi similarly, though under radically different circumstances, seemed to initially take this route to the surprise of many given his popularity but returned in other guises later in his post-prime ministerial afterlife.

Death and illness are the primary reasons prime ministers do not continue to pursue political aims and ambitions as a former prime minister. All three periods display in-post deaths from natural causes or illnesses that force a prime minister to step down and result in their passing not long after. However, assassinations and executions of in-post prime ministers are specific to the tumultuous political contexts of the Taishō and early Shōwa periods, as illustrated in Chapter 3. Ultranationalist disillusionment with the governments of the day proved particularly deadly, ultimately taking the lives of three serving prime ministers between 1921 and 1932. Although the assassination of Abe in 2022 drew worldwide attention, it is not the sole example of the assassination of a former prime minister truncating their afterlife. Japan's first prime minister, Itō, was also the first, and not the last, former prime minister to be assassinated.

Political Dabblers

The opposite of an Exhausted Volcano is the Political Dabbler, who maintains a keen interest in influencing day-to-day party political matters and decision-making but does not occupy an official position that the Still Ambitious former prime minister would seek out. Like the extant analyses of former leaders in other countries, the Japanese case shows that many former prime ministers are involved in intervening in political and party affairs, either for or against the government of the day and often to their disappointment. As Dobson and Rose (2019) noted, this is an especially populated category in Japan due to the structural peculiarities of Japanese politics. The empirical chapters fleshed out the point that the dominance of the Liberal Democratic Party (LDP, *Jiyū Minshutō*) since the mid-20th century and its factional nature make this category ripe for former prime ministers' meddling. As noted in Chapter 2, the term *kuromaku* (literally, black curtain) connotes an image of a puppet master, and across the history of Japanese politics, influential power brokers have been credited with exerting greater authority than their official political positions might suggest. Some former prime ministers like Tanaka, Kishi and Abe, among others, have been given nicknames like *yami shōgun* (shadow shogun) and *Shōwa no yōkai* (monster of the Shōwa era) that reflect the public perception.

The empirical chapters develop this category with further detail than the extant literature. Specifically, they point to a considerable overlap between Political Dabblers with other categories and activities engaged in by former prime ministers explored later in more detail. As political creatures, several former premiers sought to maintain power and influence as an end in itself. However, for many it was also a mechanism to support other aims. As seen in Chapter 3 in the cases of Saionji Kinmochi, Katsura Tarō and Yamagata Aritomo and in Chapter 4 with Ashida Hitoshi's anti-Yoshida efforts, those who were ambitious for a return to the top job intervened in both party political matters and diplomatic affairs (to greater or lesser degrees of success) in order to maintain their own political cachet or undermine that of their rivals. Political dabbling may also be a means of promoting one's own acolytes and protégés, or advancing a particular cause or policy direction. The latter was certainly true for those former prime ministers frustrated with the direction taken by Japan, as was the case for Tōjō in the final months of WW2 as the incumbent government sought to end the war.

While the function of political dabbling has remained broadly similar through time, the form and extent has changed according to structural changes in the Japanese political system. In the early 20th century, the role of an elder statesman in advising and selecting members of the incumbent government was much more institutionalized. As mentioned in the previous Still Ambitious section, the oligarchical nature of the political class enabled a greater proportion of former leaders to successfully return to the prime ministership. The structure is also reflected in the more personal form of political meddling taken by Itō, for example, who sought to directly influence Japan's foreign affairs.

By contrast, changes to the political system after WW2 are evident in the form and extent of political dabbling. On the one hand, the longer lifespans and appointment of younger prime ministers have led to longer afterlives as former leaders. At the same time, short premierships in recent decades, with the exception of Abe's second term, have increased the number of former prime ministers still exercising their influence. On the other hand, postwar democratization has changed the scope and mechanism of political dabbling. As it has become necessary to build viable coalitions whether within or between parties, political machinations have become predominantly domestic and internal to the party. Former prime ministers may act as a representative of the government of the day in foreign affairs, but there is little opportunity to directly shape foreign policy in the same manner.

The primary mechanism of political dabbling for former prime ministers is through their factions. Former prime ministers have become powerful kingmakers as leaders of factions. In this role, they may support or resist bids by aspiring party leaders, who would then become the next prime minister by virtue of the LDP's dominance since the 1950s. For extending support to successful aspirants, the former prime minister may have preferential access and influence over the incoming government as a *quid pro quo*. This was abundantly evident through the latter part of the Shōwa era, for example Tanaka's influence over Nakasone's first cabinet earned it the moniker *Tanakasone*. While reforms in the 1990s dampened some factional influence, this dynamic has still been evident in more recent years as seen in Chapter 5, particularly with the powerful Abe and Asō factions. As of the time of writing, we are yet to witness the full consequences of the LDP slush-fund scandal of late 2023, which led to the dissolution of most factions and will shape the premiership of Ishiba Shigeru, who was elected in September 2024.

First Citizens

The extant literature in Chapter 2 discusses how former leaders take up the role of a dignified public servant or elder statesman, possibly involving some kind of humanitarian work. Taking after Theakston (2010), we have used the label of First Citizen, indicating a sense of public duty above the minutiae of partisan politics and personal ambitions. Here we might point to Nelson Mandela as a First Citizen recognized on a global scale, who successfully achieved his political goals and exuded the halo effect. At the same time, in terms of a pathway, think of Jimmy Carter who, despite being widely regarded as a failed president, embraced several specific causes in his post-presidency and ended up securing the status of a First Citizen. Distinctive to the case of Japan in this context is the extent to which the role of the former prime minister was historically institutionalized. As illustrated in Chapter 3, First Citizens, although elder statesmen is a more appropriate and commonly used term, are salient in the prewar period in the institutionalized form of the *genrō* and *jūshin*. However, this is a temporally specific example. In the democratic postwar period, once the *genrō* and *jūshin* had disappeared, few prime ministers were able to acquire the status of First Citizen in the way it is understood as previously discussed.

The political upheaval of the early postwar years meant few former premiers were able to take on the role of a First Citizen, as they were either active in Japan's reconstruction, purged from public office or convicted of war-crimes. Yoshida's post-premier afterlife in the postwar period represents a turning point for the First Citizen category, as the last of the *genrō*-esque First Citizens and the first who harnessed more informal and ceremonial aspects. His ability to act as an unofficial *genrō* to incumbent governments resulted from a combination of his own agency and external circumstances, as he stepped down from the top job into a paucity of elder statesmen. Given the political instability of his times, rivals required his input for coalition building thus raising him above petty partisan politics despite his active political dabbling in party political matters. With his protégés Ikeda and Satō secured in consecutive premierships, Yoshida guaranteed his legacy as a modern (and perhaps only) postwar *genrō*.

More recently, however, no other former prime minister seems to have reached the same stature in both political weight *and* public imagination that earlier elder statesmen had achieved, making them 'aspiring', or quasi-, First Citizens. A handful of subsequent leaders have sought to act in ways commensurate to a First Citizen through various advisory, humanitarian and diplomatic activities, as well as benefiting sheer political longevity both during and after their premiership. Yet, none have been able to achieve the stature as a kind of consensus figure who operated *above* the specific institution and cause to which he was associated. There is a temporal factor at play here. First, the memory of more recent premiers may be too fresh in public memory and not (yet) enshrined in national history. Second, an extended post-premiership is required to elevate the individual beyond the Embracer of a Cause (as discussed later) to the status of a First Citizen. While Satō and his great-nephew Abe wielded significant influence, their post-premierships were simply too short. Illustrative of these factors is the memorialization of the (would-be) First Citizen after death. Nakasone's and Abe's funerals in 2020 and 2022, respectively, the former sponsored by the LDP and the latter Japan's second postwar state funeral, were mired in controversy for the two former leaders' nationalist ideologies (*Asahi Shimbun*, 2020; Yamaguchi, 2022). By comparison, though Yoshida's state funeral (the first in postwar Japan) faced some opposition from the Japan Communist Party and trade unions, the incumbent premier Satō was able to garner a broad coalition to positively burnish Yoshida's legacy (Tsuda, 2023: 20; cf *The Japan Times*, 1967).

One key way that First Citizens (or aspiring First Citizens) demonstrate their status is as a national representative on the international stage. Like Mandela's group, The Elders, or Fukuda Takeo's InterAction Council, former leaders self-identify not only as national but *international* leaders in policy and ethical values. As such, they may consider themselves as guardians of high-minded guidance to the incumbent national and international leaders of the day. At the same time, they may harness these opportunities and personal connections with political elites to advance substantive policy positions, as we saw in Chapters 4 and 5, showing a close relationship between the First Citizen and Political Dabbler categories. However, even if these informal diplomatic spaces provide an opportunity, they are often highly Western-centric and place Japanese former leaders on the back foot as '…English is a key to exploiting this advantage. Meetings of ex-leaders were traditionally dominated by leading figures from the United States, and much of the agenda had to do with transatlantic relations' (Paterson, 2012: 121).

Across the historical spectrum – from prewar *genrō* to the more contemporary quasi-First Citizen – former prime ministers are able to act as such in accordance with their contemporary environment. Most clearly, the prewar elder statesmen required a political structure which allowed for extra-constitutional political influence. After WW2, for Yoshida the fact that his protégés Ikeda and Satō were at the helm of leadership for a sustained duration of his post-prime ministerial life enabled him to act in broad and influential ways. But even without the direct personal relationship of mentor and mentee, the ability of a former prime minister to act as a First Citizen in representing Japan was dependent on his relationship with the individuals and factions (especially within the LDP) who were in power at the time. This is true for Fukuda Takeo, who had been ousted from the premiership as a result of his long-standing rivalry with Tanaka Kakuei. However, because the proceeding administration of Suzuki Zenkō did not freeze him out – and, in fact, dispatched him on diplomatic missions – Fukuda could be seen to act as a First Citizen. In the post-Cold War context of rising international tensions in the region, the dispatch of former prime ministers as special envoys or cultural envoys, for example, enabled the government of the day to capitalize on the connections and relationships developed by their predecessors. Mori's close links with India and Russia, Fukuda's and Hatoyama's ties with China, and Suga's connections with Southeast Asia, among others, helped to maintain continuity or demonstrate ongoing commitments to bilateral relations. The symbolic nature of dispatching such individuals, albeit in an informal capacity, speaks to their perceived ongoing value and influence.

Embracing a humanitarian cause is another path to first citizenship, as was the case for Carter. However, this is a high bar to pass. As mentioned previously, the closest to achieving the status of a First Citizen in the postwar period is possibly Yoshida. He was associated with political dabbling in his retirement and was thus closer to a prewar *genrō*, rather than embracing a specific cause. However, one could argue that his broader aim which spanned from before to after his premiership was aligning Japan with the liberal capitalist order. As discussed in Chapter 4, he had an important role in smoothing over relations with Taiwan while Japan improved relations with Beijing during the Cold War. By comparison, subsequent former leaders like Nakasone, Murayama and Hatoyama have been unable to shake their association with the specific causes they championed as will be discussed in the next section. The scale and success of the cause may then have a bearing on whether its champion is remembered as a First Citizen. Nevertheless, there is no Japanese Mandela. Thus, while a lowered threshold and the ever extending afterlives of former prime ministers may afford greater opportunities to seek a First Citizen status, this is a category that may be experiencing a decline or transformation.

Embracers of a Cause

As outlined in Chapter 2, an Embracer of a Cause devotes their energies and resources to a specific issue or cluster of inter-related concerns. Although this category overlaps with the previous category of First Citizen, it can be distinguished by the specificity of the cause(s). It may be that embracing a cause can be a pathway to the exalted status of First Citizen but that latter category requires a higher degree of recognition, either nationally or internationally, gravitas and expertise. We might think of the difference between John Major as the embracer of the European cause during the Brexit debates in the UK, for example, and, once again, Mandela.

Several prime ministers across the three periods under examination in this book have embraced a specific cause that is close to their hearts. Chapter 3 pointed to some examples of prewar former prime ministers who pursued educational and humanitarian causes. Ōkuma Shigenobu is probably one of the highest profile examples as a result of the many causes he embraced but particularly his close association with Waseda University, one of Japan's leading private institutions with an international reputation, and his nominative footprint on the main campus. Chapter 4 highlighted the continuing importance of Katayama Tetsu's faith and sense of social justice that ran through his life and career. Although of a more liberal–conservative orientation than Katayama's socialism, Ishibashi Tanzan shared with him an embrace of normalization with the communist world as a cause in his post-premiership. Ashida was similarly a liberal-leaning conservative, but his stance on relations with the communist world differed greatly from Ishibashi as he advocated for a unilateral peace treaty with the West and Japanese rearmament so that it could defend itself against the communist threat. Ashida's position was closer to that of arch-conservative Kishi. In both cases, the two causes muddies the picture of neat ideological divides. Rather, these causes were supported by advocates from different ideological camps but who converged over their interpretation of Japan's position in Cold War Asia.

Chapter 5 highlights further passion projects pursued by former prime ministers. Whether it be Murayama's efforts to promote normalization of relations with North Korea, or advocacy on behalf of the comfort women or the people of Okinawa, or Fukuda's promotion of Sino-Japanese reconciliation specifically and Hatoyama in the case of East Asia more broadly, or Koizumi's non-nuclear stance, these activities never quite elevated any of them to a position of a First Citizen or elder statesman as defined previously. Certainly, these former prime ministers can claim the age and seniority that one might associate with a First Citizen/elder statesman, but these two aspects do not automatically merit the application of this category. Their activities have been associated with one cause or set of issues, lacking the broad scope (and often, the concrete successes) associated with a First Citizen/elder statesman and are thus more closely aligned with an Embracer of a Cause.

It is also clear that the specific cause matters in terms of whether its embrace can provide a pathway to the status of First Citizen. As mentioned previously, the cause may not always be virtuous and the Japanese case illustrates this point well over the three historical periods under examination, although context matters in terms of the opportunities available. For example, the ideological causes embraced in Chapter 3 were often associated with the

Japanese colonies, as seen in the case of Katsura. Chapters 4 and 5 offer examples of former prime ministers embracing ideological causes linked with the colonial period but framed by postwar decolonization and displaying a historical revisionist tone. Kishi is a good example of this, as his crusade for rearmament has coloured his legacy and scuppered his chances of being categorized as a First Citizen as a result.

The historical context can also help explain Takeshita Noboru's engagement with global climate change activism; this would not have been a cause available to prewar and most postwar former prime ministers. It does appear to have been heartfelt but has also been regarded as an attempt to rehabilitate his own reputation and a scandal-ridden LDP, as seen in Chapter 4. In short, embracing a cause is not always neutral, and this category can overlap with the next category of Seekers of Vindication.

Seekers of Vindication

As outlined in Chapter 2, Seekers of Vindication want to present their side of the story of their time in power. This suggests that a controversial event, political scandal or policy failure has damaged their reputation to the extent that a former prime minister feels the need to seek this vindication. As is often quoted, '[a]ll political lives, unless they are cut off in midstream at a happy juncture, end in failure, because that is the nature of politics and of human affairs' (Powell, 1977: 151). This is regularly observed in the US and UK, and Japan is no different across the historical periods in question. Chapter 3 pointed to Ōkuma's efforts to reestablish his image after his second period in office was tainted by scandal. Fast forward almost 100 years and Chapter 5 discussed the example of Kan Naoto, prime minister at the time of the triple disasters of 11 March 2011, who was widely criticized for failing to respond swiftly and adequately to the Great East Japan Earthquake, tsunami and Fukushima nuclear accident, and resigned six months later. Kan continued to play a formal political role as a Diet member, embracing the anti-nuclear cause, but also explaining and justifying his past decisions to national and international audiences.

Kan engaged with the media to set the record straight, which is an extension of the traditional means employed by former prime ministers across space and time, the memoir. Again, the Japanese case is no different as seen in the empirical chapters across three periods. Some former prime ministers have been prolific writers. For example, Chapter 4 focused on Nakasone and the active role he played in constructing a heroic narrative of his life and career through a body of work that expanded prolifically during his afterlife from 1987, and especially after his forced retirement in 2004, through to his death in 2019. However, it is difficult to discern in Japan the same kind of publishing industry, money-making opportunities and public interest (whether it be frenzied or cynical) that exist in the UK and US around the release of ex-leaders' memoirs.

In terms of agency, it need not always be the former prime minister in question. Chapter 4 points to the case of Tanaka as a preeminent example of a former prime minister whose reputation was tarnished by scandal. It also highlights his daughter Makiko as the relatively rare example of a woman playing the role of Seeker of Vindication. Chapter 5 highlights Abe's efforts before, during and after his time in power to normalize the reputation of his grandfather Kishi, damaged by the anti-Japan–US Security Treaty protests mentioned in Chapter 4. In these cases and others, the Japanese case provides a salient example of this category intersecting with that of Family Affair, explored later in more detail.

The question raised in Chapter 2 around the point at which vindication has been achieved remains a challenging one to answer. The example of Nakasone, and more recently Kan, who have continued to dabble and publish, suggests that this vanishing point is elusive.

Acolytes and Protégés

As discussed in Chapter 2, supporting a protégé's ascent to power is neither unique to Japan nor limited to any one political system. Like other democratic societies, former leaders in Japan have readily campaigned in elections on behalf of their party. In fact, Abe was on the campaign trail, giving a stump speech on behalf of a local LDP candidate, when he was fatally shot in July 2022. However, as critics have pointed out, the practice of a former leader actively supporting a protégé may pose a challenge to democratic principles (Anderson, 2010: 71). As readily seen with Political Dabblers, much of their activities seek to ensure that one's protégés gain privileges or higher office through backroom machinations.

Such concerns were of little consequence in the imperial era. Chapter 3 shows that the Meiji oligarchs, like Yamagata and his rival Itō, nurtured political acolytes from within the Chōshū clan. Not only did they secure the line of succession through this lineage, as a result Yamaguchi Prefecture (present-day Chōshū) is vastly overrepresented as the place of origin for Japanese prime ministers: 8 out of 65 prime ministers, across 47 prefectures. By comparison, Chapters 4 and 5 show that place of origin has less importance in the years since WW2. Instead, there are a variety of other factors that serve as the foundation of the mentor and mentee relationship. In some cases it has been familial, as was the case with Kishi and his son-in-law Abe Shintarō. In other cases, the protégé came though similar government posts: for Kishi, Shiina Etsusaburō was his junior (*kōhai*) in the colonial government in prewar Manchuria. While ideological alignment may not be the central factor, in many instances the protégés will carry on the same policy direction as their mentor. Ikeda and Satō – who have come to be known as the two so-called 'honours students' (*yūtōsei*) of the Yoshida school of politics – carried on their mentor's foreign policy footsteps (Edström, 1999b: 68).

Compared to the factional politics of the Political Dabbler, the relationships between the former leader and his acolytes and protégés are characteristically and understandably more personal. Nonetheless, these are instrumental relationships on both sides. Generally, installing a trusted follower gains the former prime minister continued access. In Yoshida's case, with his protégés in power, he was enabled to act as a modern day *genrō* and was memorialized as a First Citizen through a state funeral as discussed previously. The acolyte has great influence over a former prime minister's legacy; however, depending on the state of the relationship, the former acolyte may negatively distort the former leader's image as Hara did to Saionji's historical reputation. Even positive accolades may be a shrewd political calculation in some instances. The example of Takaichi Sanae is illustrative as discussed in Chapter 5. A conservative with hawkish military policies, she is sometimes regarded as Abe's protégé as he supported her run as candidate for the LDP presidency in 2021. Finding difficulty gaining internal allies in the absence of her mentor after his death in 2022 – especially in the 2024 LDP presidential elections – she styled herself as Abe's natural successor and in the process burnished his legacy. However, her shock defeat to Ishiba in the second round was a clear indication that she had failed to secure the confidence of the party to take Abe's project forward.

Fostering one's succession has evidently been a key preoccupation for former Japanese leaders and has led them to engage in various forms of political dabbling to ensure power for their chosen acolytes and protégés. As argued previously, this category highlights the deep personal character of Japanese politics. The Japanese case also shows the agency of the so-called acolytes to influence or harness the former leader's reputation to their own political advantage. Ward pointed out some years ago that a new politician will 'join someone rather than something, [and] select a protector and a leader rather than a cause' (1965: 71). This does seem to broadly hold true through to the present, although some shared policy views do help make the case for a succession.

Family Affair

As mentioned in Chapter 2, generational politics is highly relevant to the case of Japan and has been highlighted as one of the most salient features of its politics, especially compared to other democracies (Itoh, 2003; Asako et al, 2015; Smith, 2018). It can allow politicians to leverage family connections for their own ends. In the case of prime ministers, Chapters 4 and 5 provide many examples of how widely this has manifested since 1945. For example, Chapter 4 highlighted the fact that 75 per cent of prime ministers under the postwar constitution have been inter-generational politicians, and it is easier to name the former prime ministers who did not have a member of their direct family (children, siblings or children-in-law) become a public official, than to namecheck those who did. Among those who did, the brothers Kishi and Satō provide a high-profile example where both became prime minister. This is even more evident at the ministerial level, and Kishi provides another example as he actively manoeuvred his son-in-law Abe Shintarō through the ranks, although he ultimately fell short of securing the top job. At a different level, the family connection has manifested through the passing of a constituency from one generation to the next, as seen in the many examples cited in Chapters 4 and 5. Comparing both periods, there appear to be fewer cases of this phenomenon over time and especially in the post-1989 period than had been the case previously. This can partly be explained by changes in political culture and election strategy within the LDP as part of an active move against hereditary seats (Smith, 2018).

Chapter 3 also demonstrates examples that could be counted under this category whereby former prime ministers actively leveraged direct members of their family, as defined previously, or even indirect family connections. This could starkly be seen in Yamagata using his family connections in tandem with a protégé to try and influence subsequent administrations. However, it should also be noted that some of the offspring and extended family of the prime ministers under examination during the Meiji, Taishō and early Shōwa periods could engage in a military career or the peerage. In the postwar context, the family of prime ministers would have had to consider the optics surrounding the former and found the latter to be unconstitutional. Chapter 3 may also represent the formative stages during which the political families and dynasties highlighted in Chapters 4 and 5 established and consolidated themselves. For example, Hosokawa was seven years old when his grandfather Konoe committed suicide in December 1945. Similarly, Hiranuma Takeo was a teenager when his grandfather Kiichirō died but both were born into a structure of power based around political heritage.

Similar cases of the descendant benefitting from the predecessor's legacy were mentioned in Chapters 4 and 5 and at times manifested themselves at the highest level. For example, Fukuda Yasuo was born into the legacy of his father Takeo, Hatoyama Yukio born into that of his grandfather Ichirō and Abe Shinzō into that of his grandfather Kishi. All six served as prime minister. Comparing across historical periods point to the importance of political structure. Whereas the prewar oligarchy systematically provided avenues for political offspring to maintain the family's influence through the peerage or the military, in contrast the name recognition, connections and access to wealth associated with political dynasties have greater significance in a democratic system. This requires a degree of definitional flexing in the category of Family Affairs to include not only how senior family members leverage junior members but how descendants regard their predecessors and their inherited legacy.

There seems to be an association between generational politics with political conservatism. The cases examined are skewed toward conservative politicians and their families given the scope of our research and the dominant LDP. With this caveat in mind, it is nevertheless notable that since 1945, non-conservative prime ministers have tended to be 'first generation' politicians (Katayama, Murayama, Kan and Noda), with the exceptions of Hatoyama Yukio and Hosokawa.

It also requires recognition that this category intersects with the category of Celebrity; a family connection from one period can play out in later historical periods in terms of the potential for political or social capital. In the case of the Hatoyamas, dubbed the Kennedys of Japan, this can be positive. Similarly, Koizumi Shinjirō, a front runner in the 2024 LDP presidential elections and touted as a future prime ministerial candidate, has benefitted from his father, Junichirō's, continued popularity. However, in the cases of Tanaka and Tōjō, celebrity and infamy are closely connected and the latter can provide the context that shapes the actions of future generations. The two examples also represent rare cases of daughters and granddaughters seeking to restore the reputation of their predecessors that highlight the gendered nature of generational politics.

Celebrity

As touched upon in Chapter 2, a literature has emerged over the last couple of decades on the topic of celebrity politics that highlights two definitions of the actors involved. On the one hand, the celebrity *politician* is either the celebrity-turned-politician who leverages their celebrity status in the service of their new-found political career or the traditional politician who associates themselves with celebrity and celebrities to promote their ideas or platform. On the other hand, the political *celebrity* reflects a more recent phenomenon whereby celebrities have ventured into politics, articulated a cause and are listened to on the basis of their fame and status (Street, 2004; Cooper, 2008; Wheeler, 2013). When considering former prime ministers, it is clear that they fall into the former category either as celebrities who move into politics, rise to the top job and then resign (think back to Ronald Reagan or ahead to Volodymyr Zelenskyy), or as former leaders who flirt with celebrity culture in retirement in order to promote a political message. In addition, when focussing on Japan, it is worth noting that it possesses a highly developed celebrity culture that has received academic attention over the years (Galbraith and Karlin, 2012). So, even if we are dealing with a small pool, namely 64 former Japanese prime ministers, opportunities exist for this exclusive group of individuals to leverage their status as former prime ministers, if they are so inclined and possess the personal skills.

Although some form of celebrity culture has existed across historical periods, in light of the recent rise of social media and reality TV, it might be expected that this category is less well populated by the former prime ministers examined in Chapter 3 and more heavily populated by those explored in Chapter 5. It is true that neither celebrity-turned-prime-minister-turned-former-prime-minister can be discerned in Chapter 3, nor can explicit examples of former prime ministers leveraging celebrity to a political end. Nevertheless, this chapter does highlight prime ministers who had a reputation or status at the time that could be viewed through the lens of celebrity, for example Hara as the 'commoner prime minister' or Ōkuma as recipient of the 'people's funeral'. However, any celebrity status, often as the 'father of' a Japanese institution, tended to be established with the passing of time and during the longer historical period that these prime ministers benefit from compared to those in Chapter 4 and certainly Chapter 5.

Although there are several celebrity-turned-politicians in Japan, it is difficult to identify any who have made it to the position of prime minister and then former prime minister in Chapters 4 and 5. Ishibashi was a renowned journalist prior to his political career, Ashida concomitantly served as an elected representative and as president and editor-in-chief of *The Japan Times* during the 1930s, and Asō's participation in the 1976 Montreal Olympics predates his election to the House of Representatives by three years. It would be difficult to describe these three as celebrities, however. Chapter 5 highlights former prime ministers who flirted with celebrity culture, ranging from the bizarre examples, such as Koizumi, who provided his vocal talents to the role of *Ultraman King in Mega Monster Battle Ultra Galaxy: The Movie*, or Hatoyama's musical theatre debut as the first female president of the US in retirement, through to the more traditional, exemplified as Hosokawa's career as a potter. However, it would be difficult to view these as attempts by former leaders to leverage celebrity to a political end. The reality is that no former prime minister in Japan has sought a career change to that of celebrity or, for the most part, used the celebrity accrued from their position to pursue a political objective. The two exceptions appear to be Nakasone and Murayama. Nakasone continued to engage with the media to convey his political views and even hosted his own TV show for a decade, as another former prime minister, Harold Wilson, had done in the UK but only for a fortnight in 1979. Murayama chose to appear in *8-gatsu no Kariyushi* (Happiness in August), an anti-war movie set in Okinawa.

Perhaps more noticeable here in the case of Japan is the process of celebritization by which prime ministerial reputations are forged in popular culture with or without the input of the former leader in question, as seen in the case of Yoshida and his acolytes, as well as Nakasone in Chapter 4, or Koizumi in Chapter 5.

Anchor Point

Focussing on Satō, Tsuda (2023) describes a much more significant role than his short post-premiership might suggest. He provided political stability during a period of instability caused by the normalization of relations with the People's Republic of China (PRC), the 1973 Oil Shock and the divisive premiership of Tanaka. This role can be captured by the term Anchor Point and all the historical periods under examination in this book include the tumultuous events that require one, whether it be periods of rapid modernization, world wars, victory and defeat, bipolar tensions, post-Cold War uncertainties, financial and economic dislocation or the more recent perma-crisis. Despite this, the examples of Anchor Points among former prime ministers are few and far between. Chapter 3 highlighted Saionji and Yamamoto as two examples out of 29 prime ministers. Out of the 17 prime ministers under examination, and in addition to Satō, Chapter 4 highlights three further but more discrete examples of Yoshida, Kishi and Nakasone, who possessed respectively the status and the reputation/skills to steer Japan through the specific challenges of their times. Chapter 5 focuses on 18 prime ministers but can only point to Miyazawa and his policy expertise that explains his return to the position of finance minister in response to the East Asian Financial Crisis. It should be noted that Anchor Points tend to have the role thrust upon them in the first instance because of circumstances – there needs to be a crisis – but then they require the status, gravitas, reputation, knowledge and/or skills to meet this crisis. Nevertheless, this category is not particularly heavily populated across time.

To understand why there are so few Anchor Points despite there being so much upheaval, we could focus on the absence of skills, knowledge and leadership traditionally associated with the Japanese prime minister, as explored in Chapter 2. However, this is only one aspect of the literature on Japanese prime ministers; as we have seen, they have come to be more proactive and capable over recent decades. It is important to make a distinction here between, what is better termed, a safe pair of hands who can provide policy expertise and bring relevant experience at a time of crisis and being a source of continuity in the eyes of the people in the way the UK monarchy has played this role. There are some, although not many, Japanese prime ministers who can act as a safe pair of hands in a specific time of need, and instead it is the imperial institution that can stand aside from the greasy pole of politics and provide the longer-term reassurance in a similar fashion to Queen Elizabeth II and, potentially, King Charles III 'at a time when the pace of change is bewildering to many' (Prescott, 2022).

As discussed in Chapter 5, similarly in Japan, in the years since the death of the Shōwa emperor in 1989 especially, the imperial court has filled this role with Akihito, Emperor Emeritus dubbed the 'consoler in chief' in the wake of crises and upheavals.

Where are we now?

To return to our original guiding questions, on the one hand, it is clear that the ten categories that we have extracted from the extant literature are all relevant in the case of Japan to varying degrees and help us understand what prime ministers have gone on to do in their afterlives. The lens of former prime ministers also allows us to see from a different angle important and well-known aspects of Japanese politics such as factions, generational politics and other informal mechanisms for continuing to exert influence. This is akin to the relationship between 'positive space' and 'negative space' in art and design. Prime ministers, periods in power, administrations and cabinets are the positive space (the actual thing we observe) and are what traditionally receive most attention. This book has looked at post-premierships or the negative space (the spaces that exist between and around the actual thing we observe) of what goes on between and after periods in power. Not only does this approach allow us to observe something that is often overlooked as negative space, it also allows us to reconsider the positive space or the features of Japanese politics that we usually focus on.

Through this lens, we get a sense of how these aspects have developed over time and where we are today. For example, whether they be between or within the Satsuma and Chōshū clans, or reaching peak influence in the postwar period, the influence of factions is a persistent aspect of Japanese politics. Many observers have hailed the recent events outlined in the vignette at the beginning of Chapter 1 around the collapse of the factional structures as representing a watershed moment. However, the longer-term view provided here suggests that factions are persistent and should never be written off. Indeed, despite heading the charge to dissolve LDP factions under his premiership in November 2024, now as a former prime minister, Kishida moved to create a new 'group' within the party to maintain his influence (*The Japan Times*, 2024b). As regards the importance of generational politics, this can be discerned across all periods but appears to have ballooned during the period covered in Chapter 4.

An additional feature of postwar Japanese politics is the dominance of the LDP. This has impacted on what prime ministers could and could not do after stepping down. For example, as regards what they can do, if their party is still in power then so will their faction, protégés, acolytes and possibly family members thereby increasing the incentives and opportunities for ex-prime ministers to continue dabbling as well as the related impact. In short, the dominance of the LDP has enabled the dominance of one category above the others, namely Political Dabblers. In contrast and as regards what they cannot do, since the creation of the LDP in 1955, only one prime minister has staged a return to the top job and this was achieved from the position of opposition. Whenever faced with the threat of losing power, the unpopular prime minister has been replaced from within the party ranks. As has been argued, the routine exchange of leaders 'like a pendulum on a grandfather clock' has enabled the ruling party to maintain dominance (Hayasaka, 1994: 26). In other words, with internal *coups d'état* the most common way for a prime minister to leave power, the structure that supports LDP dominance makes a return to power unlikely.

On the other hand, the case of Japan highlights aspects of the literature on former leaders that require some reconsideration. The first thing to highlight is that a single action alone does not qualify a former prime minister for inclusion in that specific, related category. Rather, the aggregate of his activities and how they are perceived also matter. Compare, for example, Kishi and Yoshida: both were eminent elder statesmen with profound influence on party political matters and policy in their post-prime ministerial afterlives. Yet, only Yoshida is remembered as a First Citizen for reasons discussed previously. Furthermore, they will be regarded differently by allies and opponents. While a former prime minister may be best associated with certain kinds of activity in retrospect (Yoshida as a First Citizen, Kishi as an Embracer of a Cause, for example), this is not necessarily reflective of their *intent*. They may have pursued other types of activities which have been subsequently overshadowed. In short, their reputation as an ex-premier is contingent on how they are memorialized in public and political consciousness.

It is also clear that nuance emerges in some of the individual categories. In other words, a continuum is clear from a close match with the definition through to a more diluted variant of the category. The result of this is that we can observe quasi-categories or one category operating as a pathway to another. For example, the First Citizen category only works in the case of Japan if it is toned down from the high international benchmark of Nelson Mandela and redefined as an elder statesman along the lines of the *genrō*. In the case of Murayama, his advocacy for peaceful regional relations blurred the line between Embracer of a Cause and First Citizen. As shown in Chapter 5, some categories seem to have become less delineated in recent years as we saw with Hatoyama Yukio moving between the Embracer of a Cause and First Citizen categories, for example. Yet it is worth noting that this may also be a function of recency. Similarly to Hatoyama, Kan Naoto's anti-nuclear activities and rhetoric speak to being both an Embracer of a Cause and a Seeker of Vindication for the decisions made during his time in power and in the middle of a crisis. As more recent prime ministers from the late 2000s and early 2010s, their actions have not yet been fully subject to memorialization and the judgement of history. As time passes, it may be the case that these former premiers and their activities will be more clearly delineated.

It is clear that very few prime ministers and their post-premier activities can be contained in a single category. Rather, the relevant categories in the case of any prime minister will often be multiple, may blur and overlap, and could possibly reinforce each other. If one were to imagine a Venn diagram of these categories across all 64 former prime ministers across time, it would be a complicated, messy and three-dimensional picture – one that is certainly beyond our technical abilities to reproduce here. However, it would be clear that one category sits at the centre of the numerous intersections: Political Dabblers. That former leaders will seek to continue to exert some influence is unsurprising but the extent to which this represents an uber-category with the other categories supporting it is illustrated clearly in the case of Japan. Often, political dabbling is both an end in itself *and* a means to various other ends. For example, at the turn of the 20th century the renowned *genrō* and First Citizen Yamagata Aritomo politically dabbled extensively both to undermine the second Saionji cabinet as an end but also to ensure his protégés' successes. An oligarchical political system enabled the extent of such interventions, to be sure. Yet, the extent and ubiquity of political dabbling discussed in Chapters 4 and 5 show the relevance of this category across history and political structure, pointing toward the influence of non-elected actors even in electoral democracies.

Given that all Japanese prime ministers to date have been men, there is little we can say as to how gender may or may not impact on whether and how former premiers may seek continued political influence. Of course, women have been important political actors in Japanese politics and diplomacy, formally and informally, as discussed in Chapter 2 (Domett, 2005; Dobson, 2012a). As we saw in Chapters 4 and 5 especially, women have played increasingly important roles in maintaining the political legacies of former prime ministers since the middle of the 20th century. As wives, daughters and sisters, women have been instrumental in the creation and maintenance of politics as a family business since before enfranchisement. Through the second half of the 20th century, the most prominent female politicians have been associated with the political left, such as the suffragist Ichikawa Fusae and Doi Takako, who became the first opposition leader as the chairwoman of the Japan Socialist Party (JSP). It has only been since the 1990s that women themselves have harnessed former prime ministers' influence and legacies in earnest to further their own political career, with Takaichi Sanae – self-proclaimed as Abe Shinzō's disciple – coming closest to the top role as the runner up to Ishiba Shigeru in the 2024 LDP presidency contest.

Another aspect that the Japanese case highlights relates to our definition of afterlives. At times, two afterlives emerge with the obvious one being the time between resignation and death, or more uncommonly a return to the top job. However, a more extended afterlife is also evident from death onwards and will often involve burnishing reputations or seeking vindication through family members or acolytes and protégés. For example, the controversy surrounding many of Japan's wartime leaders and attempts towards rehabilitating their reputations demonstrates this extended reputational afterlife. Abe Shinzō's efforts to promote historical revisionism include not only Japan's wartime actions but also the reputation of his grandfather Kishi. As a result, these activities would now become an important aspect of any future biography of the latter. Less controversial examples could be seen in the many museums, parks, statues and residences that exist across Japan and beyond to memorialize, and even presidentialize, Japan's prime ministers since their death. Again, using the example of Abe, since his assassination a statue has been erected in Kaohsiung, Taiwan, and a park created in Pristina, Kosovo, in memory of his contribution to bilateral relations between Japan and the two countries. Clearly, mortality does not limit the extent of a leader's afterlife.

Where do we go from here?

The research and writing of this book have acted as a catalyst to identify intriguing avenues of future research. As regards Japanese politics and its prime ministers, deeper dives and more detailed empirical research into the afterlives of individual ex-prime ministers would be welcome. Tsuda (2023) provides an important example of the richer understanding this kind of approach can result in. At the time of writing, all eyes have been on the two leadership contests in the LDP and Constitutional Democratic Party of Japan (CDP, *Rikken Minshutō*). Former prime ministers have played a salient role in both these contests, which is not unusual in the Japanese context, but potentially provides a neatly framed and specific case study to explore their afterlives further.

Thinking beyond Japan, several comparative projects can be highlighted. As mentioned in Chapter 1, there has been an uptick in research comparing the UK and Japanese prime ministers over recent years (Burrett, 2023; Dobson et al, 2023). Although the afterlives of the former have been thoroughly explored thanks to the work of Kevin Theakston, the latter has traditionally been overlooked as outlined in Chapter 1. With the publication of this first research monograph, and when added to earlier isolated work (Dobson and Rose, 2019; Tsuda, 2023), there is now a solid base upon which a more systematic comparative analysis of UK and Japanese ex-prime ministers can be conducted. Comparison with and between former leaders in modern democracies is a fruitful research agenda; however, the focus has mostly been placed on western democracies with a tendency to focus on Europe or North America (Theakston and de Vries, 2012). A similar project that looks beyond these well-worn regions, builds on the focus on Japanese democracy presented here and extends across Asian democracies would fill an obvious gap in the literature. Alternatively, a comparative focus on newly emerging democracies in which former leaders are still a novelty might provide an original twist.

Several thematic possibilities have emerged. As leaders become younger, their afterlives will become extended providing more opportunities for activity when still in good health. The gender aspects of their afterlives have been touched on in this book but require further thought. Taking an even more extended view, this book has demonstrated that reputations of leaders can be forged or memorialized years, decades or centuries after their deaths. In other words, we also need to understand their post-afterlives.

Finally, on a practical level, there is a degree of formalization of former leaders' roles across several countries, or at least there are debates surrounding the associated pros and cons, as mentioned in Chapter 2. In the UK, an association of former parliamentarians was established in 2003 to make their expertise available to the government of the day. A more streamlined group could be created at the leaders' level with the same objective in the UK, Japan or elsewhere. However, in the case of Japan, it is highly unlikely that any formalization of the role will happen anytime soon. Former prime ministers will, for the most part, continue to dabble politically and in a range of ways – including formal but mostly informal – motivated by a variety of factors: short-term, longer term, personal, reputational and generational.

References

Abe, S. (2006) *Utsukushii kuni e* [Towards a Beautiful Country], Bungei Shunjū.

Abe, S. (2013) 'Japan Is Back: A Conversation With Shinzo Abe', *Foreign Affairs*, 92(4): 2–8.

Akimoto, D. (2022) *Japanese Prime Ministers and Their Peace Philosophy: 1945 to the Present*. Springer Singapore.

Allen, R. (1981) Memorandum for the President. 19 March. Folder Japan (03/19/1981-04/03/1981), RAC Box 8, Executive Secretariat NSC Country Files. Ronald Reagan Library. Available at: https://www.reaganlibrary.gov/public/2022-03/40-748-12026383-R8-031-2022.pdf?y_b9729sMbuiFKCY20FerEd72N73twca

Amakawa, A. (2016) 'Shidehara Kijūrō: His "Final Public Duty" and the Draft Constitution', in A. Watanabe and R.D. Eldridge (eds), *The Prime Ministers of Postwar Japan, 1945–1995: Their Lives and Times*, Lexington Books, pp 9–19.

Amyx, J. (2002) 'Moving Beyond Bilateralism? Japan and the Asian Monetary Fund', *Asia Pacific Economic Papers*, 331 (September), https://openresearch-repository.anu.edu.au/server/api/core/bitstreams/2261f209-1072-4c79-9c75-83fcc9901fa5/content

Anderson, L. (2010) 'The Ex-Presidents', *Journal of Democracy*, 21(2): 65–78.

Armstrong, J.D. (1996) 'The Group of Seven Summits', in D.H. Dunn (ed), *Diplomacy at the Highest Level: The Evolution of International Summitry*, Macmillan, pp 41–52.

Asahi Shimbun (2014) 'Top Abe Adviser Dispatched for Secret Talks in China between Fukuda, Xi', 12 October, http://ajw.asahi.com/article/behind_news/politics/AJ201410120020

Asahi Shimbun (2020) 'Joint Funeral for Nakasone Held; Some Schools Fly Flags at Half-Mast', 18 October, https://www.asahi.com/ajw/articles/13840925

Asahi Shimbun (2021) 'Abe Disciple Takaichi Throws Hat into LDP Leadership Race', 9 September, https://www.asahi.com/ajw/articles/14436859

Asahi Shimbun (2023a) 'In Yamaguchi, Picking Someone to Take Abe's Seat Proves Difficult', 20 January, https://www.asahi.com/ajw/articles/14819373

Asahi Shimbun (2023b) 'Shinji or Shinzo? Spirit of Abe Haunts Elections in Yamaguchi', 12 April, https://www.asahi.com/ajw/articles/14883772

Asahi Shimbun (2023c) 'Mori's Influence Seen in Bulky New Leadership of Abe Faction', 1 September, https://www.asahi.com/ajw/articles/14995200

Asahi Shimbun (2024a) 'As Many Nuclear Reactors Sit Idle, Inexperienced Workforce Grows', 5 March, https://www.asahi.com/ajw/articles/15166618

Asahi Shimbun (2024b) 'Suga Calls on Kishida to Take Responsibility for Funding Scandal', 24 June, https://www.asahi.com/ajw/articles/15317178

Asahi Shimbun (2024c) '"Wakaki rīdā motomerareru": Jimin Fukuda moto sōmu kaichō-ra ga kaikaku shian o kōhyō' ['Younger Leaders Needed': Former LDP Chairman Fukuda and Others Release Draft Reform Plan], 10 August, https://www.asahi.com/articles/ASS8930W6S89UTFK008M.html

Asahi Shimbun (2024d) 'Koizumi to Run in LDP Election, Expected to Gain Suga's Support', 21 August, https://www.asahi.com/ajw/articles/15395771

Asahi Shimbun (2024e) 'Survey: Public Prefers Ishiba or Koizumi in LDP Election', 26 August, https://www.asahi.com/ajw/articles/15401521

Asahi Shimbun (2024f) 'Shadow of Abenomics Clouds BOJ's Rate Hike Path', 25 September, https://www.asahi.com/ajw/articles/15440109

Asako, Y., T. Iida, T. Matsubayashi and M. Ueda (2015) 'Dynastic Politicians: Theory and Evidence from Japan', *Japanese Journal of Political Science*, 16(1): 5–32.

Ashida, H. (1956) 'The Realities of Japan's Foreign Policy: The Conservative View', *Japan Quarterly*, 3(2): 145–60.

Ashida, H. (1986) *Ashida Hitoshi Nikki*, vol. 7, Iwanami Shoten.

Asia Times (2024) 'Why Japan's Kishida Finally Called It Quits', 14 August, https://asiatimes.com/2024/08/why-japans-kishida-finally-called-it-quits

Asō, K. (1992) 'Chichi no Omoide' [Memories of my Father], in Yoshida Shigeru Memorial Foundation (ed), *Ningen Yoshida Shigeru* [Yoshida Shigeru, the Human], Chūō Kōronsha, pp 503–11.

Aspinall, R. and Cave, P. (2008) 'Lowering the Flag: Democracy, Authority and Rights at Tokorozawa High School', *Social Science Japan Journal*, 4(1): 77–93.

Azzi, S. (2012) 'The Strange Afterlives of Canadian Prime Ministers', in K. Theakston and J. de Vries (eds), *Former Leaders in Modern Democracies: Political Sunsets*, Macmillan, pp 54–77.

Babb, J. (2000) *Tanaka: The Making of Postwar Japan*, Longman.

Bailey, J. (1965) 'The Origin and Nature of the Genro', *Studies on Asia*, 1(6): 125–41.

Bailey, T.A. (1978) *Presidential Greatness: The Image and the Man from George Washington to the Present*, Appleton-Century.

Barr, M.D. (2011) 'Singapore Without Lee Kuan Yew', *East Asia Forum*, 23 June, http://www.eastasiaforum.org/2011/06/23/singapore-without-lee-kuan-yew

BBC News (2007) 'How to Be an Ex-Prime Minister', 27 June, http://news.bbc.co.uk/1/hi/uk/6233470.stm

BBC News (2018) 'Japan's Finance Minister Returns Part of Salary over Land Scandal', 4 June, https://www.bbc.co.uk/news/world-asia-44355770

BBC News (2019) 'Akihito: The Japanese Emperor with the Human Touch', 30 April, https://www.bbc.co.uk/news/world-asia-48093668

Beckmann, G.M. (1957) *The Making of the Meiji Constitution: The Oligarchs and the Constitutional Development of Japan, 1868–1891*, University of Kansas Press.

Belenky, I. (1999) 'The Making of the Ex-Presidents, 1797–1993: Six Recurrent Models', *Presidential Studies Quarterly*, 29(1): 150–65.

Bell, D.S. (2012) 'Former Leaders in France', in K. Theakston and J. de Vries (eds), *Former Leaders in Modern Democracies: Political Sunsets*, Macmillan, pp 124–45.

Benardo, L. and Weiss, J. (2009) *Citizen-in-Chief: The Second Lives of the American Presidents*, William Morrow.

Brinkley, D. (1998) *The Unfinished Presidency: Jimmy Carter's Journey Beyond the White House*, Viking.

Browne, C. (1967) *Tōjō: The Last Banzai*, Angus and Robertson.

Burrett, T. (2017) 'Abe Road: Comparing Japanese Prime Minister Shinzo Abe's Leadership of his First and Second Governments', *Parliamentary Affairs*, 70(2): 400–29.

Burrett, T. (2023) *Contemporary Prime Ministerial Leadership in Britain and Japan*, Palgrave Macmillan.

Bush, G.H.W. (2000) '10 Rules for Former Presidents', *Forbes*, 18 September, https://www.forbes.com/forbes-life-magazine/2000/0918/114.html

Butow, R. (1961) *Tōjō and the Coming of War*, Princeton University Press.

Cameron, R. (2008) 'Václav Havel – "Leaving", but also Returning', *Radio Prague International*, 23 May, http://www.radio.cz/en/print/article/104330

Cha, M.S. (2003) 'Did Takahashi Korekiyo Rescue Japan from the Great Depression?', *Journal of Economic History*, 63(1): 127–44.

Chambers II, J.W. (1979) 'Presidents Emeritus', *American Heritage*, 30(4): 16–22, https://www.americanheritage.com/presidents-emeritus

Chambers II, J.W. (1998) 'Jimmy Carter's Public Policy Ex-Presidency', *Political Science Quarterly*, 113(3): 405–25.

China Daily (2012) 'Beijing, Tokyo to Strengthen Ties, Work Through Differences', 10 May, http://www.chinadailyasia.com/news/2012-05/10/content_113700.html

Clark, J.C. (1985) *Faded Glory: Presidents Out of Power*, Praeger.

Club de Madrid (2024) *Homepage*, https://clubmadrid.org

CNBC (2014) 'Japan's Obuchi: Political "Princess" Could Be First Female PM', 2 October, https://www.cnbc.com/2014/10/02/japans-obuchi-political-princess-could-be-first-female-pm.html

Colegrove, K. (1931) 'The Japanese Privy Council', *American Political Science Review*, 25(4): 881–905.

Connors, L. (1976) 'Saionji Kinmochi and the Paris Peace Conference', *Proceedings of the British Association for Japanese Studies*, 1(2): 26–47.

Connors, L. (1987) *The Emperor's Adviser: Saionji Kinmochi and Prewar Japanese Politics*, Croom Helm.

Cooper, A.F. (2008) *Celebrity Diplomacy*, Paradigm.

Cooper, A.F. (2014) *Diplomatic Afterlives*, Polity.

Coox, A.D. (1975) *Tojo*, Random House.

Cunningham, H.F. (1989) *The Presidents' Last Years: George Washington to Lyndon B. Johnson*, McFarland & Company.

De Vries, J., 't Hart, P. and Onstein, H. (2012) 'From Oblivion to Limelight: Stability and Change in Dutch Post-Prime Ministerial Careers', in K. Theakston and J. de Vries (eds), *Former Leaders in Modern Democracies: Political Sunsets*, Macmillan, pp 161–85.

De Winter, L. and Rezsöhazy, I. (2012) 'The Afterlives of Belgian Prime Ministers', in K. Theakston and J. de Vries (eds), *Former Leaders in Modern Democracies: Political Sunsets*, Macmillan, pp 186–211.

Delury, J. (2015) 'The Kishi Effect: A Political Genealogy of Japan-ROK Relations', *Asian Perspective*, 39(3): 441–60.

Dickinson, F.R. (1999) *War and National Reinvention: Japan in the Great War, 1914–1919*, Harvard University Press.

Dittmer, L. (2000) 'Conclusion: East Asian Informal Politics in Comparative Perspective', in L. Dittmer, H. Fukui and P.N.S. Lee (eds), *Informal Politics in East Asia*, Cambridge University Press, pp 290–308.

Dittmer, L., Fukui, H. and Lee, P.N.S. (eds) (2000) *Informal Politics in East Asia*, Cambridge University Press.

Dobson, H. (2004) *Japan and the G7/8: 1975 to 2002*, Routledge.

Dobson, H. (2012a) 'Where Are the Women in Global Governance? Leaders, Wives and Hegemonic Masculinity in the G8 and G20 Summits', *Global Society*, 26(4): 429–49.

Dobson, H. (2012b) 'Japan's Diplomatic Double Whammy: Hosting TICAD-IV and the G8 Hokkaidō Tōyako Summit', *Japanese Studies*, 32(2): 237–53.

Dobson, H. (2017) 'Is Japan Really Back? The "Abe Doctrine" and Global Governance', *Journal of Contemporary Asia*, 47(2): 199–224.

Dobson, H. (2019) 'Abe's Lasting Legacy', *East Asia Forum*, 24 November, https://eastasiaforum.org/2019/11/24/abes-lasting-legacy

Dobson, H. and Rose, C. (2019) 'The Afterlives of Post-War Japanese Prime Ministers', *Journal of Contemporary Asia*, 49(2): 127–50.

Dobson, H., Heppell, T. and Polanco Leal, P. (2023) 'Understanding Prime Ministerial Leadership in the United Kingdom and Japan in the 21st Century: Introduction to a Special Issue', *Asian Journal of Comparative Politics*, 8(1): 5–17.

Domett, T. (2005) 'Soft Power in Global Politics? Diplomatic Partners as Transversal Actors', *Australian Journal of Political Science*, 40(2): 289–306.

Dower, J.W. (1979) *Empire and Aftermath: Yoshida Shigeru and the Japanese Experience, 1878–1954*, Harvard University Press.

Duus, P. (1968) *Party Rivalry and Political Change in Taisho Japan*, Harvard University Press.

East Asia Community Institute (2024) '*Go-aisatsu*' [Welcome], https://www.eaci.or.jp/greeting.html

The Economist (1998) 'Leaving It to the Old Man', 30 July, https://www.economist.com/asia/1998/07/30/leaving-it-to-the-old-man

The Economist (2011a) 'Not Fade Away', 17 September, https://www.economist.com/asia/2011/09/17/not-fade-away

The Economist (2011b) 'Politics This Week', 15 October, https://www.cconomist.com/the-world-this-week/2011/10/15/politics-this-week

The Economist (2011c) 'Not Fade Away', 19 May, https://www.economist.com/asia/2011/05/19/not-fade-away

The Economist (2011d) 'The Distaff of Office', 7 July, https://www.economist.com/international/2011/07/07/the-distaff-of-office

The Economist (2011e) 'Bold, or Plain Reckless', 3 February, https://www.economist.com/asia/2011/02/03/bold-or-plain-reckless

e-Gov (1946) 'Nihonkoku Kenpō' [The Constitution of Japan], 3 November, https://elaws.e-gov.go.jp/document?lawid=321CONSTITUTION_19470503

e-Gov (1954) 'Jieitaihō' [The Japan Self-Defence Forces Law], 26 May, https://elaws.e-gov.go.jp/document?lawid=329AC0000000165

Edström, B. (1996) 'Prime Ministerial Leadership in Japanese Foreign Policy', in I. Neary (ed), *Leaders and Leadership in Japan*, Japan Library, pp 243–64.

Edström, B. (1999a) *The Foreign Policy Doctrines of Prime Minister Fukuda Takeo*, Stockholm University/ArcoMedia.

Edström, B. (1999b) *Japan's Evolving Foreign Policy Doctrine: From Yoshida to Miyazawa*, St Martin's Press.

Edström, B. (2009) 'Problems and Perils of a Prime Minister: Asō Tarō and Japan's Political Autumn', *Asia Paper*, Institute for Security and Development Policy, February 2009, https://isdp.eu/wp-content/uploads/publications/2009_edstrom_problems-and-perils-of-a-prime-minister.pdf

The Elders (2024) *Homepage*, https://theelders.org

Fahey, R. (2017) 'Why Is Shinzo Abe's Protege Being Used as a Trial Balloon?', *Japan Forward*, 12 January, https://japan-forward.com/why-is-shinzo-abes-protege-being-used-as-a-trial-balloon/

Fahey, R.A. (2021) 'Social Media in the 2021 Election Campaign', in R.J. Pekkanen, S.R. Reed and D.M. Smith (eds), *Japan Decides 2021: The Japanese General Election*, Palgrave Macmillan, pp 183–201.

Farnsworth, L. (1974) 'Hirota Koki: The Diplomacy of Expansionism', in R.D. Burns and E.M. Bennett (eds), *Diplomats in Crisis: United States-Chinese-Japanese Relations, 1919–1941*, ABC-CLIO, pp 227–49.

Financial Times (2018) 'Junichiro Koizumi: "I'm not Strange. I'm Extraordinary"', 10 August, https://www.ft.com/content/5b5a7770-9a3d-11e8-9702-5946bae86e6d

Finn, R.B. (1992) *Winners in Peace: MacArthur, Yoshida and Postwar Japan*, University of California Press.

Ford, G. (1990) 'Personal Reflections on My Experiences as a Former President', in R.N. Smith and T. Walch (eds), *Farewell to the Chief: Former Presidents in American Public Life*, High Plains Publishing, pp 169–77.

Foreign Correspondents' Club of Japan (2022) 'Press Conference: Denouncing Europe's Plan to Label Nuclear as Sustainable Energy by Junichiro Koizumi and Naoto Kan', 27 January, https://www.fccj.or.jp/event/press-conference-denouncing-europes-plan-label-nuclear-sustainable-energy-junichiro-koizumi

Fukai, S.N. (1999) 'The Missing Leader: The Structure and Traits of Political Leadership in Japan', in O. Feldman (ed), *Political Psychology in Japan: Behind the Nails That Sometimes Stick Out (and Get Hammered Down)*, Nova Science Publishers, pp 171–91.

Fukuda, T. (1995) *Kaiko Kyūjūnen* [Ninety-Year Retrospective], Iwanami Shoten.

Fukui, H. (2000) 'Introduction: On the Significance of Informal Politics', in L. Dittmer, H. Fukui and P.N.S. Lee (eds), *Informal Politics in East Asia*, Cambridge University Press, pp 1–19.

Fukui, H. and Fukai, S.N. (2000) 'The Informal Politics of Japanese Diet Elections: Cases and Interpretations', in L. Dittmer, H. Fukui and P.N.S. Lee (eds), *Informal Politics in East Asia*, Cambridge University Press, pp 23–41.

Fukunaga, F. (2016) 'Katayama Tetsu: The First Batter under the New Constitution', in A. Watanabe and R. Eldridge (eds), *The Prime Ministers of Postwar Japan, 1945–1995: Their Lives and Times*, Lexington Books, pp 47–54.

Galbraith, P.W. and Karlin, J.G. (eds) (2012) *Idol and Celebrity in Japanese Media Culture*, Palgrave Macmillan.

Gaunder, A. (2007) *Political Reform in Japan: Leadership Looming Large*, Routledge.

Green, M. and Szechenyi, N. (2009) 'A Fresh Start', *Comparative Connections*, 11(1), https://cc.pacforum.org/2009/04/a-fresh-start/

Grew, J.C. (1940) 'The Ambassador in Japan (Grew) to the Secretary of State', *Foreign Relations of the United States Diplomatic Papers, The Far East*, Volume IV, 16 August, Document 1083.

Hackett, R.F. (1971) *Yamagata Aritomo in the Rise of Modern Japan, 1838–1922*, Harvard University Press.

Hamada, K. (1936) *Prince Ito*, Sanseidō.

Hamilton, A., Madison, J. and Jay, J. (1948) *The Federalist or The New Constitution*, Everyman's Library.

Hara, Y. (2005) *Yoshida Shigeru: Sonnō no Seijika* [Yoshida Shigeru: The Emperor's Politician], Iwanami Shoten.

Harris, T. (2020) *The Iconoclast: Shinzō Abe and the New Japan*, Hurst and Company.

Harris, T. (2022) 'Abe's Legacy', in R.J. Pekkanen, S.R. Reed and D.M. Smith (eds), *Japan Decides 2021: The Japanese General Election*, Palgrave Macmillan, pp 87–102.

Harris, T. (2024) 'The True Believer', *Observing Japan*, 9 September, https://observingjapan.substack.com/p/the-true-believer

Hatoyama, Y. (2017) *Datsu dai Nihon shugi: 'Seijuku no jidai' no kuni no katachi* [Escaping Great Japanism: The Shape of the Nation in an Age of Maturity], Heibonsha.

Hatoyama Yūai-Juku (2024) *Homepage*, https://yuai-love.com/yuaijuku/index.html

Hattori, R. (2021a) *Japan at War and Peace: Shidehara Kijūrō and the Making of Modern Diplomacy*, Australian National University Press.

Hattori, R. (2021b) *Eisaku Satō, Japanese Prime Minister, 1964–1972: Okinawa, Foreign Relations, Domestic Politics and the Nobel Prize*, Routledge.

Hattori, R. (2023) *Fighting Japan's Cold War: Prime Minister Yasuhiro Nakasone and His Times*, Routledge.

Havel, V. (2008) *Leaving*, Faber and Faber.

Hayao, K. (1993) *The Japanese Prime Minister and Public Policy*, University of Pittsburgh Press.

Hayasaka, S. (1994) *The Making of a Japanese Prime Minister: How to Become No. 1 in Japan*, Sekai no Ugokisha.

Hecht, M.B. (1976) *Beyond the Presidency: The Residues of Power*, Macmillan.

Hiraizumi, E. (1983) 'A Winter Moon: The Legacy of Tōjō Hideki', *Japan Quarterly*, 30(3): 266–69.

Hirasawa, K. (1972) 'Politics in Review: When Will Sato Retire?', *The Japan Times*, 24 March.

Hofmann, R. (2021) 'The Conservative Imaginary: Moral Re-Armament and the Internationalism of the Japanese Right, 1945–1962', *Japan Forum*, 33(1): 77–102.

Hook, G.D., Gilson, J., Hughes, C.W. and Dobson, H. (2011) *Japan's International Relations: Politics, Economics and Security*, Routledge.

Horie, S. (1992) 'Yoshida-san no Omoide' [Memories of Mr Yoshida], in Yoshida Shigeru Memorial Foundation (ed), *Ningen Yoshida Shigeru* [Yoshida Shigeru the Human], Chūō Kōronsha, pp 512–25.

Hosokawa, M. (2008) *Futōan Nichijō* [Day to Day in Futōan], Shogakukan.
Hosokawa, M. (2010) *Naishōroku: Hosokawa Morihiro Sōridaijin Nikki* [An Internal Record: Prime Minister Hosokawa's Dairies], Nihon Keizai Shimbun Shuppansha.
Hosokawa, M. (2011) *Kotoba o Tabisuru* [A Journey Around Language], Bungeishunjū.
Hosoya, C. (1984) 'Japan, China, the United States and the United Kingdom, 1951–2: The Case of the "Yoshida Letter"', *International Affairs*, 60(2): 247–59.
Hufbauer, B. (2005) *Presidential Temples: How Memorials and Libraries Shape Public Memory*, University Press of Kansas.
Hughes, C.W. (2000) 'Japanese Policy and the East Asian Currency Crisis: Abject Defeat or Quiet Victory?', *Review of International Political Economy*, 7(2): 219–53.
Hughes, C.W. (2015) *Japan's Foreign and Security Policy Under the 'Abe Doctrine': New Dynamism or New Dead End?*, Palgrave Macmillan.
Hyung, G.L. (2005) 'Malthusian Dreams, Colonial Imaginary: The Oriental Development Company and Japanese Emigration to Korea', in C. Elkins and S. Pedersen (eds), *Settler Colonialism in the Twentieth Century: Projects, Practices, Legacies*, Routledge, pp 25–40.
Idditti, S. (1940) *The Life of Marquis Shigenobu Okuma: A Maker of New Japan*, The Hokuseidō Press.
Igarashi, T. (1985) 'Peace-Making and Party Politics: The Formation of the Domestic Foreign-Policy System in Postwar Japan', *Journal of Japanese Studies*, 11(32): 323–56.
The Independent (1998) 'Obituary: Sosuke Uno', 20 May, https://www.independent.co.uk/news/obituaries/obituary-sosuke-uno-1158611.html
Independent Investigation Commission on the Fukushima Daiichi Nuclear Accident (2012) *Fukushima genpatsu jiko dokuritsu kenshō iinkai chōsa kenshō hōkokusho* [Independent Investigation Commission on the Fukushima Daiichi Nuclear Accident Report on the Inquiry and Investigation], Rebuild Japan Initiative Foundation.
Inoguchi, T. (2011) 'Prime Ministers', in T. Inoguchi and P. Jain (eds), *Japanese Politics Today: From Karaoke to Kabuki Democracy*, Palgrave Macmillan, pp 11–28.
Inoki, T. (2016) 'Ishibashi Tanzan: A Coherent Liberal Thinker', in A. Watanabe and R.D. Eldridge (eds), *The Prime Ministers of Postwar Japan, 1945–1995: Their Lives and Times*, Lexington Books, pp 87–96.
InterAction Council (2024) 'About Us', https://www.interactioncouncil.org/index.php/about-us
Ishibashi, M. and Reed, S. (1992) 'Second-Generation Diet Members and Democracy in Japan: Hereditary Seats', *Asian Survey*, 32(4): 366–79.

Itoh, M. (2003) *The Hatoyama Dynasty: Japanese Political Leadership Through the Generations*, Palgrave MacMillan.

Jack, A. (2007) 'Into the Sunset: How Ex-Leaders Adjust to Life with Less Power', *Financial Times*, 26 December, https://www.ft.com/content/dc1e1682-b3e4-11dc-a6df-0000779fd2ac

Japan Forward (2022) 'Interview. Junichiro Koizumi on Nuclear Power Risks and Better Alternatives', 13 December, https://japan-forward.com/interview-junichiro-koizumi-on-nuclear-power-risks-and-better-alternatives/

Japan Times (1948) 'Liberals Take Step to Win Democrats', 3 February.

Japan Times (1950) 'Reds Threatening Japan, Ashida Says; Unity Urged', 28 December.

Japan Times (1954) 'Japan Democrats Approve Roster of Leaders', 25 November.

Japan Times (1967) 'Sohyo Hits Government on State Funeral', 31 October.

Japan Times (1969) 'Nixon-Kishi Meeting Announced in D.C.', 2 April.

Japan Times (1976) 'Scandal Tarnished Figures Returned Despite Outcry', 6 December.

Japan Times (1983) 'Tanaka Found Guilty, Given 4 Years', 13 October.

Japan Times (1992) 'Share Our Pollution-Control Technology', 11 March.

Japan Times (1998a) 'Hata Leads Official Launch of Minseito', 23 January, https://www.japantimes.co.jp/news/1998/01/23/national/hata-leads-official-launch-of-minseito/

Japan Times (1998b) 'Hosokawa Announces Resignation from Diet', 30 April, https://www.japantimes.co.jp/news/1998/04/30/national/hosokawa-announces-resignation-from-diet/

Japan Times (1998c) 'Business Responds with Hope to New Lineup', 30 July.

Japan Times (2000) 'Murayama Offered Pyongyang Compromise for Past', 10 December, p 2.

Japan Times (2001) 'Japan, India Forging a Counterbalance', 18 December, https://www.japantimes.co.jp/opinion/2001/12/18/commentary/world-commentary/japan-india-forging-a-counterbalance

Japan Times (2003) 'LDP, NCP Ink Absorption Agreement', 18 November, https://www.japantimes.co.jp/news/2003/11/18/national/ldp-ncp-ink-absorption-agreement

Japan Times (2004) 'Koizumi: Robot? Dummy? Dictator? All Three?', 1 August, https://www.japantimes.co.jp/news/2004/08/01/national/media-national/koizumi-robot-dummy-dictator-all-three

Japan Times (2005) 'Kono Warns Koizumi about Yasukuni Visits', 8 June, http://www.japantimes.co.jp/news/2005/06/08/national/kono-warns-koizumi-about-yasukuni-visits/#.WFfJkpImNE4

Japan Times (2007) 'Karel Van Wolferen: Insights into the New World Disorder', 6 May, https://www.japantimes.co.jp/life/2007/05/06/people/karel-van-wolferen

Japan Times (2008a) 'Public Hits Fukuda's Move', 2 September, http://www.japantimes.co.jp/news/2008/09/02/news/public-hits-fukudas-move/#.WFeqStwmNE4

Japan Times (2008b) 'Koizumi to Exit Political Stage', 26 September, https://www.japantimes.co.jp/news/2008/09/26/national/koizumi-to-exit-political-stage

Japan Times (2009a) 'Koizumi Enters Postal Fray, Fires Shot at Aso', 13 February, https://www.japantimes.co.jp/news/2009/02/13/national/koizumi-enters-postal-fray-fires-shot-at-aso

Japan Times (2009b) 'Aso Decides to Step Down', 31 August, https://www.japantimes.co.jp/news/2009/08/31/national/aso-decides-to-step-down

Japan Times (2013) 'Murayama: China Seeks Resolution', 1 April, pp 1–2.

Japan Times (2015a) 'Ex-PM Murayama Lashes Out at Abe's War Statement as Lacking Clarity', 14 August, http://www.japantimes.co.jp/news/2015/08/14/national/politics-diplomacy/ex-pm-murayama-lashes-out-at-abes-war-statement-as-lacking-clarity

Japan Times (2015b) 'Ex-Prime Minister Murayama Lauds "Comfort Women" Accord Reached with Seoul', 29 December, http://www.japantimes.co.jp/news/2015/12/29/national/politics-diplomacy/ex-prime-minister-murayama-lauds-comfort-women-accord-reached-seoul/#.VpACdPHIRxJ

Japan Times (2021) 'How "Indispensable" Mori Came to Enjoy Huge Influence in Politics and Sport', 12 February, https://www.japantimes.co.jp/news/2021/02/12/national/mori-influence-politics-sport

Japan Times (2022) 'Hosokawa Family's 500-Year Cultural Labor of Love', 22 September, https://sustainable.japantimes.com/magazine/vol16/16-01

Japan Times (2023a) 'Yamaguchi By-Election Puts Spotlight on Dynastic Politics', 27 February, https://www.japantimes.co.jp/news/2023/02/27/national/politics-diplomacy/nobuchiyo-kishi-political-dynasties-backlash

Japan Times (2023b) 'LDP Power Struggle in Yamaguchi Shows Waning Influence of Abe Faction', 20 June, https://www.japantimes.co.jp/news/2023/06/20/national/politics-diplomacy/yamaguchi-ldp-power-struggle

Japan Times (2023c) 'Yoshiro Mori's Image as LDP Kingmaker Rubs Up Against Reality', 29 September, https://www.japantimes.co.jp/news/2023/09/29/japan/politics/yoshiro-mori-ldp-influence

Japan Times (2024a) 'The Second Act of the Koizumi Theater', 20 September, https://www.japantimes.co.jp/news/2024/09/20/japan/politics/koizumi-junichiro-shinjiro

Japan Times (2024b) 'Former Prime Minister Kishida Launches New Group in Ruling LDP', 24 November, https://www.japantimes.co.jp/news/2024/11/24/japan/politics/former-pm-kishida-new-group

Jiji Press (2014) 'Hosokawa Morihiro moto-shushō intabyū' [Interview with former prime minister Hosokawa Morihiro,], 17 February, https://www.jiji.com/jc/v4?id=seikaiinterview-hosokawa-01_201402170001

Jiji Press (2024a) 'Abe Yōko-san Shikyo, 95-sai Shinzō-shi Haha "Seikai no Goddomaza-"' [Abe Yōko Passes at age 95, Shinzō's Mother and 'Godmother of politics'], 4 February, https://www.jiji.com/jc/article?k=2024020400484&g=pol

Jiji Press (2024b) 'Rimin Noda-shi, daihyō-sen shutsuba ni shinchō "hoshu-kei" nozomashī' [CDP's Noda cautious about running for party leader: 'Conservative candidates preferred'], 22 July, https://www.jiji.com/jc/article?k=2024072200722&g=pol

Johnson, C. (1986) 'Tanaka Kakuei, Structural Corruption, and the Advent of Machine Politics in Japan', *The Journal of Japanese Studies*, 12(1): 1–28.

Johnston, D.M. (1971) 'Marginal Diplomacy in East Asia', *International Journal*, 26(3): 469–506.

Josselin, D. and Wallace, W. (eds) (2001a) *Non-State Actors in World Politics*, Palgrave.

Josselin, D. and Wallace, W. (2001b) 'Non-State Actors in World Politics: A Framework', in D. Josselin and W. Wallace (eds), *Non-State Actors in World Politics*, Palgrave, pp 1–20.

Just, P. (2004) 'United Kingdom: Life after Number 10 – Premiers Emeritus and Parliament', *The Journal of Legislative Studies*, 10(2/3): 66–78.

Kabashima, I. and Steel, G. (2007) 'How Junichirō Koizumi Seized the Leadership of Japan's Liberal Democratic Party', *Japanese Journal of Political Science*, 8(1): 95–114.

Kabashima, I. and Steel, G. (2010) *Changing Politics in Japan*, Cornell University Press.

Kaifu, T. (2010) *Seiji to Kane: Kaifu Toshiki Kaikoroku* [Politics and Money: The Memoirs of Kaifu Toshiki], Shinchōsha.

Kamata, J. (2023) 'Will Suga Yoshihide Make a Comeback?', *The Diplomat*, 1 February, https://thediplomat.com/2023/02/will-suga-yoshihide-make-a-comeback/

Kan, N. (2012) *Tōden Fukushima Genpatsu Jiko Sōridaijin Toshite Kangaeta Koto* [My Thoughts on the Fukushima Incident], Gentōsha.

Kan, N. (2017) *My Nuclear Nightmare: Leading Japan Through the Fukushima Disaster to a Nuclear-Free Future*, Cornell University Press.

Kan, N. (2024) *Shimin Seiji 50 nen: Kan Naoto Kaikoroku* [50 Years of Civil Politics: The Memoirs of Kan Naoto], Chikuma Shobō.

Kanda, Y. (2016) 'The Transformation of a Manchukuo Imperial Bureaucrat to Postwar Supporter of the Yoshida Doctrine: The Case of Shiina Etsusaburō', in B. Kushner and S. Muminov (eds), *The Dismantling of Japan's Empire in East Asia*, Routledge, pp 182–98.

Kantei (2005) 'Koizumi Cabinet E-mail Magazine No. 192', 16 June, https://japan.kantei.go.jp/m-magazine/backnumber/koizumi/2005/0616.html

Kantei (2008) 'Press Conference by Prime Minister Yasuo Fukuda', 1 September, https://japan.kantei.go.jp/hukudaspeech/2008/09/01kaiken_e.html

Kapur, N. (2018) *Japan at the Crossroads: Compromise and Conflict After Anpo*, Harvard University Press.

Katayama, T. (1954) *Minshu Seiji no Kaiko to Tenbō: Nihon ni okeru Minshushugi to Kiki* [Retrospective and Outlook on Democratic Politics: The Crisis of Democracy in Japan], Minshu Hyōronsha.

Katayama, T. (1967) *Kaiko to Tenbō* [Retrospective and Outlook], Fukumura Shuppan.

Keane, J. (2009) 'Life after Political Death: The Fate of Leaders after Leaving High Office', in J. Kane, H. Patapan and P. 't Hart (eds), *Dispersed Democratic Leadership: Origins, Dynamics and Implications*, Oxford University Press, pp 279–96.

Kets de Vries, M. (2003) 'The Retirement Syndrome: The Psychology of Letting Go', *European Management Journal*, 21(6): 707–16.

Kim, C. (2009) 'Politics and Pageantry in Protectorate Korea (1905–1910): The Imperial Progresses of Sunjong', *The Journal of Asian Studies*, 68(3): 835–59.

Kim, D.J. (1993) 'Korean Reunification: A Rejoinder', *Security Dialogue*, 24(4): 409–14.

Kim, M.S.H. (2008) 'Ume Kenjirō and the Making of Korean Civil Law, 1906–1910', *The Journal of Japanese Studies*, 34(1): 1–31.

Kingston, J. (ed) (2012) *Natural Disaster and Nuclear Crisis in Japan: Response and recovery after Japan's 3/11*, Routledge.

Kingston, J. (2019) 'Filling the Post-Heisei Void', 27 April, https://eastasiaforum.org/2019/04/27/filling-the-post-heisei-void

Kirk-Greene, A.H.M. (1991) 'His Eternity, His Eccentricity, or His Exemplarity?', *African Affairs*, 90(359): 163–87.

Kishi, N. (1965) 'Political Movements in Japan', *Foreign Affairs*, 1 October. Available at: https://www.foreignaffairs.com/articles/asia/1965-10-01/political-movements-japan

Kitaoka, S. (2016) 'Kishi Nobusuke: Frustrated Ambition', in A. Watanabe and R.D. Eldridge (eds), *The Prime Ministers of Postwar Japan, 1945–1995: Their Lives and Times*, Lexington Books, pp 97–118.

Kitaoka, S. (2019) 'Tsuito Ogata Sadako-shi: Sekai ga Keiai shita Jindō to Kokusai kyōryku no Kyojin' [In Memoriam: Ogata Sadako. A Giant of Humanity and International Cooperation, Loved and Respected by the World], *Gaikō* [Diplomacy], 58 (November/December): 68–73.

Korn, D. (2012) 'The Once and Future Prime Ministers of Israel', in K. Theakston and J. de Vries (eds), *Former Leaders in Modern Democracies: Political Sunsets*, Macmillan, pp 212–32.

Krauss, E. and Nyblade, B. (2005) '"Presidentalization" in Japan? The Prime Minister, Media and Elections in Japan', *British Journal of Political Science*, 35(2): 357–68.

Krauss, E. and Pekkanen, R. (2011) *The Rise and Fall of Japan's LDP: Political Party Organizations as Historical Institutions*, Cornell University Press.

Krebs, G. (1990) 'Admiral Yonai Mitsumasa as Navy Minister (1937–9): Dove or Hawk?', in P. Lowe and H. Moeshart (eds), *Western Interactions with Japan: Expansion, the Armed Forces and Readjustment 1859–1956*, Japan Library, pp 74–83.

Kristof, N.D. (1999) 'Mr "Cold Pizza" Earns Respect in Japan with Deft Tinkering', *New York Times*, 1 April, https://www.nytimes.com/1999/04/01/world/mr-cold-pizza-earns-respect-in-japan-with-deft-tinkering.html

Kumagai, N. (2014) 'Asia Women's Fund Revisited', *Asia-Pacific Review*, 21(2): 117–48.

Kuramatsu, T. (1999) 'A Great Ordinary Man: Saitō Makoto (1858–1936) and Anglo-Japanese Relations', in J.E. Hoare (ed), *Britain and Japan: Biographical Portraits, Volume III*, Japan Library, pp 182–94.

Kusunoki, A. (2016) 'Ashida Hitoshi – Tai-Bei Kyōchōronshano "Kokusai Kōken" ron' [Ashida Hitoshi – an Advocate of US Cooperation's Theory of "International Contribution"], in H. Masuda (ed) *Sengo Nihon Shushō no Gaikō Shisō: Yoshida Shigeru kara Koizumi Junichirō made* [Postwar Japanese Prime Ministers' Foreign Policy: From Yoshida Shigeru to Koizumi Junichirō], Mineruva Shobō.

Kuwahara, S. (1992) 'Ōiso Yoshida-tei no Bokuyūkai Reikai' [A Social Calligraphy Gathering at the Yoshida Residence in Ōiso], in Yoshida Shigeru Memorial Foundation (ed), *Ningen Yoshida Shigeru* [Yoshida Shigeru the Human], Chūō Kōronsha, pp 210–20.

Kyodo News (2019) 'Koizumi seeks further innovation in Japan to fight climate change', 12 September, https://english.kyodonews.net/news/2019/09/325043876f99-koizumi-seeks-further-innovation-in-japan-to-fight-global-warming.html

Kyodo News (2021) 'Ex-PMs Kan, Koizumi Urge Japan to Quit Nuclear Power Generation', 1 March, https://english.kyodonews.net/news/2021/03/6b3c5a6b5519-ex-pms-kan-koizumi-urge-japan-to-quit-nuclear-power-generation.html

Kyodo News (2024) 'Japan PM Forced to Rely More on "kingmaker" Aso Amid Funds Scandal', 7 January, https://english.kyodonews.net/news/2024/01/e184d5518edf-japan-pm-forced-to-rely-more-on-kingmaker-aso-amid-funds-scandal.html

Kyōwa Research Centre (2024) '*Kyōwa Risāchi Sentā to wa*' [About], https://www.kyowa-research.center/共和バンドとは

Lebra, J.C. (1973) *Ōkuma Shigenobu: Statesman of Meiji Japan*, ANU Press.

Lee, J.H. (2011) 'Normalization of Relations with Japan: Toward a New Partnership', in B.K. Kim and E. Vogel (eds), *The Park Chung Hee Era: The Transformation of South Korea*, Harvard University Press, pp 430–56.

Lee, P.N.S. (2000) 'The Informal Politics of Leadership Succession in Post-Mao China', in L. Dittmer, H. Fukui and P.N.S. Lee (eds), *Informal Politics in East Asia*, Cambridge University Press, pp 165–82.

Levidis, A. (2020) 'Politics in a Fallen Empire: Kishi Nobusuke and the Making of the Conservative Hegemony in Japan', in Barak Kushner and Andrew Levidis (eds), *In the Ruins of Japanese Empire: Imperial Violence, State Destruction, and the Reordering of Modern East Asia*, Hong Kong University Press, pp 161–84.

Levidis, A. (2023) 'The War Is Not Over: Kishi Nobusuke and the National Defense Brotherhood, 1944–45', *The Journal of Japanese Studies*, 49(1): 1–30.

Lincoln, E.J. (2002) 'Japan in 2001: A Depressing Year', *Asian Survey*, 42(1): 67–80.

Lone, S. (2000) *Army, Empire and Politics in Meiji Japan: The Three Careers of General Katsura Tarō*, Macmillan.

Maeda, Y. (2024) 'Shushō e no kōo kara miru "bunkyokuka no kiten"' [The Origin of Polarization as Seen from Likes and Dislikes of the Prime Minister], Smart News Media Research Institute, 1 April, https://smartnews-smri.com/smppsurvey/media_value_research-1733

Mainichi (2020) 'Suga-shi hatsu no "muhabatsu tatakiage" sōsai senshutsu' [The First 'Non-Factional, Self-Made' Candidate, Suga, Elected as Party Leader], 14 September, https://mainichi.jp/articles/20200914/k00/00m/010/001000c

Mainichi (2021a) 'Cursed Olympics? With Mori Out, All 4 Tokyo Bid Leaders Now Gone', 13 February, https://mainichi.jp/english/articles/20210213/p2a/00m/0sp/005000c

Mainichi (2021b) '5 Ex-Japan PMs Call for Country to end Nuclear Power Use on Fukushima 10th Anniversary', 12 March, https://mainichi.jp/english/articles/20210312/p2a/00m/0na/019000c

Mainichi (2021c) 'Gaffe-Prone Aso Leaves Legacy, Challenges After Nearly 9-Yr Tenure as Japan Finance Czar', 5 October, https://mainichi.jp/english/articles/20211005/p2a/00m/0na/016000c

Mainichi (2021d) 'Can Former PM Shinzo Abe Become Japanese Politics' Kingmaker?', 19 October, https://mainichi.jp/english/articles/20211019/p2a/00m/0na/029000c

Mainichi (2024) 'Individual Dignity on the Ballot in Japan Ruling Party Leadership Race', 19 September, https://mainichi.jp/english/articles/20240919/p2a/00m/0op/012000c

Martin, A.E. (1951) *After the White House*, Penns Valley Publishers.

Masuda, H. (2012) 'Fear of World War III: Social Politics of Japan's Rearmament and Peace Movements, 1950–3', *Journal of Contemporary History*, 47(3): 551–71.

Masuda, H. (2016) 'Ashida Hitoshi: The Intellectual and Cultured Man as Politician', in A. Watanabe and R.D. Eldridge (eds), *The Prime Ministers of Postwar Japan, 1945–1995: Their Lives and Times*, Lexington Books, pp 55–69.

Matsuoka, H. (1967) 'Daiichiji Katsura Naikaku to Rikken Seiyūkai' [The First Katsura Cabinet and the Association of Friends of Constitutional Government], *Tōyō Hōgaku* [Tōyō University Law Review], 10(3): 1–32.

McNeill, D. (2012) 'Naoto Kan: The Man Who Says He Saved the World', *The Independent*, 23 April, https://www.independent.co.uk/news/world/asia/naoto-kan-the-man-who-says-he-saved-the-world-7669097.html

Melber, H. and Southall, R. (2006) 'Introduction: About Life After Presidency', in R. Southall and H. Melber (eds), *Legacies of Power: Leadership Change and Former Presidents in African Politics*, Nordic Africa Institute, pp xv–xxvi.

Mendel, D.H. Jr (1964) 'Japan's Taiwan Tangle', *Asian Survey*, 4(10): 1073–84.

Metzler, M. (2006) *Lever of Empire: The International Gold Standard and the Crisis of Liberalism in Prewar Japan*, University of California Press.

Mikanagi, K. (1992) 'Bannen no Yoshida Shigeru-shi' [Mr Yoshida Shigeru in his Later Years], in Yoshida Shigeru Memorial Foundation (ed), *Ningen Yoshida Shigeru* [Yoshida Shigeru the Human], Chūō Kōronsha, pp 578–603.

Mikuriya, T. and Nakamura, T. (2017) *Politics and Power in 20th-Century Japan: The Reminiscences of Miyazawa Kiichi*, Bloomsbury.

Miyazawa, K. (1998) 'Towards a New International Financial Architecture', Speech at the Foreign Correspondents Club of Japan, 15 December, https://www.mof.go.jp/english/policy/international_policy/new_international_financial_architecture/e1e057.htm

MOFA (1999) 'Statement of Prime Minister Keizo Obuchi', 9 August, https://www.mofa.go.jp/announce/announce/1999/8/809.html

MOFA (2006) 'Speech by Mr Taro Aso, Minister for Foreign Affairs on the Occasion of the Japan Institute of International Affairs Seminar "Arc of Freedom and Prosperity: Japan's Expanding Diplomatic Horizons"', 30 November, http://www.mofa.go.jp/announce/fm/aso/speech0611.html

MOFA (2010a) 'Press Conference by Minister for Foreign Affairs Katsuya Okada', 13 August, http://www.mofa.go.jp/announce/fm_press/2010/8/0813_01.html

MOFA (2010b) 'Visit to the Federative Republic of Brazil and the Republic of Ecuador by Mr Taro Aso, Former Prime Minister of Japan', 24 December, http://www.mofa.go.jp/announce/event/2010/12/1224_01.html

MOFA (2011a) 'Press Conference by the Deputy Press Secretary, 3 February 2011', http://www.mofa.go.jp/announce/press/2011/2/0203_01.html

Morgan, I. (2012) 'After the White House: The Modern US Post-Presidency', in K. Theakston and J. de Vries (eds), *Former Leaders in Modern Democracies: Political Sunsets*, Macmillan, pp 12–32.

Morris, E. (2010) *Colonel Roosevelt*, Random House.

Morton, W.F. (1980) *Tanaka Giichi and Japan's China Policy*, Dawson.

Mulgan, A.G. (2018) *The Abe Administration and the Rise of the Prime Ministerial Executive*, Routledge.

Najita, T. (1967) *Hara Kei in the Politics of Compromise, 1905–1915*, Harvard University Press.

Nakagawa, Y. (2022) *Seshū: Seiji•Kigyō•Kabuki* [Inheritance: Politics, Business, Kabuki], Gentōsha.

Nakamura, K. (1910) *Prince Ito: The Man and Statesman: A Brief History of his Life*, Japanese-American Commercial Weekly and Anraku Publishing Company.

Nakamura, T. (2016) 'Ikeda Hayato: The Man Who Created the "Economic Era"', in A. Watanabe and R.D. Eldridge (eds), *The Prime Ministers of Postwar Japan, 1945–1995: Their Lives and Times*, Lexington Books, pp 119–139.

Nakasone, Y. (1992) *Seiji to Jinsei: Nakasone Yasuhiro Kaikoroku* [My Memoirs: Politics and Life], Kōdansha.

Nakasone, Y. (1996) *Tenchi Yūjō: 50–nen no Sengo Seiji o Kataru* [The Nature of Heaven and Earth: On Fifty Years of Postwar Politics], Bungeishunjū.

Nakasone, Y. (2002) *Japan: A State Strategy for the Twenty-First Century*, L. Connors and C. Hood (trans), RoutledgeCurzon.

Nakasone, Y. (2004) *Jishuroku: Rekishi Hōtei no Hikoku to shite* [Meditations: As a Defendant in the Court of History], Shinchōsha.

Nakasone, Y. (2006) *Meditations: On the Nature of Leadership*, PHP Institute.

Nakasone, Y. (2008) 'Fukuda Shushō ni "Kokueki" no Shugoshataru Jikaku ha aru ka' [Is Prime Minister Fukuda Aware of His Role as Defender of the National Interest?], *Seiron* [Sound Debate], August: 50–55.

Nakasone, Y. (2010) 'Gaikō no Yōtei wo Hanasō' [Let's Discuss the Key Points of Diplomacy], *Gaikō* [Diplomacy], 1: 85–96.

Nakasone, Y. (2011) 'Nihonjin-yo, Motto Donyoku ni Nare!' [People of Japan, Become Greedier!], *nippon.com*, 10 October, www.nippon.com/ja/people/e00002/

Nakasone, Y. (2015) *Nakasone-sō* [Nakasone villas], Sekai-Bunkasha.

Nakasone, Y. and Umehara, T. (2010) 'Hatoyama-kun ni Oshietai "Ridashippu no Joken"' [What I Would Like to Teach Hatoyama About Leadership], *Voice*, July: 94–100.

NBC News (2007) 'Tojo's Granddaughter Runs for Office', 11 June, https://www.nbcnews.com/id/wbna19173184

Neary, I. (1996) 'Leaders and Leadership in Japan', in I. Neary (ed), *Leaders and Leadership in Japan*, Japan Library, pp 1–13.

New York Times (1960) 'Vacation Meeting', 8 June, https://nyti.ms/41foewF

New York Times (1962) 'Japanese Borrow at German Banks', 9 February, https://nyti.ms/49fL3C3

New York Times (1964a) 'Yoshida Confers with Chiang', 25 February, https://nyti.ms/4fQmrlX

New York Times (1964b) 'Japan Reaffirms Ties to Taiwan But Will Keep Up China Trade', 8 March, https://www.nytimes.com/1964/03/08/archives/japan-reaffirms-tie-to-taiwan-but-will-keep-up-china-trade.html

New York Times (2008) 'Japanese Prime Minister Resigns Unexpectedly', 1 September, http://www.nytimes.com/2008/09/02/world/asia/02japan.html

NHK (2021) 'Japan's Prime Minister Under Pressure After Son Embroiled in Ethics Breach', 24 February, https://www3.nhk.or.jp/nhkworld/en/news/backstories/1525/

Nikkan Sports (2024) 'Hatoyama Kiichirō-shi "Nippon o hinshi kara sukū" Kokumin Minshutō Taikai de ohirome jiki Shūin-sen shutsuba yotei, chichi wa moto-shushō' ['We Will Rescue Japan from the Brink of Death'. Hatoyama Kiichirō debuts at the Democratic Party for the People convention, plans to run in next Lower House Election, father Is former Prime Minister], 2 February, https://www.nikkansports.com/general/nikkan/news/202402120000887.html

Nikkei Asia (2021) 'Kishida's Foreign Minister Pick Rankles Kingmakers Abe and Aso', 11 November, https://asia.nikkei.com/Politics/Kishida-s-foreign-minister-pick-rankles-kingmakers-Abe-and-Aso

Nikkei Asia (2024) 'Behind the Scenes: How Former Japanese PMs Swayed Ishiba's Election', 2 October, https://asia.nikkei.com/Politics/Japan-s-new-PM/Behind-the-scenes-How-former-Japanese-PMs-swayed-Ishiba-s-election

Nikkei Shimbun (2020) 'Suga-shi, Hosoda Asō-ha ga shiji, shushō no ikō han'ei' [Hosoda and Asō Factions Back Suga, Reflecting PM's Wishes], 9 September, https://www.nikkei.com/article/DGXMZO63274690R30C20A8EA2000

Nikkei Shimbun (2024) 'Jimintō no Asō Tarō-shi, Ishiba Shigeru sōsai to no kinen satsuei ni sanka sezu' [LDP's Asō Tarō Does Not Participate in Commemorative Photo with LDP President Ishiba Shigeru], 30 September, https://www.nikkei.com/article/DGXZQOUA30BGL0Q4A930C2000000

Nish, I. (1984) 'Itō Hirobumi in St Petersburg, 1901', in G. Daniels (ed), *Europe Interprets Japan*, Paul Norbury Publications, pp 90–95.

Nish, I. (1996) 'The Leadership of Admiral Katō Tomosaburō', in I. Neary (ed), *Leaders and Leadership in Japan*, Japan Library, pp 147–54.

Nolte, S.H. (1987) *Liberalism in Modern Japan: Ishibashi Tanzan and his Teachers*, University of California Press.

Noda, Y. (2024) 'Kawaraban Leaflets', https://www.nodayoshi.gr.jp/leaflet/

Notehelfer, F.G. (1971) *Kotoku Shusui: Portrait of a Japanese Radical*. Cambridge University Press.

Nuckolls, C.W. (2006) 'The Banal Nationalism of Japanese Cinema: The Making of *Pride* and the Idea of India', *Journal of Popular Culture*, 39(5): 817–37.

Nuke0 Re100 (2021) 'Global Conference for a Nuclear Free, Renewable Energy Future', https://20210311.genjiren.com/en/

Obuchi, K. (1998) Transcript of Prime Minister Obuchi Keizo's Press Conference, 31 July, https://japan.kantei.go.jp/980818press.html

Oka, Y. (1983) *Konoe Fumimaro: A Political Biography*, University of Tokyo Press.

Oka, Y. (1986) *Five Political Leaders of Modern Japan: Itō Hirobumi, Ōkuma Shigenobu, Hara Takashi, Inukai Tsuyoshi and Saionji Kinmochi*, University of Tokyo Press.

Okinawa Taimusu (2003) 'Murayama motoshushō ga ginmaku debyū' [Former Prime Minister Murayama Makes Silver Screen Debut], 24 May, evening edition, p 5.

Ōhira, M. (1978) *Brush Strokes: Moments From my Life*, Foreign Press Centre.

Ōhira, M. (1983) *Ōhira Masayoshi Kaisōroku* [The Memoirs of Ōhira Masayoshi], Kajima Shuppankai.

Ohta, H. (2000) 'Japanese Environmental Foreign Policy', in T. Inoguchi and J. Purnendra (eds), *Japanese Foreign Policy Today: A Reader*, St Martin's Press.

Okuma, S. (1910) *Fifty Years of New Japan, Vols 1 and 2*, Smith, Elder and Company.

O'Malley, E. (2012) 'Outside the Bubble: The Activities and Influence of Former Taoisigh', in K. Theakston and J. de Vries (eds), *Former Leaders in Modern Democracies: Political Sunsets*, Macmillan, pp 146–60.

O'Shea, P. (2014) 'Overestimating the "Power Shift": The US Role in the Failure of the Democratic Party of Japan's "Asia Pivot"', *Asian Perspective*, 38 (3): 435–59.

O'Toole, P. (2005) *When Trumpets Call: Theodore Roosevelt after the White House*, Simon and Schuster.

Panda, Ankit (2014) 'Former Japanese Prime Minister Meets Comfort Women', *The Diplomat*, 15 February, http://thediplomat.com/2014/02/former-japanese-prime-minister-meets-comfort-women

Paterson, W.E. (2012) 'The Political Afterlives of German Chancellors', in K. Theakston and J. de Vries (eds), *Former Leaders in Modern Democracies: Political Sunsets*, Macmillan, pp 103–23.

Pharr, S. and Kishima, T. (1987) 'Japan in 1986: A Landmark Year for the LDP', *Asian Survey*, 27(1): 23–34.

Pike, D. (2000) 'Informal Politics in Vietnam', in L. Dittmer, H. Fukui, and P.N.S. Lee (eds), *Informal Politics in East Asia*, Cambridge University Press, pp 269–89.

Pollmann, M. (2022) 'Abe Shinzo's Political Faction to Select a New Leader', *The Diplomat*, 8 October, https://thediplomat.com/2022/10/abe-shinzos-political-faction-to-select-a-new-leader

Powell, J. (2010) *The New Machiavelli: How to Wield Power in the Modern World*, The Bodley Head.

Powell, J.E. (1977) *Joseph Chamberlain*, Thames and Hudson.

Prescott, C. (2022) 'Charles III and the Future of the UK Monarchy: Looking Abroad for Clues', *The Conversation*, 9 September, https://theconversation.com/charles-iii-and-the-future-of-the-uk-monarchy-looking-abroad-for-clues-174074

The Print (2023) 'PM Modi, Former Japan PM Yoshihide Suga Hold Discussions on Deepening Special Strategic, Global Partnership', 6 July, https://theprint.in/world/pm-modi-former-japan-pm-yoshihide-suga-hold-discussions-on-deepening-special-strategic-global-partnership/1658199

Pyle, K.B. (1987) 'In Pursuit of a Grand Design: Nakasone Betwixt the Past and the Future', *The Journal of Japanese Studies*, 13(2): 243–70.

Pyle, K.B. (2018) 'Japan's Return to Great Power Politics: Abe's Restoration', *Asia Policy*, 13(2): 69–90.

Radtke, K.W. (2003) 'Nationalism and internationalism in Japan's economic liberalism: The case of Ishibashi Tanzan', in D. Stegewerns (ed), *Nationalism and Internationalism in Imperial Japan: Autonomy, Asian Brotherhood, or World Citizenship?*, Routledge Curzon, pp 169–95.

Reuters (2009) 'After Quitting Politics, Japan's Koizumi Turns Superhero', 13 October, https://www.reuters.com/article/lifestyle/after-quitting-politics-japan-s-koizumi-turns-superhero-idUSTRE59C0QH

Richards, C. (2014) 'A Former Japanese PM "Feels Sad" for Putin', *The Diplomat*, 11 September, https://thediplomat.com/2014/09/former-japanese-pm-feels-sad-for-putin-delivers-abes-message/

Richardson, B. (1997) *Japanese Democracy: Power, Coordination and Performance*, New Haven: Yale University Press.

Saito, M. (1922) 'Yamagata: Life and Death', *The Japan Times & Mail*, 2 February, p 4.

Sakata, M. and Murayama, T. (2009) *'Murayama Danwa' to wa Nani ka* [What is the 'Murayama Statement'?], Kadokawa Shoten.

Samuels, R.J. (2003) 'Leadership and Political Change in Japan: The Case of the Second Rinchō', *The Journal of Japanese Studies*, 29(1): 1–31.

Sankei (2015) 'Fukushima genpatsu meguru Abe shushō merumaga soshō' [Lawsuit over Prime Minister Abe's email newsletter regarding the Fukushima nuclear plant], 3 December, https://www.sankei.com/article/20151203-XJYWBROIOBJVNOM35LLKNGZ7PA/

Sankei (2024) 'Suga zen shushō to Asō fukusōsai: Jimin sōsai-sen wa shushō keikensha futari ni yoru kingumēkā arasoi no yōsō' [Former Prime Minister Suga and Deputy Prime Minister Asō: The LDP Leadership Race Takes on the Appearance of a Kingmaker Battle Between Two Former Prime Ministers], 2 July, https://www.sankei.com/article/20240702-CPJYBVTKHVLZHO6AJPE5R4MCQI/?dicbo=v2-bJe3sAE

Schaller, T.F. and Williams, T.W. (2003) 'The Contemporary Presidency: Postpresidential Influence in the Postmodern Era', *Presidential Studies Quarterly*, 33(1): 188–200.

Schenker, A.E. (1982) 'Former Presidents: Suggestions for the Study of an Often Neglected Resource', *Presidential Studies Quarterly*, 12(4): 545–51.

Schenker, A.E. (1985) 'Former Prime Ministers and Presidents: Suggestions for Study and Comparison', *Presidential Studies Quarterly*, 15(3): 498–511.

Scherer, J.A.B. (1936) *Three Meiji Leaders: Itō, Tōgō, Nogi*, The Hokuseidō Press.

Shapiro, M. and Hiatt, F. (1989) 'Takeshita Announces Resignation', *Washington Post*, 24 April.

Sheldon, W.D. (1925) *The Ex-Presidents of the United States: How Each Played a Role*, Philadelphia, http://hdl.handle.net/2027/mdp.39015059428725

Shidehara Heiwa Zaidan (1955) *Shidehara Kijūrō*, Shidehara Heiwa Zaidan.

Shima, N. (2000) *Shunō Gaikō: Senshinkoku Samitto no Rimenshi* [Leaders' Diplomacy: History of the Summit of the Most Industrialized Nations], Bungeishunjū.

Shimizu, I. (1960) 'Anpo Tōsō no "Fukō na Shuyaku" – Anpo Tōsō wa naze zasetsu shitaka' [The 'Unfortunate Protagonist' of the Anti-Security Treaty Protests – Why Did the Anti-Security Treaty Protests Fail?], *Chūō Kōron* [Central Debate], 75(9): 179–89.

Shimizu M. (2005) *Kantei shudō: Koizumi Junichirō no kakumei* [Cabinet leadership: Koizumi Junichirō's revolution], Nihon Keizai Shimbunsha.

Shimota, T. (1992) 'Yoshida-san Bannen no Omokage' [Vestiges of Mr Yoshida in his Later Years], in Yoshida Shigeru Memorial Foundation (ed), *Ningen Yoshida Shigeru* [Yoshida Shigeru the Human], Chūō Kōronsha, pp 572–77.

Shinoda, T. (1998) 'Japan's Decision Making Under the Coalition Governments', *Asian Survey*, 38(7): 703–23.

Shinoda, T. (2000) *Leading Japan: The Role of the Prime Minister*, Praeger.

Shinoda, T. (2007) *Koizumi Diplomacy: Japan's* Kantei *Approach to Foreign and Defense Affairs*, University of Washington Press.

Shiroyama, S. (1977) *War Criminal: The Life and Death of Hirota Kōki*, Tokyo Kōdansha.

Shūkan Ekonomisuto (2022) 'Tokubetsu rensai: Sandē Mainichi ga mita 100-nen no sukyandaru [Special Series: One Hundred Years of Scandals Seen by the Sunday Mainichi], 17 January, https://weekly-economist.mainichi.jp/articles/20220117/se1/00m/020/001000d

Skidmore, M.J. (2004) *After the White House: Former Presidents as Private Citizens*, Palgrave Macmillan.

Smethurst, R.J. (1998) 'The Self-Taught Bureaucrat: Takahashi Korekiyo and Economic Policy during the Great Depression', in J. Singleton (ed), *Learning in Likely Places: Varieties of Apprenticeship in Japan*, Cambridge University Press, pp 226–38.

Smethurst, R.J. (2007) *From Foot Soldier to Finance Minister: Takahashi Korekiyo, Japan's Keynes*, Harvard University Press.

Smith, D.M. (2018) *Dynasties and Democracy: The Inherited Incumbency Advantage in Japan*, Stanford: Stanford University Press.

Smith, R.N. and Walch, T. (eds) (1990) *Farewell to the Chief: Former Presidents in American Public Life*, High Plains Publishing.

Soble J. and Dickie, M. (2010) 'Revolving Door Keeps Turning in Japan', *Financial Times*, 2 June, https://www.ft.com/content/4a401eb8-6e2c-11df-ab79-00144feabdc0

Southall, R. and Melber, H. (eds) (2006) *Legacies of Power: Leadership Change and Former Presidents in African Politics*, Nordic Africa Institute.

Southall, R., Simutanyi, N. and Daniel, J. (2006) 'Former Presidents in African Politics', in Roger Southall and Henning Melber (eds), *Legacies of Power: Leadership Change and Former Presidents in African Politics*, Nordic Africa Institute, pp 1–25.

Stathis, S.W. (1983) 'Former Presidents as Congressional Witnesses', *Presidential Studies Quarterly*, 13(3): 458–81.

Sterngold, J. (1993) 'Kakuei Tanaka, 75, Ex-Premier and Political Force in Japan, Dies', *New York Times*, 17 December.

Stockwin, J.A.A. (1991) 'The Influential Ōhira Masayoshi', *Japan Quarterly*, 38(1): 90–94.

Strangio, P. (2012) 'The Evolution of Prime Ministerial Afterlives in Australia', in K. Theakston and J. de Vries (eds), *Former Leaders in Modern Democracies: Political Sunsets*, Macmillan, pp 78–102.

Street, J. (2004) 'Celebrity Politicians: Popular Culture and Political Representation', *The British Journal of Politics and International Relations*, 6(4): 435–52.

Suga, Y. (2024) 'Suga Yoshihide Ofisharu Burogu' [Suga Yoshihide Official Blog], https://ameblo.jp/suga-yoshihide/

Suginohara, M. (2004) 'Handling Japan's Banking Crisis, 1997–98: Gaiatsu or not?', Discussion Paper Series F-115, Institute of Social Science, University of Tokyo, https://www.iss.u-tokyo.ac.jp/publishments/dpf/pdf/f-115.pdf

Suzumura, Y. (2014) 'Ishibashi Tanzan no tai-Chugoku Seijōka e no Torikumi' [Ishibashi Tanzan's Efforts to Normalize Relations with China], *Kokusai Nihongaku* [International Japan Studies], 11: 109–24.

't Hart, P. and Tindall, K. (2009) 'Leadership by the Famous: Celebrity as Political Capital', in J. Kane, H. Patapan and P. 't Hart (eds), *Dispersed Democratic Leadership: Origins, Dynamics and Implications*, Oxford University Press, pp 255–78.

Tadokoro, R. (2024) 'Shi o mae ni "Eien no Heiwa" Kurikaeshita Sofu, Taiheiyōsensō Saigo no Shushō' ['Eternal Peace': The Last Words of my Grandfather, Japan's Last Wartime Prime Minister], *Mainichi Shimbun*, 17 April, https://mainichi.jp/articles/20240417/k00/00m/040/297000c.

Takayasu, K. (2001) 'Prime-ministerial Power in Japan: A Re-examination', *Japan Forum*, 17(2): 163–84.

Takayasu, K. (2009) *Shushō no Kenryoku: Nichiei Hikaku kara miru Seikentō to no Dainamizumu* [The Power of Prime Ministers in Japan and Britain: Dynamics of Their Relationships with the Governing Party], Sōbunsha.

Takeshita, N. (2001) *Seiji to wa nani ka: Takeshita Noboru Kairoku* [What Is Politics? Takeshita Noboru's Memoir], Kōdansha.

Takeuchi, K. (2023) *Miki Takeo to Sengo Seiji* [Miki Takeo and Postwar Politics], Yoshida Shoten.

Takeuchi, Y. (2021) 'Abe to Lead LDP's Biggest Faction, Cementing Role as Kingmaker', *Nikkei Asia*, 9 November, https://asia.nikkei.com/Politics/Abe-to-lead-LDP-s-biggest-faction-cementing-role-as-kingmaker

Takii, K. (2014) *Itō Hirobumi: Japan's First Prime Minister and Father of the Meiji Constitution*, Routledge.

Tanaka, M. (1989) *Toki no Sugiyuku mama ni* [As Time Passes by], Shufu to Seikatsusha.

Tanaka, M. (2005) *Watashi no Saijiki* [My Chronicles], Kairyūsha.

Tanaka, M. (2017) *Chichi to Watashi* [My Father and I], Nikkan Kōgyō Shimbunsha.

Tanaka, M. (2019) *Kaku-san to Jajauma* [Kaku-san and the Unruly Girl], Kadokawa.

Tanaka, S. (2004) *Nihon Riberaru to Ishibashi Tanzan: Ima Seiji ga Hitsuyō to Shiteru koto* [Japan Liberalism and Ishibashi Tanzan: What Politics Needs Now], Kōdansha.

Taylor, H. (1957) *The Statesman*, W. Heffer and Sons.

Taylor, A.J.P. (1977) *The War Lords*, Hamish Hamilton.

TBS Newsdig (2023) 'Kan Naoto moto sōri, jiki shūinsen fushutsuba o seishiki hyōmei' [Former Prime Minister Naoto Kan Officially Announces That He Will Not Run in the Next House of Representatives Election], 5 November, https://newsdig.tbs.co.jp/articles/-/818660?display=1

Truman, H.S. (1961) *Mr Citizen*, Hutchinson.

Theakston, K. (2006) 'After Number Ten: What Do Former Prime Ministers Do?', *The Political Quarterly*, 77(4): 448–56.

Theakston, K. (2010) *After Number 10: Former Prime Ministers in British Politics*, Palgrave.

Theakston, K. (2012) 'Former Prime Ministers in Britain Since 1945', in K. Theakston and J. de Vries (eds), *Former Leaders in Modern Democracies: Political Sunsets*, Macmillan, pp 33–53.

Theakston, K. and de Vries, J. (2012a) 'Introduction', in K. Theakston and J. de Vries (eds), *Former Leaders in Modern Democracies: Political Sunsets*, Macmillan, pp 1–11.

Theakston, K. and de Vries, J. (eds) (2012b) *Former Leaders in Modern Democracies: Political Sunsets*, Macmillan.

Theakston, K. and de Vries, J. (2012c) 'Conclusion', in K. Theakston and J. de Vries (eds), *Former Leaders in Modern Democracies: Political Sunsets*, Macmillan, pp 233–49.

Theakston, K., Gouge, E. and Honeyman, V. (2007) *Life After Losing or Leaving: The Experience of Former Members of Parliament: A Report Prepared for the Association of Former Members of Parliament by the University of Leeds*, October.

Tiberghien, Y. and Schreurs, M. (2010) 'Climate Leadership, Japanese Style: Embedded Symbolism and Post-2001 Kyoto Protocol Politics', in K. Harrison and L. Sundstrom (eds), *Global Commons, Domestic Decisions: The Comparative Politics of Climate Change*, MIT Press, pp 139–68.

Time (1994) 'How Scandal Finally Outran the Reformer', 18 April, https://time.com/archive/6725140/how-scandal-finally-outran-the-reformer

Togawa, I. (1971) *Shōsetsu Yoshida Gakkō* [The Yoshida School: A Novel], Ryūdō.

Topping, A. (2022) 'Margaret Thatcher to Theresa May: Dramatic Prime Ministerial Resignations', *The Guardian*, 7 July, https://www.theguardian.com/politics/2022/jul/07/margaret-thatcher-to-theresa-may-dramatic-prime-ministerial-resignations

Tsuda, T. (2023) 'Elder Statesman as a Jack-of-all-Trades: The Case of Satō Eisaku in 1970s Japan', *Contemporary Japan*, DOI: 10.1080/18692729.2023.2247735

Tsuda, T. (2024) 'High Modernism and Populism in Post-War Japan: Tanaka Kakuei's Plan for Remodelling the Japanese Archipelago', *Journal of Contemporary Asia*, 54(3): 453–77.

Uchida, J. (2005) 'Brokers of Empire: Japanese and Korean Business Elites in Colonial Korea', in C. Elkins and S. Pedersen (eds), *Settler Colonialism in the Twentieth Century: Projects, Practices, Legacies*, Routledge, pp 153–70.

Uchiyama, Y. (2023) 'Japanese Prime Ministers and Party Leadership', *Asian Journal of Comparative Politics*, 8(1): 83–94.

Uji, T. (ed) (2001) *Shushō Retsuden: Itō Hirobumi kara Koizumi Junichirō made* [Prime Ministerial Biographies: From Itō Hirobumi to Koizumi Junichirō], Tokyo Shoseki.

Updegrove, M.K. (2006) *Second Acts: Presidential Lives and Legacies After the White House*, The Lyons Press.

van Boven, T. (1998) 'A Universal Declaration of Human Responsibilities?', in B. van der Heijden and B. Tahzib-Lie (eds), *Reflections on the Universal Declaration of Human Rights*, Brill Nijhoff, pp 73–79.

van Wolferen, Karel G. (1989) *The Enigma of Japanese Power*, Alfred A. Knopf.

Vietnam Plus (2024) 'President Receives Japanese PM's Special Envoy in Hanoi', 25 July, https://en.vietnamplus.vn/president-receives-japanese-pms-special-envoy-in-hanoi-post290823.vnp

VoV World (2023) 'PM Meets Former Japanese PM Suga Yoshihide, Singapore PM Lee Hsien Loong', 18 December, https://vovworld.vn/en-US/news/pm-meets-former-japanese-pm-suga-yoshihide-singapore-pm-lee-hsien-loong-1257019.vov

Wada, S. (1992) 'Yoshida Shigeru to Nichi-Bei Kyōkai' [Yoshida Shigeru and the Japan–America Society], in Yoshida Shigeru Memorial Foundation (ed), *Ningen Yoshida Shigeru* [Yoshida Shigeru the Human], Chūō Kōronsha, pp 480–98.

Wall Street Journal (2015) 'Former PM Yukio Hatoyama Makes Musical Debut', 15 January, https://www.wsj.com/articles/BL-JRTB-18916

Ward, R. (1965) 'Japan: The Continuity of Modernization', in S. Verba and L. Pye (eds), *Political Culture and Political Development*, Princeton University Press, pp 27–82.

Watanabe, A. and Eldridge, R. (eds) (2016) *The Prime Ministers of Postwar Japan, 1945–1995: Their Lives and Times*, Lexington Books.

Watson, D. (2002) *Reflections of a Bleeding Heart: A Portrait of Paul Keating, PM*, Knopf.

Wheeler, M. (2013) *Celebrity Politics: Image and Identity in Contemporary Political Communications*, Wiley.

Wice, P.B. (2009) *Presidents in Retirement: Alone and Out of Office*, Rowman and Littlefield.

Wittner, L.S. (1997) *Resisting the Bomb: A History of the World Nuclear Disarmament Movement, 1954–1970*, Stanford University Press.

Wong, E. (2002) *Restrictions on Activities of Former Heads of Government and Former Senior Members of Government*, Research and Library Services Division, Legislative Council Secretariat, www.legco.gov.hk/yr01-02/english/sec/library/0102rp02e.pdf

Yakushiji, K. (ed) (2012) *Murayama Tomiichi Kaikoroku* [Murayama Tomiichi's Memoirs], Iwanami Shoten.

Yamaguchi, E. (2022) 'A Jester and His Kings: Nakai Hiromu and the Meiji Elite', *Kyōtofuritsu Daigaku Gakujutsu Hōkoku* [The Scientific Reports of Kyoto Prefectural University], 74(December): 1–30, https://kpu.repo.nii.ac.jp/records/6337

Yamaguchi, M. (2022) 'Why Is Japan Split Over Abe's State Funeral?', *Associated Press*, 26 September, https://apnews.com/article/shinzo-abe-japan-tokyo-assassinations-state-funerals-b634f870bc0480457f63876394728e7f

Yasko, R.A. (1973) *Hiranuma Kiichirō and Conservative Politics in Prewar Japan*, PhD Thesis, University of Chicago.

Yasui, K. (2016) *Yoshida Shigeru to Kishi Nobusuke: Jimintō Hoshu Ni-Dai Chōryū no Keifu* [Yoshida Shigeru and Kishi Nobusuke: The Lineage of Two Great Tides of Liberal Democratic Party Conservatism], Iwanami Shoten.

Yomiuri Shimbun (2021) 'Kiretsu o kaihishita Asō-ha, ipponka o miokuri… Kōno, Kishida ryōshi o shiji ' [Asō Faction Avoids Split and Decides Not to Unify, Supports Both Kōno and Kishida], 14 September, https://www.yomiuri.co.jp/politics/20210914-OYT1T50060/

Yomiuri Shimbun (2022) 'Former Leaders Can Offer Perspective, and Should Model Magnanimity', 26 November, https://japannews.yomiuri.co.jp/editorial/political-pulse/20221126-73283/

Yomiuri Shimbun (2024) 'Kishida Appears Before Ethics Council: Mere Holding of Council Brings No Clarity to Funds Scandal', 1 March, https://japannews.yomiuri.co.jp/editorial/yomiuri-editorial/20240301-172066/

Yoshida, S. (1957a) *Kaisō Jūnen, Dai 1-kan* [A Decade of Recollections, Volume 1], Shinchōsha.

Yoshida, S. (1957b) *Kaisō Jūnen, Dai 2-kan* [A Decade of Recollections, Volume 2], Shinchōsha.

Yoshida, S. (1957c) *Kaisō Jūnen, Dai 3-kan* [A Decade of Recollections, Volume 3], Shinchōsha.

Yoshida, S. (1958) *Kaisō Jūnen, Dai 4-kan* [A Decade of Recollections, Volume 4], Shinchōsha.

Yoshida, S. (1961) *The Yoshida Memoirs: The Story of Japan in Crisis*, Heineman.

Yoshida, S. (1967a) *Nihon o Kettei shita Hyakunen* [Japan's Decisive Century], Nihon Keizai Shimbunsha.

Yoshida, S. (1967b) *Japan's Decisive Century 1867–1967*, Frederick A. Praeger.

Yoshida, S. (1992 [1963]) *Sekai to Nihon* [The World and Japan], Chūō Kōronsha.

Yoshida, S. (2007) *Yoshida Shigeru: Last Meiji Man*, Rowman and Littlefield.

Yoshida, R. (2022) 'The Demise of the Rearmament Movement in the Aftermath of the San Francisco Peace Conference', in Y. Sugita and V. Teo (eds), *Rethinking the San Francisco System in Indo-Pacific Security: Enduring Legacies, Structural Contradictions and Geopolitical Rivalry*, Palgrave Macmillan, pp 41–60.

Yoshitake, N. (2016) 'Nōberu-shō no Kokusaiseiji – Nōberu Heiwa-shō to Nihon: Yoshida Shigeru Moto Sōri no Suisen o Meguru 1966-nen no Himitukōsaku' [International Politics of the Nobel Prize: The Nobel Peace Prize and Japan, Covert Actions in 1966 and the Nomination of Former Prime Minister Yoshida Shigeru], *Chiiki Seisaku Kenkyū*, 19(1): 1–25.

Yoshitake, N. (2017) 'Nōberu-shō no Kokusaiseiji – Nōberu Heiwa-shō to Nihon: Yoshida Shigeru Moto Sōri no Suisen o Meguru 1966-nen no Himitukōsaku to Sono Kiketsu' [International Politics of the Nobel Prize: The Nobel Peace Prize and Japan, Covert Actions in 1966 and Consequences of Nominating Former Prime Minister Yoshida Shigeru], *Chiiki Seisaku Kenkyū*, 19(4): 43–69.

Zaidan Hōjin Satō Eisaku Kinen Kokuren Daigaku Kyōsan Zaidan [Satō Eisaku Memorial Foundation for Cooperation with the United Nations University] (2021), https://satoeisaku.com

Zakowski, K. (2011) 'Kōchikai of the Japanese Liberal Democratic Party and Its Evolution After the Cold War', *The Korean Journal of International Studies*, 9(2): 179–205.

Index

References to tables appear in **bold** type.

A

Abe Kan 30, 92
Abe Nobuyuki **38**, 42
Abe Shintarō 30, 80, 81, 83, 84, 85, 92, 138, 140
Abe Shinzō 1, 26, 56, 66, 84, **94**, 111, 118–19, 121–3, 127, 129, 134
 Abenomics 91, 93, 97, 119
 and Acolytes/Protégés 119–20, 123, 138–9
 ambitious efforts 92–6, 129–30
 assassination of 41, 102, 105, 122–3, 131, 138, 147
 family connections 30, 83–4, 92, 140
 and factions 1, 96, 105–6, 133
 grandfather's influence (Kishi Nobusuke) 30, 75–6, 92–3, 138, 147
 political dabbling 104–6
 second premiership 93–6
Abe Yōko (Kishi's daughter) 85
Acolytes and Protégés 21, 23, 30, 138–9, 147
 Meiji period to World War Two examples 52–3, 57
 1945 to 1989 period examples 62, 80–2
 post-1989 period examples 118–20, 123, 127
Adenauer, Konrad 70
administrative reforms 29, 79, 91, 98
African states 19
Akao Bin 75
Akihito, Emperor 125, 144
Alexandra, Princess, of Kent 70
Allen, Richard 71
Amari Akira 106
Anami Korechika 46
Anchor Point 22, 23–4, 143–4
 Meiji Period to World War Two examples 56–7
 1945 to 1989 period examples 81, 87–8
 post-1989 period examples 124–7
Anderson, Lisa 14, 15, 21
An Jung-geun 40

Anpo protests 59, 74, 81, 110, 118
Asanuma Inejirō 63, 102
Ashida Hitoshi **60**
Asian Financial Crisis 91, 125–6, 143
Asian Population and Development Association (APDA) 82, 112
Asian Women's Fund (AWF) 109, 110–11
Asō Tarō 1, 85, 92, **95**, 103, 104, 112, 116, 120, 121, 127, 133, 142
 anime envoy role 96, 129
 family connections 85, 122
 as finance minister 97
 kingmaker role 106–7
 political ambitions 96–7
 political dabbling 106–7, 108
assassination 35, 43–4, 102, 131
 of Abe Shinzō 102, 131, 138, 147
 attempt on Crown Prince Hirohito 57
 of Hara Takashi 41, 43
 of Hamaguchi Osachi 43
 of Inukai Tsuyoshi 43
 of Itō Hirobumi 40, 47, 131
 in 26 February Incident 41

B

Bailey, Thomas A. 16, 47
Belenky, I. 18, 22
Benardo, Leonard 14
Ben-Gurion, David 72
Blair, Tony 3
Boao Forum 112, 113
Brinkley, Douglas 11, 13
Brown, Gordon 2–3
bubble economy, collapse of 91, 124–5
Buchanan, Frank 73
Burundi 17
Bush, George H.W. 15, 16, 30

C

Cabinet Secretariat 26
Cameron, R. 2

INDEX

Carter, Jimmy 11, 13, 15, 23, 133, 135
Carter Centre 13
Celebrity 21, 127, 141–3
  celebritization process 142–3
  early period examples 55–6
  media engagement 86–7, 123–4
  1945 to 1989 period examples 86–7
  popular culture appearances 124, 142
  post-1989 period examples 123–4
  social media use 123
celebrity diplomacy 24
Chambers, John Whiteclay, II 13
Charles III, King 143
Chiang Kai-shek 87
Chiang Mai Initiative 126
Chiba Kō 83
China 19–20, 69, 73–4, 77, 87, 91, 93, 98, 109, 111–14, 129, 135, 136
Chinese Communist Party (CCP) 74, 113
Chōshū clan 52, 53, 57, 138, 144
Clark, James C. 13
Clinton, Bill 13, 15, 16
Club de Madrid 20
Cold War 8, 62–3, 70–1, 73–8, 135, 136
  end of 58, 62, 89–91, 100
  impact on former PM activities 87, 89–90
colonialism 33, 50, 73, 75, 80, 137, 138
Communist Party (JCP, *Kyōsantō*) 63, 134
Connors, Lesley 47, 49, 56
Constitutional Council (France) 17
Constitutional Democratic Party (CDP, *Rikken Minshutō*) 92, 98, 99, 117, 122, 127, 147
Cooper, A.F. 6, 24–5
Council for Protecting the Constitution (*Kenpō-yōgo Kokumin Rengō*) 73
Council of Elders (*jūshin*) 44, 46–7, 50, 57, 70, 109, 133
COVID-19 pandemic 4, 97, 101, 108, 116, 122, 125
Cunningham, Homer F. 13

D

de Gaulle, Charles 71
democracy 15, 33, 57–8, 62–4, 67, 70, 75, 83, 89–90, 130, 132, 138, 141, 148
Democratic Liberal Party (*Minshu Jiyūtō*) 64, 68
Democratic Party 63, 64, 79
Democratic Party for the People (DPFP, *Kokumin Minshutō*) 84, 92
Democratic Party of Japan (DPJ, *Minshutō*) 93, 96, 98, 100, 101, 112, 113, 117, 118, 120, 122, 130
Democratic Socialist Party (DSP, *Minshatō*) 68
de Vries, Jouke 3, 18
de Vries, Manfred Kets 11, 148

Dittmer, L. 24
Dobson, Hugo 21, 25, 131, 147
Doi Takako 86, 110, 146
Dokō Toshio 29
Domett, T. 25
Dower, J.W. 64

E

East Asian Financial Crisis 143
Edström, B. 27
Eisenhower, Dwight 15, 16, 72
Elders, The 20, 134
Elizabeth II (Queen) 25, 125, 143
Embracers of a Cause 18, 23, 50–1, 73–8, 89, 104, 107, 115–16, 117, 127, 134, 135–7, 145
European Economic Community 71
Exhausted Volcanoes 18, 22
  death and illness causes 130–1
  Meiji period to World War Two examples 43–5
  1948 to 1989 period examples 65–6
  post-1989 examples 101–4

F

factions (*habatsu*), 21, 22, 26, 29–30, 62, 82, 91–2, 104, 144–5
  Abe faction (*Seiwakai*) 105–6
  Asō faction 106–7
  as mechanism for influence 68–70, 108–9, 127, 132–3
  role in political dabbling 131–3
Family Affair 21, 23, 127, 139–41, 147
  Meiji period to World War Two examples 53–5
  gender aspects 84–5, 141
  hereditary politicians 120–1
  1945 to 1989 period examples 83–6
  post-1989 examples 120–3
15 May Incident (1932) 43
First Citizens 18, 22, 145–6
  difficulty achieving status 133–5
  diplomatic activities 70–2, 114–15
  Meiji period to World War Two examples 47–50
  1945 to 1989 period examples 70–2
  post-1989 examples 109–15
Foreign Correspondents' Club of Japan 116
Former Presidents' Act (1958), US 16
Fourth Tokyo International Conference on African Development (TICAD-IV) 111, 112
France 17, 18, 30, 71, 72, 87
From Five group 100, 101
Fukai, S.N. 24, 27
Fukuda Takeo **61**, 64, 66, 68, 71, 80, 81, 83, 84, 111, 134, 135
Fukuda Tatsuo 121–2

175

Fukuda Yasuo 83, **95**, 96, 105, 109, 112–13, 120, 121, 140
Fukui, H. 24
Fukushima disaster 93, 98, 104, 115, 116, 117, 118, 137
Furusato Sōsei 76

G

G20 4, 29
G7 1, 5, 29, 77
Garden Club of America 70
gender aspects 25, 146, 148
generational politics 23, 139, 140, 141, 144
genrō (elder statesmen) 22, 35, 41, 70, 72, 109, 139, 145–6
 as First Citizens 47–50, 133–4
 institutional role 46–7
 members who were former prime ministers 47
 Saionji as last 48–9
 Yamagata as 47–8
Genron-NPO Tokyo-Beijing Forum 112
Germany 42, 70, 73
Global Environmental Action (GEA) 77
Good Governance Party (*Minseitō*) 100
Gorbachev, Mikhail 72
Grand Cordon of the Order of the Chrysanthemum (*Daikun'i Kikka Saijushō*) 72
Great Depression 41
Great East Japan earthquake 91, 137
Great Hanshin earthquake 91, 124
Great Kantō Earthquake 44, 56, 58
Green Initiative fund 108

H

Habitat for Humanity programme 13
Hallstein, Walter 71
Hamaguchi Osachi **38**, 43, 62, 53
Hamilton, Alexander 17
Hara Takashi 33, 41, 43, 48–9, 51, 53–4, 57, 70, 132, 139, 142
Harris, T. 119
Hashimoto Gaku 98, 122
Hashimoto Ryūtarō 77, 80, 83, 92, **94**, 97–8, 102, 103, 104, 107, 108, 109, 115, 117, 118, 120
Hata Tsutomu 80, 82, 92, **94**, 99, 100, 101, 118, 120, 122
Hata Yūichirō 101, 122
Hatoyama family 23, 30, 54, 109, 124
 Hatoyama Ichirō 29, **60**, 66, 83–4, 130, 140
 Hatoyama Yukio 83–4, **95**, 101, 109, 113–15, 117, 120, 124, 127, 140–1, 145
 Hatoyama Jirō 84
 Hatoyama Kiichirō 38, 54, 84, 140
 Hatoyama Kunio 84, 114

 as "Kennedys of Japan", 84, 141
 political dynasty 83–4, 120, 140–1
Hattori Ryūji 6, 88
Havel, Václav 2, 4
Hayao Kenji 28–9
Hayasaka, S. 103, 129
Hayashi Senjūrō **38**, 123
Hayashi Yoshimasa 105
Hecht, Marie B. 13, 17
Heisei Kenkyūkai faction 109
hereditary politics 30, 127, 139–41
 see also Family Affair
Higashikuni Naruhiko 41, 42, 43, **60**, 63, 64, 65, 83, 89, 130
Hiranuma Kiichirō **38**, 40–1, 42–3, 50, 54
Hiranuma Takeo 54, 140
Hirohito
 Crown Prince 57
 Emperor 90
Hirota Kōki 34, **38**, 42, 56
HIV-contaminated blood scandal 117
Hoover, Herbert 13
Horie Shigeo 70
Hosoda Hiroyuki 105, 106
Hosokawa Morihiro 5, 54, 91, 92, **94**, 99, 100–1, 113, 115, 116, 118, 120, 123–4, 140, 141, 142
House of Councillors 54, 56, 93, 100, 101, 102, 103, 107, 112, 114, 122
House of Peers 48, 54
House of Representatives 1, 41, 54, 63, 96, 97, 102, 103, 104, 107, 110, 113, 117, 122, 142
Hu Deping 113
Hu Jintao 20
Hussein, Saddam 88
Hu Yaobang 113

I

Ichikawa Fusae 146
Ikeda Hayato **60**, 66, 76, 80, 81, 82, 83, 87, 118, 133, 134, 139
Ikeda Yukihiko 83
Imperial Household Law 35
Imperial Rescript on Education 40
Imperial Rule Assistance Association 42, 45
IMTFE (International Military Tribunal for the Far East) 34, 44, 45, 52, 56
Inada Tomomi 119
Inoue Kaoru 47
Inoue Kazuko 114
InterAction Council 71, 112, 113, 134
International Institute for Global Peace 76
International Manga Award 96
International Martial Arts Federation 65
Inukai Takeru 54
Inukai Tsuyoshi **38**, 41, 43, 54
Iron triangle 28

INDEX

Ishiba Shigeru 5, 6, 80, 93, 97, 106–7, 108, 119–20, 121, 133, 139, 146
Ishibashi Tanzan **60**, 67, 73–4, 75, 77, 80, 81, 83, 86, 87, 89, 100, 136, 142
Ishihara Shintarō 86, 113
Israel 18, 72
Itō Hirobumi 7–8, 34, 35, **36**, 40, 41, 46, 47, 48, 51, 52, 53, 129, 131, 132, 138
Itō Hirokuni 54
Izumi Kenta 99

J

Jack, Andrew 12
Japanese Antarctic expedition (1910–1911) 50
Japanese Constitution
  Meiji Constitution (1889) 35
  Constitution of Japan (1947) 25, 59, 73, 75–6, 140
Japanese Imperial Army 40, 54
Japanese Imperial Navy 43, 54
Japan-Holland Society 50
  Japan Inc. (iron triangle) 28
Japan-India Society 50
Japan Innovation Party (*Ishin no Kai*) 92, 98
Japan International Cooperation Agency 54
Japan-Korea Parliamentary Friendship League 115
Japan New Party (*Nihon Shintō*) 92, 100
Japan Red Cross Society 50
Japan Socialist Party (JSP, *Nihon Shakaitō*) 59, 63, 64, 67, 68, 75, 86, 87, 89, 110, 146
Japan-UK summit 98
Japan-US Security Treaty 59, 74, 81, 110, 138
Japan-Vietnam Parliamentary Friendship Alliance 115
Jiang Zemin 20
Johnson, Chalmers 69, 78
Johnson, Lyndon B. 13, 66
Johnston, D.M. 24
jūsen (housing loan companies) 110

K

Kabashima, I. 103
Kabaya Ryōichi 104
Kaifu Toshiki 6, 29, 30, 80, 82, 92, **94**, 97, 99–100, 118
Kaikoku Gojūnenshi (*Fifty Years of New Japan*) 51
Kamei Shizuka 103
Kamikawa Yōko 97
Kanba Michiko 75
Kan Gentarō 122
Kan Naoto 93, **95**, 98, 101, 113, 114, 116–18, 137, 138, 141, 145
Katayama Tetsu **60**, 64, 67, 68, 73, 77, 80, 83, 87, 89, 100, 110, 136, 141
Katō Kōichi 109
Katō Takaaki **37**, 41, 44, 46, 48, 49, 53, 62

Katō Tomosaburō 33, **37**, 44, 49, 56
Katsura Tarō 35, **36**, 44, 45–6, 47, 48, 50, 52, 53, 54, 132, 137
Keane, John 3, 12
Keating, Paul 12
keien period 35, 41, 45
Kennedy, John F. 71
Khrushchev, Nikita 73
kickback scandal 67, 97, 99, 105, 108, 126
Kim Dae-jung 72, 88
Kingston, J. 117
Kishida Fumio 1, 8, **95**, 97, 99, 105, 106, 107, 108, 116, 119, 121, 122, 126, 144
Kishida Shōtarō 122
Kishi Nobuchiyo 84
Kishi Nobuo 84
Kishi Nobusuke 29, **60**, 64, 67, 79–84, 136–8, 140, 145
  and Acolytes/Protégés 80–2, 138
  as Anchor Point 87–8, 143
  family connections 83–4, 140
  influence on Abe 92–3, 147
  political dabbling 68, 81, 131
  postwar activities 74–6
Kissinger, Henry 27, 66
Kitaoka Shinichi 76
Kiyoura Keigo **37**
KK sensō 109
Kobayashi Takayuki 106
Kōchikai faction 108, 109
Koike Yuriko 28, 120
Koiso Kuniaki **39**, 42, 44, 46
Koizumi Junichirō 5, 26, 28, 79, 90, 91–2, **94**, 127, 136, 141–3
  and Acolytes/Protégés 80
  ambitious efforts 93, 96, 97, 98
  anti-nuclear activism 115–16, 136
  celebrity activities 104, 124, 141–2
  as Exhausted Volcano 101, 103–4, 130
  family connections 120–1
  media skills 103–4, 123
  political dabbling 107
  son as protégé 120–1
Koizumi Shinjirō 30, 104, 108, 116, 120, 121, 141
Kokovtsov, Vladimir 40
Kōmei Party 92, 97, 102
Konoe Fumimaro 34, **38**, 40, 42, 43, 44, 45, 50, 51, 53, 54, 100, 120, 130, 140
Kōno Tarō 106, 119, 121
Kōno Yōhei 97, 109
Korea 40, 42, 46, 50, 74, 79, 87–8, 102, 115, 136
Krauss, E. 26
Kuroda Kiyotaka 33, **36**, 41, 47
kuromaku (black curtain) 22, 29, 131

177

Kyōwa Research Centre 114
Kyōwatō (Republican Party) 114

L

Leaving (play) 2, 4
Lee, P.N.S. 24, 88
Lee Kuan Yew 20
Le Pen family 25, 30
Liberal Democratic Party (LDP, *Jiyū Minshutō*) 1, 54, 59, 62, 64, 74–5, 79, 81, 83, 89–92, 96–109, 116, 119–21, 140–1, 144–7
  dominance of 144–5
  factions within 68–70, 104–9, 131–3, 144
  formation of 59, 68
  presidential elections 106–8, 119, 127, 147
  reforms affecting 91, 108, 127
  slush-fund scandal 133
Liberal Party (*Jiyūtō*), 63–4, 81, 84, 102, 117
Lockheed scandal 59, 69, 78
Lula da Silva, Luiz Inácio 4, 28

M

MacArthur, Douglas 63
Machimura Nobutaka 107
Major, John 3, 11, 136
Malik, Jacob 42
Manchukuo 80, 82
Manchurian Incident (1931) 67
Mandela, Nelson 20, 133, 134, 135, 136, 145
Mao Zedong 73
marginal diplomacy 24, 72
Martin, Asa E. 12
Matsukata Haru 55
Matsukata Masayoshi **36**, 41, 47, 50, 51, 53, 55
Matsumura Kenzō 74
Meiji (period) 33, 35–6, 46–7, 52–3, 57, 140
  Constitution 35
  oligarchs 52, 55, 57, 129, 138
  Restoration 33, 52
Meiji Emperor 53, 58
Mejiro Palace 85
Melber, H. 19
memoirs 10, 14–16, 51, 65, 79–80, 85, 118, 137–8
memorialization 134, 139, 145, 146, 147, 148
Michiko, Empress 125
Miki Takeo **61**, 64, 68, 69, 78, 79, 80, 82, 85, 89, 118
Mikuriya Takashi 6
militarism 33, 55, 56, 64, 70, 73
Ministerial Code (UK) 17
Ministry of International Trade and Industry (MITI) 82, 88, 103, 107
Minshintō 98
Mitterand, François 72

Miyake Yukiko 112
Miyazawa Kiichi 86, **94**, 103, 104, 107, 108–9, 118, 120, 122, 125–6
Miyazawa Yōichi 122
Modi, Narendra 115
Moral Re-Armament 73
Mori no Seidan (series) 123
Mori Yoshirō 1, 86, **94**, 98, 104, 105, 107–8, 115, 120, 121, 122, 125
Mori Yūki 122
Morris, Edmund 13
Motegi Toshimitsu 106
Murayama Statement (*Murayama danwa*) 110
Murayama Tomiichi **94**, 97, 100, 107, 109, 110–11, 116, 124, 127, 135, 136, 141, 142, 145

N

Nakai Hiromu 54
Nakaoka Konichi 43
Nakasone Hirofumi 83
Nakasone Peace Institute 76
Nakasone-Sō (TV show) 86
Nakasone Yasuhiro **61**, 76, 97, 107, 134–5, 142–3
  celebrity activities 86–7, 123, 142
  diplomatic missions 72, 88, 90
  family connections 83
  political influence 68–9, 72
  seeking vindication 79–80, 137
Nakasone Yasutaka 83
National Citizens' Council to Enact an Independent Constitution 76
National Organization for the Promotion of Normalization between Japan and North Korea 110
National Security Council 26–7
Neary, Ian 27
Neuffer, John F. 102
New Armament Promotion Association 75
New Frontier Party (*Shinshintō*) 100, 101
New Party Sakigake (*Shintō Sakigake*) 101, 110, 113, 117
Nikolayevsk Incident (1920) 43
Nixon, Richard 11, 15, 66, 72
Nixon Shocks 62, 66
Nobel Peace Prize 13, 72
Noda Yoshihiko 92, 93, **95**, 98–9, 113, 141
non-nuclear energy movement 101, 104, 115–16, 117, 118, 136
Northeast Asia Trilateral Forum (NATF) 112
North Korea 4, 13, 91, 102, 110, 136
Nyblade, B 26

O

Obuchi Keizō 80, 82, 92, **94**, 98, 101, 102, 107, 118, 120, 121, 125
Obuchi Yūko 102, 107, 120, 121

Ogata Sadako 54
Ōhira Masayoshi 29, **61**, 65, 69, 71, 83, 97, 102
Oil Shock (1973) 22, 143
Okada Keisuke **38**, 41, 50
Okamoto Mitsunori 100
Okinawa 59, 62, 66, 72, 93, 107, 109, 114, 122, 124, 136, 142
Okinawa Kyōsōkyoku (Okinawa Rhapsody) 124
Okinawa Rape Incident (1995) 124
Ōkuma Nobutsune 54
Ōkuma Nobuyuki 54
Ōkuma Shigenobu **36**, 46, 48, 50, 51, 54, 55, 57, 136, 142
Olympics (Tokyo 1964, 2020/2021) 97, 108, 116, 142
Oriental Development Company (ODC) 50
Oriental Society 50
Ōta Takafumi 124
O'Toole, Patricia 13
Ōyama Iwao 47
Ozawa Ichirō 99, 102, 114, 117

P

Paris Peace Conference 47, 49
Park Chung Hee 87, 88
Peace Society of Japan 50
Persian Gulf War 88, 99
Pike, D. 24
Political Dabblers 18, 22, 145–6
  factional politics role 68–70, 131–3
  Meiji period to World War Two examples 45–7, 57
  1945 to 1989 period examples 62, 67–70, 82, 90
  post-1989 examples 92, 104–9, 127
  as uber-category 145–6
Polk, James K. 15
post-premierships 7, 21, 31, 34, 44, 50, 55–6, 87, 109–11, 128, 134, 143, 144
Potsdam Declaration 45
Powell, Charles 11
presidentialization 26, 147
Presidential Libraries Act (1955), US 16
Privy Council (*sūmitsuin*) 35, 40, 45, 129
Privy Council (UK) 16
Progressive Party (*Shinpotō*) 63
Puraido (*Pride*) (biopic) 56
Putin, Vladimir 115

Q

Quadrilateral Peace Alliance 74

R

Reagan, Ronald 15, 71, 79, 141
Recruit scandal 59, 76–7, 88, 103
Reform Party (*Kaishintō*) 67

Reischauer, Edwin 55
Renhō (Saitō) 99
retirement syndrome 11
Rikken Dōshikai (Association of Comrades of the Constitution) 44
Rikken Seiyūkai (Association of Friends of Constitutional Government) 35, 36
Roosevelt, Theodore 13, 15
Rose, Caroline 21, 22, 131
Rugby World Cup 116
Russia 47, 91, 115, 135
Russo-Japanese War (1904–05) 47

S

Sagoya Tomeo 43
Saigō Tsugumichi 47
Saionji Kinmochi 35, **37**, 45–6, 47, 48–9, 50, 51, 53, 54, 56, 124, 132, 139, 143, 146
Saitō Makoto **38**, 41, 50, 52, 102
Samuels, Richard 29
Sanaenomics 119
San Francisco Peace Treaty 85
Sanjō Sanetomi 33
sarin gas attack (1995) 110
Satō Eisaku 6, 21–2, 24, 29, 30, **61**, 75, 76, 79–84, 87, 89, 92, 133, 134, 140
  as Anchor Point 56, 65–6, 87, 124, 143
  family connections (Kishi) 83–4
  Nobel Peace Prize 72
  postwar influence 65–6, 68–9
  relationship with Yoshida 80–1, 139
Satō Kei 102
Satō Shinji 83
Satsuma clan 52, 144
Schaller, Thomas F. 14
Schenker, Alan Evan 13–14, 16
Schmidt, Gerhard 20
Schreurs, Miranda 77
Seekers of Vindication 18, 23, 109, 145, 147
  Meiji period to World War Two examples 50–2
  memoirs as method 137–8
  1945 to 1989 period examples 78–80
  post-1989 examples 115, 116–18, 127
Seiwa Seisaku Kenkyūkai (*Seiwakai*) faction 96, 105, 107
Seiyūhontō (Orthodox Friends of Government Party) 41
Self-Defence Forces (SDF) 25, 75, 110, 119
Senkaku/Diaoyu islands 98, 112, 113
Sheldon, Winthrop Dudley 13, 16
Shidehara Kijūrō 6, 42, 43, 49, 53, **60**, 62–3, 64, 67–8, 80, 83, 87, 89, 125
Shiina Etsusaburō 80, 81–2, 88, 138
Shikōkai faction 106
Shimoda Takesō 70
Shinoda Tomohito 26, 29, 67

Shinshintō (New Frontier Party) 100, 101
Shōsetu Yoshida Gakkō (The Yoshida School: A Novel) 86
Shōwa Denkō scandal (1948) 64, 67, 78
Shōwa era 53, 54, 62, 64, 75, 129, 131, 132, 140, 144
Sino-Japanese War (1894–95) 35, 52
Skidmore, Max 14
slush fund scandal 108, 119, 122, 133
Smith, D.M. 120
Social Democratic Party (*Shakai Minshūtō*) 73, 100, 110
Social Democratic Party of Japan (SDP, *Shakai Minshutō*) 100, 110
social media 23, 93, 123, 142
Southall, R. 19
Soviet Union 29, 42, 43, 45, 73, 75
Sports Promotion Act 96
Stathis, Stephen W. 16
Steel, G. 103
Still Ambitious 18, 21, 22, 131, 132
 democratization impact 129–30
 Meiji period to World War Two examples 35–43, 57
 1945 to 1989 period examples 62–5
 post-1989 examples 92–101, 106, 127
Stockwin, Arthur 28
Strauss-Kahn, Dominique 3
Student Defense Research Association 75
Suga Seigo 122
Suga Yoshihide 1, 84, 93, **95**, 97, 104, 105, 106, 108, 115, 116, 119, 121, 122, 135
Sunjong, Emperor 40
Sun Party (*Taiyōtō*) 101
Suzuki Kantarō **39**, 41, 42, 45, 46
Suzuki Naoto 85
Suzuki Shunichi 107, 122
Suzuki Zenkō 29, **61**, 69, 71, 79, 89, 96, 107, 122, 135

T

Taiwan 87, 135, 147
Taiwan Association School (Takushoku University) 50
Takahashi Iwao 124
Takahashi Kiseko 85
Takahashi Korekiyo 33, **37**, 41–2, 49, 102, 125
Takaichi Sanae 105, 106, 107, 108, 119–20, 121, 123, 139, 146
Takasaki Tatsunosuke 74
Takayasu Kensuke 29
Takeshita Noboru 27, 29, **61**, 65, 68, 69, 72, 76–8, 80, 82, 83–4, 89, 90, 99, 102, 103, 118, 125, 137
Tanaka Giichi **38**, 41, 44, 52, 54
Tanaka Kakuei 5, 22, 30, **61**, 64, 74–6, 82, 89, 102, 143

corruption scandals 78–9, 138
family connections 84–5, 141
Lockheed scandal 59, 69, 78
political influence 68–9, 131–2
relationship with Fukuda 64, 68–9, 135
Tanaka Makiko 83, 84–5, 138
Tanaka Natsuo 54
Tanakasone 30, 69, 132
Tanigaki Sadakazu 93, 96
Taylor, A.J.P. 55
Taylor, Henry 17–18
Terauchi Hisaichi 54
Terauchi Masatake **37**, 44, 46, 52
Thatcher, Margaret 2
Theakston, Kevin 3, 6, 12, 18, 20, 22, 133, 147
Tiberghien, Yves 77
Tōjō Hideki 34, **39**, 42, 45, 46, 50, 51–2, 55–6, 130, 132, 141
Tōjō Katsu 55
Tōjō Yūko 56
Tokiwakai poetry group 51
Tokudaiji family 54
Tokyo Electric Power Company (TEPCO) 118
Tomabechi Gizō 63
Toranomon Incident (1923) 56–7
Tōyō Keizai Shinpō 74
Trilateral Commission 71
Tripartite Pact 42
triple disaster (2011) 91, 104, 115, 117, 130, 137
Truman, Harry S. 13, 14, 15, 16
Tsuda, Taro 21, 22, 24, 29, 56, 66, 72, 79, 87, 105, 134, 143, 147
26 February Incident (1936) 41, 49
Twenty-One Demands 47

U

Uchida Kōsai 33
Uehara Yūsaku 46
Uji, T. 6
UK (United Kingdom) 2–3, 6, 17–18, 73, 136, 137, 138, 142, 143, 147, 148
Ukraine 91, 114, 124
Unification Church 102, 105
Uno Osamu 122
Uno Sōsuke 5, 65, **94**, 101, 102–3, 122, 130
Updegrove, Mark K. 13, 15, 16
US Occupation 34, 51, 64, 65, 67, 74, 75–6, 89

V

Vail Group 20
Vajpayee, Atal Bihari 115
van Boven, Theo 72
Vietnam War 59, 71

INDEX

W

waka poetry 51
Wakatsuki Reijirō **37**, 50, 52, 53, 62
Wall Street Journal 124
war criminals 35, 43, 51, 56, 75, 133
War on Terror 91, 104, 115
Waseda University 50, 51, 55, 82, 136
Washington, George 13, 14, 15
Washington Naval Conference 41
Watson, Don 12
Weiss, Jennifer 14
Wen Jiabao 113
Wice, Paul B. 14
Widner, Jennifer 19
Williams, Thomas W. 14
Wilson, Harold 142
Wilson, Woodrow 16
Wolferen, Karel van 28, 103
Wong, E. 17
World Conference Against Atomic and Hydrogen Bombs 73
World War Two 55–6, 73, 75, 80, 100, 130, 132, 138
  defeat's impact 35, 42–5, 59, 70
  end marking transition 42–3, 59, 88–9
  occupation period 43–5, 59
  war crimes trials 35, 43, 51–2, 56

X

Xi Jinping 20, 112, 113, 114

Y

Yachi Shōtarō 113
Yamagata Aritomo 35, **36**, 40–1, 45, 46, 47–8, 49, 51, 52–3, 57, 132, 138, 140, 146
Yamagata Isaburō (Yamagata's adopted son) 53
Yamamoto Gonbei **37**, 49, 51, 54, 56–7, 124, 143
Yasui Kōichirō 76
Yasukuni Shrine 56, 79, 104, 111, 119
Yeltsin, Boris 72
Yi Wanyong 50
Yonai Mitsumasa **38**, 42
Yoshida Gakkō (Yoshida School) 81, 86, 139
Yoshida Shigeru 42, 54, 56, **60**, 62–4, 67–9, 76, 80–3, 85–7, 89, 109, 114, 118, 129, 143
  comeback success 64, 129–30
  diplomatic activities 70–1, 87
  family connections 85, 96
  as First Citizen 70–2, 133–5, 145
  Ōiso residence activities 70, 81
  and protégés 80–1, 118, 139
Yoshida Shinji 122, 123
Yoshitake Nobuhiko 6
yūai (fraternity)
  Hatoyama Yūai Juku (Hatoyama Friendship Academy) 114
  World Yūai (fraternity) Forum 114
Yunoki Michiyoshi 122

Z

Zakowski, K. 109
Zelenskyy, Volodymyr 141
Zhang Zuolin 44
Zhou Enlai 73, 74
Zhu Rongji 20